Sources Of American Spirituality

Joseph Smith
SELECTED SERMONS & WRITINGS

Edited by Robert L. Millet

PAULIST PRESS
New York ◊ Mahwah

The publisher gratefully acknowledges permission to quote from designated pages of *Personal Writings of Joseph Smith,* edited by Dean Jessee granted by Deseret Book in Salt Lake City, Utah.

Library of Congress Cataloging-in-Publication Data

Smith, Joseph, 1805–1844.
    [Selections. 1990]
    Joseph Smith : selected sermons and writings / by Robert L.
Millet.
      p.   .cm.—(Sources of American spirituality)
    Bibliography: p.
    Includes index.
    ISBN 0-8091-0427-X
    1. Smith, Joseph, 1805–1844—Correspondence. 2. Mormons—United
States—Correspondence. 3. Church of Jesus Christ of Latter-Day
Saints—Sermons. 4. Mormon Church—Sermons. 5. Sermons, American.
6. Church of Jesus Christ of Latter-Day Saints—Doctrines.
7. Mormon Church—Doctrines. I. Millet, Robert L. II. Title.
III. Series.
BX8695.S6A4 1990
289.3′2—dc20
                                                89-35835
                                                  CIP

Published by Paulist Press
997 Macarthur Boulevard
Mahwah, N.J. 07430

Printed and bound in the United States of America

CONTENTS

GENERAL INTRODUCTION

In the history of American religion there are few more intriguing and perplexing characters than Joseph Smith. Born in Vermont in 1805, he was the son of a farmer whose bad luck in New England caused him to move to the region of Palmyra in western New York. Joseph's humble origins were indistinguishable from those of scores of farm boys from the vast stretches of western New York State bordering the Erie Canal. There he heard the revivalists repeatedly ignite the burned-over region with their message announcing the dawning of a new millennial age of unbounded prosperity for true believers. It dovetailed with the hopes of land speculators and farmers, merchants, and displaced factory workers who flooded the western frontier in search of a better life. At age fourteen, without ever having received much formal education, Joseph had a vision of angelic beings who announced to him that he would be the prophet of God's new revelation to the whole world. That experience was followed by other visions in which he received engraved plates on which were written the history of God's dealings in North America. The Book of Mormon was to tell of the epic exploits of the Lamanites, the Nephites and the Jaredites and of heroes like Mormon and Moroni.

The Prophet Joseph, as his followers came to call him, set out to reveal more than just the history of the original inhabitants of the continent, however. He founded a new religion, based on Christianity to be sure, but with a number of unique aspects that gave it a distinct cast. The religious revelation was matched by a revolutionary vision for the reordering of society to conform with the values of the Gospel.

Many of his claims were highly controversial, even scandalous. His insistence on the ongoing nature of revelation, his claim to have received a further revelation than what is contained in the Bible, his defense of polygamy and his defiant, critical posture toward the outside world all contributed to the opposition that led in 1844 to his lynching by a mob in Carthage, Illinois.

1

Yet the movement he founded was clearly the most successful communitarian experiment of the nineteenth century in America, when judged by the number of people it has involved, its prosperity, and the contribution to American society its followers have made. Moreover, it must also qualify as the most enduring of the religious innovations of an age in which change was commonplace. Joseph Smith was able to capture the pulse of frontier America. He embodied the eagerness for experimentation, the desire to build a new world, and the concrete sense of practicality that Americans of his century were famous for. In an age of sectarianism, he announced the revelation of the one, true church. In a time of social upheaval, he gave travelers to the frontier forms and structures that encompassed all of life. In a time of unbridled individualism in which greed and self-interest animated much of the new industrial order, he preached community that integrated the person with the larger group and indeed with a whole cosmological order. His appeal went beyond a narrow constituency and touched the chords of the American spirit.

Yet, while all of this helps us to understand the enigma of the man, it does not solve it. Nor, to be candid, does this volume. While the introduction and notes rigorously adhere to the standards of modern scholarship, they nevertheless are without the kind of critical distance that would facilitate an interpretation of the writings of Joseph Smith that viewed his words as symbols of something more or less than what their author intended. No, we have here instead a faithful presentation of the tradition. The care with which the original texts have been preserved and here rendered by Professor Millet is admirable and is in accord with the spirit of the Introduction. All of this works together to bring before us forcefully the historic reality: Joseph Smith was a prophet who was believed and is believed still by Americans in other ways indistinguishable from their fellow citizens. To those of us who are not believers, that reality cannot simply be passed over in one great syncreilstic nod, nor can it he buried in a barrage of bigotry. We must listen to the many voices of America's religious past that find in these writings new forms and new futures. To that end I am happy to present this work as a fitting contribution to the *Sources of American Spirituality.*

John Farina

PREFACE

At the time of the publication of this book over six million members of the Church of Jesus Christ of Latter-day Saints acknowledge Jospeh Smith as the "Prophet of the Restoration," the latter-day founder of a Christian movement which grows at a surprising rate each year. Joseph Smith spoke of having been informed by an angel in 1823 that his name "should be had for good and evil among all nations, kindreds and tongues, or that it should be both good and evil spoken of among all people." Believing Mormons are eager to point out the prophetic nature of that declaration, particularly during the last decade or so when the amount of polemical material regarding the Mormon origins and intentions has risen in almost proportionate fashion with Church membership. Unfortunately, the polarization of people by available literature on Joseph and the Mormons—whether antagonistic or apologetic—has prevented many who have sincere interest in the Mormon experience from receiving a balanced perspective.

This work is an attempt to help meet a need—to make available a collection of some of the more prominent writings and sermons of the Latter-day Saint Prophet-Leader. Where possible, it seems appropriate to let a public figure speak for himself. As a student of the life of Joseph Smith for the past twenty years, I have always felt his contributions to be significant. In preparing this work, however, it has been necessary for me to look beyond the bounds of Mormonism and attempt to assess Joseph Smith's place and impact upon the larger spectrum of religion and spirituality in America. The labor has been its own reward.

I have retained original spelling and punctuation in this collection, except in those sources now canonized or published officially by the Church—this in order that the reader might gain more of a contemporary feel for the parties as well as the documents themselves. In a number of the documents Joseph Smith lined out or crossed out words or phrases. The lined-out words have been retained.

3

There are many persons to whom I owe a significant amount of gratitude. My thanks go first to Religious Education at Brigham Young University for making available time and research funds to undertake the project. For their specific assistance, whether in the form of suggestions or in providing documents, I express appreciation to a number of my colleagues in Religious Education: to Professors Richard L. Anderson, Milton V. Backman, Jr., George A. Horton, Jr., Kent P. Jackson, Robert J. Matthews, Joseph F. McConkie, Keith W. Perkins and Larry C. Porter. Professor Paul H. Peterson made a number of helpful suggestions regarding the Introduction. I also acknowledge the assistance of Professor Ronald K. Esplin of the Joseph Fielding Smith Institute of Church History at BYU. I am particularly indebted to Dean C. Jessee, research historian at the Joseph Fielding Smith Institute, for his seminal work on the original documents written by or under the direction of Joseph Smith. Jessee's recent publication, *The Personal Writings of Joseph Smith* (Salt Lake City: Deseret Book Co., 1984) is the definitive and exhaustive treatment in this field to date. The reader will readily realize my debt to Professor Jessee. Appreciation is also expressed to Deseret Book Company in Salt Lake City for their permission to quote extensively from *Personal Writings*. For their superb editorial and typing skills, I offer thanks to Christine M. Purves and Lanise Porter, both able and conscientious secretaries. In spite of my substantial debt to many persons, however, I alone am responsible for the conclusions drawn from the evidence cited in this work.

Special thanks are due to John Farina and his associates at Paulist Press for their encouragement and expert assistance throughout the preparation of these materials for publication.

I.

INTRODUCTION

"I intend to lay a foundation that will revolutionize the whole world," Joseph Smith the Mormon Prophet declared in May of 1844. "It will not be by sword or gun that his kingdom will roll on; the power of truth is such that all nations will be under the necessity of obeying the Gospel."[1] The work and religious system set in motion in the early nineteenth century—known today as the Church of Jesus Christ of Latter-day Saints—continues in a healthy and unhindered fashion to impact upon American spirituality. For Joseph Smith, spirituality was a state of being, a condition achieved through the merging of the temporal and the spiritual, the finite and the infinite. Spirituality was essentially the result of a righteous life coupled with heightened perspective, an increased sensitivity to the things of God among men. To possess spirituality was to recognize that in the end "all things are spiritual," and that God had never given a purely temporal (time-bound or physical) command or directive.

In a sense, Joseph Smith and the Mormons sought to reconcile the irreconcilable. Indeed, the growth and spread of the Church may be attributed largely to what some might consider to be competing or contradictory processes: (1) constancy and adherence to the "ancient order of things"; and (2) development and change, according to needs and circumstances. Mormonism may thus be characterized as a religious culture with both static and dynamic—priestly and prophetic—

---

[1]*History of the Church of Jesus Christ of Latter-day Saints,* 7 Vols., ed. B. H. Roberts (Salt Lake City: Deseret Book Co., 1957), 6:365; cited hereafter as *History of the Church,* followed by appropriate volume and page numbers. This is the official history of the Church through the Joseph Smith era and into the administration of Brigham Young. See also *The Words of Joseph Smith,* ed. Andrew F. Ehat and Lyndon W. Cook (Provo, Utah: Religious Studies Center, Brigham Young University, 1980), p. 367.

elements, a movement acclimated to both conservative and progressive postures. Joseph Smith, known simply as "the Prophet," or "the Prophet Joseph" or "Brother Joseph" by his people, in his quest to establish Zion—the holy city, the New Jerusalem—held tenaciously to and grounded people of the faith in what he perceived to be the particular beliefs and rites of both ancient Israel and first-century Christianity. At the same time, Mormonism, through a belief in modern and continuing revelation, has undergone change and development when such have seemed essential to the perpetuity and preservation of the vision of the holy city.

Spirituality consisted of tying the heavens to the earth, imbuing man with the powers of God, and thereby elevating society. In the words of Ezra Taft Benson, thirteenth president of the LDS Church and successor to the position of Joseph, "the Lord works from the inside out. The world works from the outside in. The world would take people out of the slums. Christ takes the slums out of the people, and then they take themselves out of the slums. The world would mold men by changing their environment. Christ changes men, who then change their environment. The world would shape human behavior, but Christ can change human nature."[2] Such a change in one's nature was to be undertaken "in the world," amidst the throes of spiritual opposition; one need not leave the world to come out of the world. It was to be accomplished by every man and woman, not just priest or minister, "for God hath not revealed any thing to Joseph," the Mormon Prophet was to observe, "but what he will make known unto the Twelve [Apostles] & even the least Saint may know all things as fast as he is able to bear them."[3] In the mind of Joseph, then, virtue and an elevated perspective were prerequisite to spiritual union with the Infinite. In 1839 Joseph Smith wrote from a prison in Liberty, Missouri, pleading with the members of the Church to let "virtue garnish thy thoughts unceasingly then shall thy confidence wax strong in the presents [presence] of God."[4] In 1840 the Prophet wrote: "Vir-

---

[2] From an address given at the Church's 155th Semiannual General Conference, October 5, 1985, in *Conference Report,* October 1985, p. 5.

[3] *Words of Joseph Smith,* p. 4.

[4] *The Personal Writings of Joseph Smith,* comp. Dean C. Jessee (Salt Lake City: Deseret Book Co., 1984), p. 402, punctuation and spelling retained as in original. See also this statement (in edited form) in the *Doctrine and Covenants of the Church of Jesus Christ of Latter-day Saints* (1981 ed.), 138 sections (Salt Lake City: The Church of Jesus Christ of Latter-day Saints, 1981), section 121, verse 45. Cited hereafter as *Doctrine and Covenants,* with appropriate section and verse numbers. The *Doctrine and Covenants* will be discussed hereafter in the section entitled "Joseph Smith and the Expanding Canon."

tue is one of the most prominent principles that enables us to have confidence in approaching our Father who is in heaven in order to ask wisdom at his hand. Therefore, if thou wilt cherish the principle in thine heart, thou mayest ask with all confidence before him and it shall be poured out upon thy head, and thou shalt not lack anything that thy soul desires in truth."[5]

In regard to the matter of one's perspective, a revelation recorded by Joseph Smith in 1832 states: "And if your eye be single to my glory, your whole bodies shall be filled with light and there shall be no darkness in you; and that body which is filled with light comprehendeth all things." (Cf. Mt 6:22.) Then comes the following verse, which indicates the transcendent heights to which Joseph Smith believed a man could ascend: "Therefore, sanctify yourselves that your minds become single to God, and the days will come that you shall see him; for he will unveil his face unto you, and it shall be in his own time, and in his own way, and according to his own will."[6]

Brigham Young, the immediate successor to Joseph, stated in regard to the Prophet's ability to communicate spiritual matters:

> When I saw Joseph Smith, he took heaven, figuratively speaking, and brought it down to earth; and he took earth, brought it up, and opened up, in plainness and simplicity, the things of God. The excellency of the glory of the character of Brother Joseph Smith was that he could reduce heavenly things to the understanding of the finite. When he preached to the people—revealed the things of God, the will of God, the plan of salvation, the purposes of Jehovah, the relation in which we stand to Him and all the heavenly things—he reduced his teachings to the capacity of every man, woman, and child, making them as plain as a well-defined pathway. This should have convinced every person that ever heard of him of his divine authority and power, for no other man was able to teach as he could, and no person can reveal the things of God, but by the revelations of Jesus Christ.
>
> When you hear a man pour out eternal things, how well you feel! To what nearness you seem to be brought to God!

---

[5]Statement written in February 1840, cited in *Church News,* June 23, 1985, p. 10.
[6]*Doctrine and Covenants,* 88:67–68.

What a delight it was to hear Brother Joseph talk upon the great principles of eternity![7]

From the time of his first experience with Deity in 1820 until the time of his death in 1844, Joseph Smith declared emphatically that it was possible for man on earth to make contact with God in heaven; that man could transcend his environment by transforming his own nature and then his environment; and that the Spirit of God would give animation and meaning and eternal context to all things—social, economic or, of course, spiritual.

BACKGROUNDS: THE RELIGIOUS CLIMATE

The early nineteenth century was a time of change, an era of movement. "It was in the early part of the nineteenth century," writes one historian, "that physical, institutional, and psychological change accelerated to a degree unknown to previous generations."[8] The population of the young nation doubled in the first quarter of the nineteenth century. Growth seemed to lead to movement—movement in values and ideology as well as topography.[9] Alexis de Tocqueville's assessment is worthy of note: "In the United States a man builds a house in which to spend his old age, and he sells it before the roof is on; he plants a garden, and leaves it just as the trees are coming into bearing."[10] Orestes Brownson, a prominent thinker of the time, remarked:

> No tolerable observer of the signs of the time can have failed to perceive that we are, in this vicinity at least, in the midst of a very important revolution; a revolution which extends to every department of thought, and threatens to change ultimately the whole moral aspect of society. Every-

---

[7]This represents a combined expression of Brigham Young from three separate addresses, as contained in *Journal of Discourses*, 26 vols. (Liverpool: F. D. Richards & Sons, 1855–86), 4:54; 5:332; 8:206; combined in Hyrum L. Andrus and Helen Mae Andrus, *They Knew the Prophet* (Salt Lake City: Bookcraft Publishers, 1974), p. 35. The *Journal of Discourses* is a collection of addresses by Church leaders between the years 1851–86.

[8]Klaus J. Hansen, *Mormonism and the American Experience* (Chicago: University of Chicago Press, 1981), p. 45.

[9]Ibid., pp. 45–47.

[10]*Democracy in America,* 2 vols. (New York: Alfred A. Knopf, 1945), 2:164.

thing is loosened from its old fastenings, and is floating no one can tell exactly whither.[11]

Ralph Waldo Emerson, in speaking of the period from 1820 to 1845, mentioned that "no one can converse with different classes of society in New England, without remarking the progress of a revolution. Those who can share in it have no external organization, no badge, no creed, no name. They do not vote, or print, or even meet together. They do not know each other's faces or names. They are united only in a common love of truth and love of its work."[12] Some scholars contend that such a social and intellectual transformation laid a foundation for a competitive, individualistic personality type that evidenced a shift from an external focus of authority and control to a personal, inner-directed and independent man.[13] The decision by some Americans to remove the "shackles" of institutional churches and to reject religious statements opened the door to Restorationist movements.

Mormonism has been identified as a religious organization tied to biblical faith—a group which was spawned in the midst of a generation bent upon the return to the simple and direct appeal of the Bible. Thomas O'Dea has written that Joseph Smith, "together with his followers, offered claims to combine a restoration of primitive Christianity as it had been lived in the time of the Apostles with modern revelation from on high."[14] An apt description of the spirit of Restorationism in the nineteenth century is given by one historian as follows:

> Like many European reformers of the sixteenth and seventeenth centuries, many Americans of the early republic earnestly sought a restoration of New Testament Christianity. These Americans determined that the leaders of the Reformation had failed to restore the fulness of the gospel and that all Christian religions had inherited from the Medieval church incorrect doctrines and practices. Such conclusions inspired the restorationists to seek the truth and to

---

[11]*Boston Quarterly Review,* 3 Vols. (Boston: Cambridge Press, 1840), 3:265.
[12]See *The Dial* (New York: Russell and Russell, Inc., 1961), 1:2.
[13]See Hansen, *Mormonism and the American Experience,* p. 47.
[14]*The Mormons* (Chicago: University of Chicago Press, 1957), p. 2.

organize eventually new religions which in their opinion more closely resembled the Primitive Church.[15]

A classic illustration of one imbued with a desire to return to the "ancient order of things" was Alexander Campbell. Thomas and Alexander Campbell came to America from Ireland. Educated and trained as Presbyterian ministers in Scotland, Thomas Campbell and his son began another of the many campaigns against creeds and a strict Calvinism. Thomas had arrived in America first and, after having obtained a pastorate in a Presbyterian parish in southwestern Pennsylvania, had managed to incur the wrath of the synod for teaching what were perceived as heretical doctrines. Campbell rejected the notion that the Church should hold the Westminster Confession of Faith as a term of communion. He denied that faith came through some mystical-emotional experience, and stressed that faith resulted rather from "an intelligent response of the mind to evidence."[16] After dismissal by the Presbyterians, Thomas continued to teach his doctrines to the farmers in western Pennsylvania and organized the "Christian Association of Washington" in 1809. This society stressed "a pure Gospel ministry, that shall reduce to practice that whole form of doctrine, worship, discipline, and government, expressly revealed and enjoined in the word of God."[17]

Alexander Campbell joined his father in America in 1809, learned of the beliefs and practices of the movement, and assumed leadership. He accepted the doctrine of believer's baptism by immersion, was baptized, and in 1811 accepted the pastorate at the Brush Run Baptist Church in what is now Bethany, West Virginia. Campbell's adherence to his restorationist beliefs proved a serious concern to the Baptists, and he was rejected by many Baptist colleagues in the ministry. In 1823 the younger Campbell began editing a magazine entitled the *Christian Baptist,* the title of which was eventually changed to the *Millennial Harbinger,* evidencing a firm belief in the imminence of Christ's Second Coming. Campbell's dissatisfaction with nominal Christianity is apparent in a statement from the first volume of the *Christian Baptist:* "We are convinced, fully convinced, that the whole head is sick, and the whole heart faint of modern

---

[15]Milton V. Backman, Jr., *American Religions and the Rise of Mormonism* (Salt Lake City: Deseret Book Co., 1970), pp. 237–38.

[16]See W. E. Garrison and A. T. DeGroot, *The Disciples of Christ* (St. Louis, Mo.: Bethany Press, 1958), pp. 133–39.

[17]See ibid., pp. 146–48.

fashionable Christianity."[18] Backman has written of Campbell: "The iconoclast condemned all beliefs and practices that could not be validated by apostolic mandates. He proclaimed that missionary societies, tract societies, Bible societies, synods, associations, and theological seminaries were inconsistent with pure religion."[19]

Alexander Campbell's disillusionment with nineteenth-century churches did not represent an isolated perception. As late as 1838 Emerson stated in his famous "Divinity School Address" at Harvard that "the need was never greater of new revelation than now." Further, "the Church seems to totter to its fall, almost all life extinct." Continuing, "I look forward for the hour when the supreme Beauty, which ravished the souls of those Eastern men, and chiefly of those Hebrews, and through their lips spoke oracles to all time, shall speak in the west also."[20]

A number of later Mormon Church leaders spoke of their own quest for truth and of the frustrations they felt before their encounter with Joseph Smith. Brigham Young states: "My mind was opened to conviction, and I knew that the Christian world had not the religion that Jesus and the Apostles taught. I knew that there was not a Bible Christian on earth within my knowledge."[21] Wilford Woodruff, an early apostle and fourth president of the Church said: "I did not join any church, believing that the Church of Christ in its true organization did not exist upon the earth."[22] Willard Richards, later a counselor to Brigham Young, became "convinced that the sects were all wrong, and that God had no church on earth, but that he would soon have a church whose creed would be the truth."[23]

Nothing of consequence arises in a social or intellectual vacuum, and Joseph Smith and Mormonism were no different. What began as a frontier faith through the experiences and practices of an obscure farm boy and later survived and blossomed into a full-scale world religious movement would not come into being in "dry ground." The ground was prepared through a general dissatisfaction of large groups of people with mainline religious bodies, and the roots of the new

---

[18]*Christian Baptist*, 7 vols., 13th ed., rev. D. S. Burnet (Bethany, West Virginia: H. S. Bosworth, 1861), 1:33.

[19]*American Religions and the Rise of Mormonism*, p. 241.

[20]"The Divinity School Address," delivered before the senior class at the Harvard Divinity School, Cambridge, Massachusetts, July 15, 1838; in Sydney E. Ahlstrom, ed., *Theology in America* (Indianapolis: Bobbs-Merrill, 1967), pp. 306, 315–16.

[21]*Journal of Discourses*, 5:75.

[22]Ibid., 4:99.

[23]*History of the Church*, 2:470.

religion would sink deep into the soil because individuals were anxious for a "new revelation."

BEGINNINGS: JOSEPH SMITH'S FIRST VISION

Joseph Smith, Jr., was born in Sharon, Vermont on December 23, 1805. His family moved thereafter to Tunbridge, Vermont; Lebanon, New Hampshire; Norwich, Vermont; and finally in 1814 settled in Western New York. After two years of hard labor and financial strain, Joseph Smith, Sr., purchased 100 acres of unimproved land two miles south of Palmyra, New York, on the Palmyra-Manchester town line.[24]

Joseph Jr. reported that some time in the second year after his family's move to Manchester, "there was in the place where we lived an unusual excitement on the subject of religion."[25] He was referring to the avid spirit of revivalism and religious fervor prevalent in New England in the early nineteenth century. Persons "chiefly concerned with the habitual revivalism occurring" in the area, wrote Whitney R. Cross, "came to call it the 'Burnt' or 'Burned-over District,' adopting the prevalent western analogy between the fires of the forest and those of the Spirit." Continuing: "Charles Grandison Finney, the greatest evangelist of the day, helped give the term its customary usage when he applied it to localities between Lake Ontario and the Adirondacks where early Methodist circuit riders had, he thought, left souls hardened against proper religious tutelage. Yet these very people proved, in fact, thoroughly adaptable to his own exhortations, as did others farther afield." Cross then added: "The history of the twenty-five years following Finney's early campaigns suggest that the burning-over process fertilized luxuriant new growths rather than merely destroying old ones."[26]

Joseph Smith observed that the religious excitement "commenced with the Methodists, but soon became general among all the sects in that region of the country, indeed the whole district of Country seemed affected by it and great multitudes united themselves to

---

[24]An excellent treatment of the formative years of Joseph Smith is Richard L. Bushman, *Joseph Smith and the Beginnings of Mormonism* (Urbana/Chicago: University of Illinois Press, 1984.)

[25]*Personal Writings of Joseph Smith*, p. 197.

[26]*The Burned-Over District* (Ithaca: Cornell University Press, 1950), pp. 3–4. See also Milton V. Backman, Jr., *Joseph Smith's First Vision*, 2nd ed. (Salt Lake City: Bookcraft Publishers, 1980).

the different religious parties."[27] Between 1816 and 1821 revivals were reported in more towns and more settlers joined churches than at any previous time in New York's history.[28] During this period of religious explosion, the Smith family—made up of Joseph Smith, Sr., his wife Lucy Mack Smith, and their nine children—was proselyted by the Presbyterian sect. Young Joseph (in his fifteenth year) leaned toward the Methodists, and felt some desire to join them. Four members of the family became officially associated with the Presbyterians. Yet Joseph, Jr., remained an interested investigator of truth without fully committing himself to any church.

Joseph's primary concern was for the salvation of his soul. "From the age of twelve years I pondered many things in my heart concerning the situation of the world of mankind the contentions and divisions the wickedness and abominations and the darkness which pervaded the minds of mankind *my mind became exceedingly distressed for I became convicted of my sins* and by searching the scriptures I found that mankind did not come unto the Lord but that they had apostatized from the true and living faith."[29] An additional concern was a doctrinal one, for "the teachers of religion of the different sects understood the same passage of scripture so differently as to destroy all confidence in settling the question [of which of all the churches was true and divinely recognized] by an appeal to the Bible."[30] And yet Smith felt himself drawn to the Bible. Impressed with the invitation in James 1:5 to ask God if one lacked wisdom, he sought answers through prayer. He walked to a grove of trees not far from his father's farm and knelt to pray. "Information was what I most desired at this time, and with a fixed determination to obtain it I called upon the Lord for the first time."[31] Concerning the events of that spring day in 1820, Joseph Smith made a remarkable claim, one which is the basis for the LDS belief in the call of a modern prophet:

> After I had retired into the place where I had previously designed to go, having looked around me and finding myself alone, I kneeled down and began to offer up the desire of my heart to God, I had scarcely done so, when

---

[27] *Personal Writings of Joseph Smith,* p. 197.

[28] See Milton V. Backman, Jr., "Awakenings in the Burned-Over District: New Light on the Historical Setting of the First Vision," *Brigham Young University Studies,* Vol. 9, no.3 (Spring 1969), p. 302.

[29] *Personal Writings of Joseph Smith,* p. 5., italics added.

[30] Ibid., p. 199.

[31] Ibid., p. 75.

immediately I was seized upon by some power which entirely overcame me and had such an astonishing influence
over me as to bind my tongue so that I could not speak.
Thick darkness gathered around me and it seemed to me for
a time as if I were doomed to sudden destruction. But exerting all my powers to call upon God to deliver me out of the
power of this enemy which had seized upon me, and at the
very moment when I was ready to sink into despair and
abandon myself to destruction, not to an imaginary ruin but
to the power of some actual being from the unseen world
who had such a marvelous power as I had never felt in any
being. Just at this moment of great alarm I saw a pillar of
light exactly over my head above the brightness of the sun,
which descended gradually until it fell upon me. It no sooner
appeared than I found myself delivered from the enemy
which held me bound. When the light rested upon me I saw
two personages (whose brightness and glory defy all description) standing above me in the air. One of them spake unto
me calling me by name and said (pointing to the other) "this
is my beloved Son, Hear him."[32]

In an earlier (1832) account of the same phenomenon, Joseph explained that "a pillar of light above the brightness of the sun at noon
day came down from above and rested upon me and I was filled with
the spirit of God and the Lord opened the heavens upon me and I saw
the Lord and he spake unto me saying Joseph my son thy sins are
forgiven thee. Go thy way walk in my statutes and keep my commandments."[33] From yet another (1842) account:

While fervently engaged in supplication my mind was
taken away from the objects with which I was surrounded,
and I was enwrapped in a heavenly vision and saw two
glorious personages who exactly resembled each other in
features, and likeness, surrounded with a brilliant light
which eclipsed the sun at noon day. They told me that all
religious denominations were believing in incorrect doctrines, and that none of them was acknowledged of God as
his church and kingdom. And I was expressly commanded to
"go not after them," at the same time receiving a promise

---

[32]Ibid., pp. 199–200.
[33]Ibid., p. 6.

that the fulness of the gospel should at some time be made known unto me.[34]

This experience has come to be known by Latter-day Saints as "Joseph Smith's First Vision" and, as indicated, is the foundational event for a belief in the calling of latter-day prophets and the reception of modern oracles.

Joseph Smith's earliest concerns seem to have been personal rather than institutional—an initial concern for the welfare of his soul. But both issues—how he could gain personal salvation and which church was approved of God—were not unrelated. "The two questions were actually one. His anguish for himself mingled with the anguish for the world, for the corruption in the churches seemed to stand in the way of his own salvation." In short, "an answer for himself must be an answer for the entire world."[35]

Though the unfolding of Joseph Smith's doctrinal beliefs and the development of Mormonism would entail a lengthy process over the next twenty-four years of his life, the Prophet and his followers came to extract definite theological principles from the First Vision, such as: (1) a belief in a literal Satanic being bent upon the overthrow of all that is good; (2) the reality of God the Father as a separate and distinct personality from the resurrected Jesus Christ;[36] (3) the con-

---

[34]Ibid., p. 213. There are four accounts of this theophany, as recorded by Joseph Smith and his scribes, and as now contained in Jessee's excellent work, *Personal Writings of Joseph Smith:* an 1832 account (pp. 4–6); an 1835 account (pp. 74–77); an 1838 account (pp. 197–201); and an 1842 account (p. 213). Some of the differences between the accounts of the First Vision have proven to be points of controversy between critics and apologists. For example, the earliest account (1832) mentions the appearance of only one heavenly personage; there is some discrepancy between the 1832 and 1838 accounts regarding the Prophet's age at the time of the theophany (14 or 16 years); and the 1835 account indicates that "many angels" were also present at the time of the vision, a detail not mentioned in the other three accounts. Critics suggest that the discrepancies point toward fabrication of the story; believers suggest that such differences no more falsify the experience than do similar differences in the accounts of Paul's conversion [Acts 9, 22, 26] or the differences in the gospel accounts of the ministry of Jesus.

[35]Bushman, *Joseph Smith and the Beginnings of Mormonism*, pp. 54–55.

[36]Joseph Smith taught in 1843: "The Father has a body of flesh and bones as tangible as man's; the Son also; but the Holy Ghost has not a body of flesh and bones, but is a personage of spirit." (*Doctrine and Covenants*, 130:22; cf. also *Words of Joseph Smith*, p. 170.) There is some question as to whether Joseph believed in 1820 (from the time of his First Vision) that God the Father had a physical body. It is possible to show that the Saints were teaching the materiality of God as early as 1836. Reverend Truman Coe, a Presbyterian minister who had lived among the Mormons in Kirtland, Ohio for four years, published the following in the August 11, 1836, *Ohio Observer:* "They [the Mormons] contend that the God worshiped by the Presbyterians and all other sectarians is no better than a wooden god. They believe that the true God is a material being

cept that a universal apostasy had taken place in the first century Christian Church, and that no religious denomination on earth had authority to act in the name of God; and (4) it was possible for man to ascend to celestial heights, to commune with holy beings, and to come to know the things of God. Some eighteen years after the initial theophany Joseph Smith would state his position in regard to the actual reality of his experience: "Though I was hated and persecuted for saying that I had seen a vision, yet it was true . . . I knew it, and I knew that God knew it, and I could not deny it, neither dare I do it, at least I knew that by so doing I would offend God and come under condemnation."[37]

As to his spiritual and emotional state following the vision, Joseph said simply: "My soul was filled with love and for many days I could rejoice with great joy and the Lord was with me but [I] could find none that would believe the heavenly vision."[38] In regard to the latter statement—that none would believe the account of the vision—Joseph described an experience with a Methodist minister some days after the vision. "I took occasion to give him an account of the vision which I had had. I was greatly surprised at his behavior, he treated my communication not only lightly but with great contempt, saying it was all of the Devil, that there was no such things as visions or revelations in these days, that all such things had ceased with the apostles and that there never would be any more of them."[39] In discussing the cause for such reaction by the clergy of the day, Richard Bushman has written:

> Newly reborn people customarily talked over their experiences with a clergyman to test the validity of the conversion. The preacher's contempt shocked Joseph. Standing on the margins of the evangelical churches, Joseph may not have recognized the ill repute of visionaries. The preacher reacted quickly, not because of the strangeness of Joseph's story but because of its familiarity. Subjects of revivals all too often claimed to have seen visions. In 1825 a teacher in the Palmyra Academy said he saw Christ descend "in a glare

---

composed of body and parts; and that when the Creator formed Adam in his own image, he made him about the same size and shape of God himself." (See Milton V. Backman, Jr., "Truman Coe's 1836 Description of Mormonism," *Brigham Young University Studies,* Vol. 17, no. 3 [Spring 1977], p. 346.)

[37]*Personal Writings of Joseph Smith*, p. 201.
[38]Ibid., p. 6.
[39]Ibid., p. 200.

of brightness exceeding the brilliancy of the meridian sun." The *Wayne Sentinel* in 1823 reported Asa Wild's vision of Christ in Amsterdam, New York, and the message that all denominations were corrupt. At various other times and places, beginning early in the protestant era, religious eccentrics claimed visits from divinity.

Bushman concluded: "The visions themselves did not disturb the established clergy so much as the messages that the visionaries claimed to receive."[40]

JOSEPH SMITH AND THE EXPANDING CANON

For Joseph Smith and his followers, the traditions of the past regarding scripture and revelations and canon were shattered by the First Vision. God had spoken again, the heavens were no longer sealed, and a new "dispensation" of truth was under way. "We believe all that God has revealed," the Mormon leader would write in 1842, "all that he does now reveal, and we believe that he will yet reveal many great and important things pertaining to the Kingdom of God."[41] As one writer has noted concerning the "dynamic scriptural process" of the Mormons:

Latter-day Saints hold a view of canon that does not restrict itself to God's revelations of the past, whether they be those which they revere in common with their fellow Christians or those believed uniquely by the Saints. Their view is broader: *the canon is not closed, nor will it ever be. To them, revelation has not ceased; it continues in the Church. Future revelation is not only viewed as theoretically possible; it is needed and expected,* as changing circumstances in the world necessitate new communication from God. This view of canon and scriptural authority is the legacy of Joseph Smith. . . .[42]

---

[40]*Joseph Smith and the Beginnings of Mormonism,* pp. 58–59.

[41]Article of Faith #9; in *Personal Writings of Joseph Smith,* p. 219. The "Articles of Faith" are thirteen statements of belief prepared by Joseph Smith in 1842 as part of a lengthier statement for John Wentworth, editor of the *Chicago Democrat.* The "Wentworth Letter" will be presented in full later in this volume.

[42]Kent P. Jackson, "Latter-day Saints: A Dynamic Scriptural Process," in *The Holy Book in Comparative Perspective,* ed. Frederick M. Denny and Rodney L. Taylor (Columbia, South Carolina: University of South Carolina Press, 1985), p. 63, italics added.

The Book of Mormon

Over three years passed from the time of Joseph Smith's first visionary experience, and during that interim he had simply refrained from joining any of the existing churches in the area. On the evening of September 21, 1823, Joseph knelt in prayer to determine his standing before God, inasmuch as he had enjoyed no further communication with the heavens since 1820. In his own words, Joseph (now seventeen years old) stated that

> while I was praying unto God, and endeavoring to exercise faith in the precious promises of scripture on a sudden a light like that of day, only of a far purer and more glorious appearance, and brightness burst into the room, indeed the first sight was as though the house was filled with consuming fire; that appearance produced a shock that affected the whole body; in a moment a personage stood before me surrounded with a glory yet greater than that with which I was already surrounded.[43]

The angel announced himself as Moroni and explained that "God had a work for me to do, and that my name should be had for good and evil among all nations kindreds and tongues, or that it should be both good and evil spoken of among all people. He said there was a book deposited written upon gold plates, giving the account of the former inhabitants of this continent and the source from whence they sprang. He also said that the fulness of the everlasting Gospel was contained in it as delivered by the Savior to the ancient inhabitants."[44] In describing the plates, as well as the manner in which he translated them, Joseph said:

> These records were engraven on plates which had the appearance of gold, each plate was six inches wide and eight inches long and not quite so thick as common tin, they were filled with engravings, in Egyptian characters and bound together in a volume, as the leaves of a book with three rings running through the whole. The volume was something near six inches in thickness, a part of which was sealed. The characters on the unsealed part were small, and beautifully engraved. The whole book exhibited many marks of antiq-

---

[43]*Personal Writings of Joseph Smith*, pp. 213–14.
[44]Ibid., p. 203.

uity in its construction and much skill in the art of engraving. With the records was found a curious instrument which the ancients called "Urim and Thummim," which consisted of two transparent stones set in the rim of a bow fastened to a breastplate.

Through the medium of the Urim and Thummin I translated the record by the gift, and power of God.[45]

For the Latter-day Saints, the Book of Mormon is an additional book of scripture, "another testament of Jesus Christ." The majority of the Book of Mormon deals with a group of Hebrews (descendants of the tribe of Joseph) who leave Jerusalem in the first year of the reign of the King Zedekiah (ca. 600 B.C.E.), anticipating (being divinely directed concerning) the overthrow of Judah by the Babylonians. These travel south and eventually set sail for a "promised land," a land "choice above all other lands." The early story highlights the dissension between Nephi, a righteous and obedient leader of his people, and his rebellious and murmuring brothers, Laman and Lemuel. Eventually the internal squabbles result in a total break of the migrants into two separate bodies of people—the followers of Nephi (Nephites) and the followers of the older brother (Lamanites). The remainder of the Book of Mormon is essentially a story of the constant rise and fall of the Nephite nation (not unlike the accounts of the children of Israel contained in 2 Kings), as the people either choose to obey God or yield to the enticings of riches and pride.

The book of 3 Nephi, chapters 11–28, contains an account of a visit and brief ministry of Jesus Christ to the Nephites in America, following his death and ascension in Palestine. While teaching and comforting these "other sheep," Jesus organizes a church and establishes standards for a Christian community. An era of peace and unity follows for almost two hundred years, as the people see to the needs of one another through having "all things in common." The misuse of material blessings eventually leads to pride and class distinctions, resulting in a continuation of the former struggles between good and evil. The story of the Book of Mormon culminates in a final battle between the Nephites and Lamanites, in which the former (who had

---

[45]Ibid., pp. 214–15. A number of persons since Joseph Smith have speculated as to the method by which the golden plates were translated. For treatments of this matter, see Richard Van Wagoner and Steven C. Walker, "Joseph Smith: The Gift of Seeing," *Dialogue*, Vol. 15, No. 2 (Summer 1982), pp. 49–68; Paul R. Chessman, *The Keystone of Mormonism: Little Known Truths About the Book of Mormon* (Salt Lake City: Deseret Book Co., 1973), pp. 33–56.

proven over time to be more wicked than their idolatrous enemies) are exterminated. The history and divine dealings of the people from the time of Nephi had been kept by the prophets or civic leaders, and the final task of completing and editing the thousand-year collection of metal plates remained for the Prophet-leader Mormon (for whom the book/collection is named) and his son, Moroni, in about 400 C.E.

In 1841 Joseph Smith "told the brethren [the Twelve Apostles] that the Book of Mormon was the most correct of any book on earth, and the keystone of our religion, and a man would get nearer to God by abiding by its precepts, than by any other book."[46] In regard to the matter of the correctness of the Book of Mormon, an Article of Faith of the LDS Church—prepared by Joseph Smith—states: "We believe the Bible to be the word of God as far as it is translated correctly; we also believe the Book of Mormon to be the word of God."[47] In an early chapter in the Book of Mormon (1 Nephi 13), the youthful prophet Nephi (ca. 600 B.C.E.) beheld in vision the coming forth of the Bible, and also saw that many plain and precious truths as well as "many covenants of the Lord" would be taken from the Bible—a "record which proceeded forth from the mouth of a Jew"—before it was fully collected and canonized. Thus Joseph Smith believed that through difficulties in both transmission and translation, the world had never had a complete Bible. He would later remark: "I believe the bible, as it ought to be, as it came from the pen of the original writers."[48] Joseph Smith loved the Bible, acknowledged it as an inspired and God-given work, quoted from it extensively, and offered scriptural exegesis upon literally hundreds of passages.[49] At the same time, he was aware of what he perceived to be its limitations, its fallibility. The Book of Mormon, a product of only one translation—a translation which he contended was accomplished via miraculous intervention—was thus more correct in the sense that it contained many of the "plain and precious truths" that had been removed during the period from original writing to eventual collection and canonization.

Today the story of Joseph Smith's First Vision is generally the beginning point of discussion on Mormonism. Such may not have always been the case. It appears that until the 1880's the missionary appeal of Mormonism was centered in the Book of Mormon, rather than in the First Vision. Many persons in the nineteenth century claimed revelation from God, claimed visions and oracles. But the

---

[46]*History of the Church,* 4:461.
[47]Article of Faith #8; in *Personal Writings of Joseph Smith,* p. 219.
[48]*Words of Joseph Smith,* p. 256.
[49]See, for example, ibid., pp. 421–25.

Book of Mormon made Joseph's claims somewhat different, inasmuch as it represented to many a tangible evidence of divine intervention in history. People "touched the book, and the realization came over them that God had spoken again. Apart from any specific content, the discovery of additional scripture in itself inspired faith in people who were looking for more certain evidence of God in their lives."[50]

Joseph Smith as Oracle

Joseph the Prophet claimed an affinity with the heavens and those who ministered there—this in spite of the fact that he maintained his humanity. In appearance, according to one associate, Joseph Smith was "in person tall and well built, strong and active; of light complexion, light hair, blue eyes, very little beard, and of an expression peculiar to himself, on which the eye naturally rested with interest, and was never weary of beholding. His countenance was ever mild, affable, beaming with intelligence and benevolence; mingled with a look of interest and an unconscious smile, or cheerfulness, and entirely free from all restraint or affectation."[51] As to Joseph's fun-loving nature, Benjamin F. Johnson noted: "As a companion, socially, he was highly endowed—was kind, generous, and mirth loving. For amusements, he would sometimes wrestle a friend, or others; would test his strength with others by sitting upon the floor with feet together and stick grasped between them. But he never found his match. Jokes, rebuses, matching couplets in rhymes, etc., were not uncommon. But to call for the singing of one or more of his favorite songs was more frequent."[52] Another member of the Church remarked that after Joseph had been in hiding for some time and thereafter came out, "he would play with the people, and he was always cheerful and happy whenever he would come out. He was different in that respect from [his older] Brother Hyrum, who was more sedate, more serious. I thought at the time that Hyrum seemed more like a

---

[50]Bushman, *Joseph Smith and the Beginnings of Mormonism,* p. 142; see also Jan Shipps, *Mormonism: The Story of a New Religious Tradition* (Urbana/Chicago: University of Illinois Press, 1985), pp. 25–39. See also an excellent discussion of the Book of Mormon in the nineteenth century in Timothy L. Smith, "The Book of Mormon in a Biblical Culture," *Journal of Mormon History,* vol. 7 (1980), pp. 3–21.

[51]Parley P. Pratt, *Autobiography of Parley P. Pratt* (Salt Lake City: Deseret Book Co., 1976), p. 45.

[52]From a letter of Benjamin Johnson to George S. Gibbs, 1903; Church Historian's Library, Salt Lake City, Utah.

prophet than Joseph did. You see, there was a great deal of sectarianism about me."[53]

The latter comment by Rachel Grant—the surprise and often shock associated with Joseph Smith's congenial manner—is worth a moment's reflection. There were some people, both within and without the Church, who had great difficulty reconciling their personal conceptions of a prophet with what they found in Joseph Smith. One investigator of Mormonism lost interest in the Church when, in his own words, he found that Joseph was "not such a looking man as I expected to see. He looked green and not very intelligent. I felt disappointed and returned home."[54] "I have played ball with him many times," observed William Moore Allred. "But it was quite a stumbling block to some. After some had found fault about it, he was preaching one day and told a story about a certain prophet who was sitting under the shade of a tree amusing himself in some way. A hunter came along and reproved him. The prophet asked the hunter if he always kept his bow strung up. 'Oh, no,' said he. 'Why not?' 'Because it would lose its elasticity.' Said the prophet: 'It is just so with my mind. I do not want it strung up all the time.' "[55]

As indicated earlier, for Joseph Smith spirituality was a state to be enjoyed in the here and now; man did not need to leave the earth to draw upon the powers and knowledge of heaven. It was essential that man as a receptacle and recipient of revelation be clean and free from contaminating influences of major sin,[56] but no man or woman was required to live either a monastic or an ascetic existence to enter into the realm of divine experience. "I have heard the Prophet say," stated Edward Stevenson, "that he did not claim perfection, but possessed human weaknesses. He said, 'When I speak as a man it is Joseph only that speaks. But when the Lord speaks through me, it is no more Joseph Smith who speaks; but it is God.' "[57]

Brigham Young described Joseph Smith under the influence of Godly powers in the following way: "Those who were acquainted

---

[53]Rachel R. Grant, *Young Woman's Journal,* XVI (December, 1905), pp. 550–51.

[54]"Journal of Luman Andrus Shurtliff," p. 19; in Special Collections, Harold B. Lee Library, Brigham Young University, Provo, Utah; see also Donna Hill, *Joseph Smith: The First Mormon* (New York: Doubleday, 1977), chapter 1; Marvin S. Hill, "Joseph Smith the Man: Some Reflections on a Subject of Controversy," *Brigham Young University Studies,* Vol. 21, No. 2 (Spring 1981), pp. 175–86.

[55]From the diary of William Moore Allred, Church Historian's Library, Salt Lake City, Utah.

[56]See, for example, *Doctrine and Covenants,* 50:26–29; 67:9–11, 93:1.

[57]From "Autobiography of Edward Stevenson," cited in Andrus, *They Knew the Prophet,* p. 87.

with him knew when the spirit of revelation was upon him, for his countenance wore an expression peculiar to himself while under that influence. He preached by the spirit of revelation, and taught in his council by it, and those who were acquainted with him could discover it at once, for at such times there was peculiar clearness and transparency in his face."[58] William E. McLellin, an early apostle who later became disaffected from the Mormon Church, wrote: "As to Joseph Smith revealing, he would usually seat himself and seem to be in deep contemplation for a few moments, then commence for a few moments, and deliver a sentence or part of a sentence to his scribe, who would write it down, then read it vocally, then Joseph Smith would deliver more—and so on until the communication was finished. Smith never wrote any himself, he always had a scribe to write for him."[59] On the occasion when Joseph Smith received a vision regarding the afterlife and the differing kingdoms or degrees of glory (called the "Vision of the Glories,"—given later in this volume under "Three Degrees of Glory: Many Mansions of the Father"), one man, Philo Dibble, recorded the following:

> The vision of the three degrees of glory which is recorded in the *Doctrine and Covenants* [section 76] was given at the house of "Father Johnson," in Hiram, Ohio, and during the time that Joseph and Sidney [Rigdon] were in the Spirit and saw the heavens open there were other men in the room, perhaps twelve, among whom I was one during part of the time—probably two-thirds of the time. I saw the glory and felt the power, but did not see the vision.
>
> Joseph wore black clothes, but at this time seemed to be dressed in an element of glorious white, and his face shone as if it were transparent, but I did not see the same glory attending Sidney.
>
> The events and conversation, while they were seeing what is written (and many things were seen and related that are not written) I will relate as minutely as is necessary.
>
> Joseph would, at intervals, say: "What do I see?" as one might say while looking out the window and beholding what all in the room could not see. Then he would relate what he had seen or what he was looking at.
>
> Then Sidney replied, "I see the same."

[58]*Journal of Discourses*, 9:89.
[59]From letter of William E. McLellin, dated May 7, 1877; cited in *Salt Lake Tribune*, December 4, 1985.

Presently Sidney would say, "What do I see?" and would repeat what he had seen or was seeing. And Joseph would reply, "I see the same."

This manner of conversation was repeated at short intervals to the end of the vision, and during the whole time not a word was spoken by any other person. Not a sound or motion was made by anyone but Joseph and Sidney, and it seemed to me that they never moved a joint or limb during the time I was there, which I think was over an hour, and to the end of the vision.[60]

Joseph Smith was known to his people as a Modern Oracle, one through whom the word of God had come in the "dispensation of fulness of time." Those who were closest to him knew that he was not perfect, but they possessed perfect confidence in his abilities to lead the people in the manner that God intended. "Joseph Smith . . . claimed for himself no special sanctity, no faultless life, no perfection of character, no inerrancy for every word spoken by him," stated one LDS historian. "Yet to Joseph Smith," he continued, "was given access to the mind of Deity, through the revelations of God to him."[61]

Joseph Smith's Translation of the Bible

In June of 1830, just three months after the publication of the Book of Mormon, Joseph Smith began a careful study of the King James Version of the Bible and prepared what came to be known as a "new translation," an "inspired translation," or an "inspired version" of the Bible.[62] This task he pursued actively through July 2, 1833. Working without the use of ancient languages or manuscripts, Joseph suggested changes in the text that ought to be made, according to what he felt to be the spirit of revelation. Recognizing (from his work with the Book of Mormon) that many truths had been taken away or

---

[60]*Juvenile Instructor,* Vol. 27, pp. 303–4.

[61]B. H. Roberts, *A Comprehensive History of the Church of Jesus Christ of Latter-day Saints,* 6 Vols. (Salt Lake City: The Church of Jesus Christ of Latter-day Saints, 1930), 2:260–61.

[62]The definitive treatment of Joseph's work with the King James Bible is Robert J. Matthews, *"A Plainer Translation": Joseph Smith's Translation of the Bible—A History and Commentary* (Provo, Utah: Brigham Young University Press, 1975). For a brief treatment of the process, see Robert L. Millet, "Joseph Smith's Translation of the Bible: A Historical Overview," in *The Joseph Smith Translation: The Restoration of Plain and Precious Things,* ed. Monte S. Nyman and Robert L. Millet (Provo, Utah: Religious Studies Center, Brigham Young University, 1985), pp. 23–49. See also Richard P. Howard, *Restoration Scriptures* (Independence, Mo: Herald Publishing House, 1969).

kept back from the Bible before its compilation, he set out to restore many of those things that were lost.

There was nothing particularly unusual about a new translation of the Bible in the 1830's. As discussed earlier, religious revivalism reached a peak in the New York area in the early nineteenth century, and with it came a heightened awareness of the need for the Bible as a divine standard for living. New England was not the only section of the country which manifested an intense interest at this time in a study and scrutiny of the Bible. Records indicate that from 1777 to 1833 more than 500 separate editions of the Bible (or parts thereof) were published in America.[63] Many of these represented new translations or "modern translations," often with an attempt to prepare paraphrased editions or alternate readings based on comparisons with Hebrew and Greek manuscripts.

Joseph Smith's "translation" was, however, quite different. Here there were no language skills and no manuscripts with which to work. Joseph believed that he had been called of God to serve as a translator, as well as a prophet, seer and revelator.[64] On October 8, 1829 Joseph Smith and an associate, Oliver Cowdery, had purchased a large pulpit-style edition of the King James Bible (containing the Old and New Testaments and Apocrypha) in Palmyra, New York. It was this Bible which was used in the translation.[65] It appears that Joseph would read the Bible aloud and dictate alterations to a scribe who then recorded the changes on manuscript pages. In all, Joseph Smith suggested changes in 3,410 verses. Some of the books which received more revisions than others were (the number indicates the number of verses which differ from the King James text):[66]

Old Testament		*New Testament*	
Genesis	662	Matthew	483
Exodus	66	Luke	563
Psalms	188	John	159
Isaiah	178	Romans	118
		I Cor.	68
		Hebrews	47
		Revelation	75

---

[63]Margaret T. Hills, *The English Bible in America* (New York: The American Bible Society, 1961); E. B. O'Callaghan, *A List of Editions of the Holy Scriptures and Parts Thereof, Printed in America Previous to 1860* (Albany: Munsell and Rowlan, 1861).

[64]See *Doctrine and Covenants*, 21:1; 107:91–92; 124:125.

[65]See Matthews, *"A Plainer Translation,"* p. 26.

[66]Ibid., pp. 424–25.

Although the most intense period of the Bible work took place between 1830 and 1833, Joseph spent the rest of his life (until 1844) preparing the manuscripts for publication. In fact, the "inspired translation" was never published during the Prophet's lifetime, but was made available to the public in complete published form in 1867.[67] Joseph Smith took this project very seriously and considered it to be a "branch of his calling"[68] as prophet and restorer of the ancient order of things. Numerous revelations in the present book of *Doctrine and Covenants* (to be discussed below) make reference to the work of translation, and Smith taught that a number of revelations came as a direct result of the translation.[69]

The Doctrine and Covenants

Inasmuch as Joseph Smith claimed divine authority to speak for God, it was but natural that revelations and oracles would be recorded by those associated with the Church he founded in 1830. In fact, in a revelation received by Joseph in November of 1831, we find a demonstration of the broadened concept of scripture, one still held by the Latter-day Saints. This revelation stated that the elders of the Church "shall speak as they are moved upon by the Holy Ghost. And whatsoever they shall speak when moved upon by the Holy Ghost shall be scripture, shall be the will of the Lord, shall be the mind of the Lord, shall be the word of the Lord, shall be the voice of the Lord, and the

---

[67]After Joseph's death the manuscripts were held by his widow, Emma. In 1866 Emma made the manuscripts and the Bible available to the Reorganized Church of Jesus Christ of Latter Day Saints, a group which was formed a number of years after the death of Joseph and which felt that the proper mode of prophetic succession was according to lineal descent. (See Matthews, "*A Plainer Translation*," chapters 4, 6–8.)

[68]*History of the Church*, 1:238.

[69]See Robert L. Millet, "Joseph Smith's Translation of the Bible and the *Doctrine and Covenants*," in *Studies in Scripture, Vol. 1: The Doctrine and Covenants*, ed. Robert L. Millet and Kent P. Jackson (Sandy, Utah: Randall Book Co., 1984), pp. 132–43. There has been much discussion in recent years as to the nature of this translation. Some scholars of the Old and New Testaments have questioned Joseph's use of the word "translation," inasmuch as the Mormon Prophet utilized neither ancient manuscripts nor ancient languages in his work with the King James Bible. While many from the more conservative element of Mormonism consider the translation to be largely an inspired restoration of ancient texts once lost before compilation, others tend to view the work as a type of prophetic paraphrase or modern midrash, inasmuch as few of the Prophet's alterations are reflected in the most ancient extant manuscripts. For examples of the former positions, see Matthews, "*A Plainer Translation*"; Millet, "The Joseph Smith Translation: A Historical Overview"; for the latter view, see Anthony A. Hutchinson, "The Joseph Smith Revision and the Synoptic Problem: An Alternative View," *John Whitmer Historical Association Journal*, Vol. 5 (1985), pp. 47–53; Kevin L. Barney, "The Joseph Smith Translation and Ancient Texts of the Bible," *Dialogue: A Journal of Mormon Thought*, Vol. 19, No. 3 (Fall, 1986), pp. 85–102.

power of God unto salvation."[70] In 1831 the leaders of the Church began to compile the revelations received by Joseph Smith to date, and by 1833 that collection was known as *A Book of Commandments for the Government of the Church of Christ,*[71] a volume consisting of approximately sixty-four of the present sections of the *Doctrine and Covenants.* Mob violence in Missouri led to the destruction of the press and the loss of all but a few copies of the *Book of Commandments.* In August of 1835 Joseph Smith published the first edition of *The Doctrine and Covenants,* an expanded form of the *Book of Commandments,* a collection which contained an additional forty-five revelations. Today the *Doctrine and Covenants* consists of 138 divisions called "sections" and two "Official Declarations."[72]

Sections 1–135 are revelations or official statements that came as a part of the ministry of Joseph Smith. One section (no. 136) is considered to be a revelation of Brigham Young, Joseph Smith's successor in the leadership of the Church (1844–77), and another (no. 138) is to Joseph F. Smith, a nephew of the founding Prophet, and President of the Church, 1901–18. Official Declarations 1 and 2 are proclamations by Wilford Woodruff (President of the Church, 1889–98) and Spencer W. Kimball (President of the Church, 1973–85), respectively. Like all who have followed Joseph Smith in the presidency of the Church, these four men are viewed by Latter-day Saints as prophets, and their canonized statements are therefore considered to be revelations of the mind of God.[73]

A glimpse through the *Doctrine and Covenants* reveals that most of the revelations recorded (over sixty) were received during the Ohio era of the Church's history, over twenty were received in Mis-

---

[70]*Doctrine and Covenants,* 68:3–4.

[71]The Church was formally organized in Fayette, New York on April 6, 1830 and was called the "Church of Christ." It was later known as the "Church of the Latter-day Saints," and was finally given its present name in a revelation received in 1838. (See *Doctrine and Covenants,* 115:4.)

[72]The most complete history of the *Doctrine and Covenants* to date is Robert J. Woodford, "The Historical Development of the *Doctrine and Covenants,*" unpublished Ph.D. Dissertation, Brigham Young University, 1974. An excellent but abbreviated publication history of the *Doctrine and Covenants* is Woodford, "The *Doctrine and Covenants:* A Historical Overview," in Millet and Jackson, *Studies in Scripture, Vol. 1: The Doctrine and Covenants,* pp. 3–22. See also a work by Lyndon W. Cook entitled *The Revelations of the Prophet Joseph Smith* (Salt Lake City: Deseret Book Co., 1985).

[73]Jackson, "Latter-day Saints: A Dynamic Scriptural Process," p. 75.

souri, and less than ten were recorded in the *Doctrine and Covenants* in Illinois. At the same time, most LDS scholars agree that the Nauvoo, Illinois period (1839–46) proved to be a time of doctrinal depth, a span of years when Joseph Smith's thought reached its peak in profundity.[74] One historian has perceived the earlier revelations (New York, Pennsylvania, Ohio) as evidence of Joseph's role as "the Lord's Spokesman," a time wherein God spoke and his mouthpiece dictated and recorded the oracles. On the other hand, the later Illinois period might be viewed as evidence of a spiritually maturing role for Joseph—"the Spokesman for the Lord," an era when the Prophet dictated some revelations but also made known the mind of the Lord through speeches, sermons, and informal doctrinal discussions.[75]

The Pearl of Great Price

In 1850 Franklin D. Richards, a young member of the Mormon Quorum of the Twelve Apostles, was called to serve as the President of the British Mission of the Church. Richards discovered a paucity of either LDS scripture or even Church literature among the Saints in England, this in spite of the fact that a larger number of members resided in the British Isles at this time than in the United States.[76] In 1851 he published a mission tract entitled "The Pearl of Great Price," a collection of translations and narrations from Joseph Smith, essentially a type of prophetic potpourri. Interest in and appreciation for Richards' tract quickly caught on, and by 1880 the entire Church voted to accept "The Pearl of Great Price" as the fourth "standard work," the fourth book of scripture in the LDS canon.

The contents of "The Pearl of Great Price" (1981 edition) are as follows:

1. "Selections from the Book of Moses." This eight-chapter section is taken directly from Joseph Smith's translation of Genesis 1:1–8:18. In addition, there is an extra-biblical account of a vision by Moses which serves as a type of preface to the entire Book of Moses. Matters discussed here include a pre-mortal existence of man; the

---

[74]See T. Edgar Lyon, "Doctrinal Development of the Church During the Nauvoo Sojourn, 1839–1846," *Brigham Young University Studies,* Vol. 15, no. 4 (Summer 1975), pp. 435–46.

[75]See James R. Christianson, "A Ray of Light in an Hour of Darkness," in Millet and Jackson, *Studies in Scripture, Vol. 1: The Doctrine and Covenants,* pp. 463–75.

[76]A brief but excellent background of the Pearl of Great Price is H. Donl Peterson, "The Birth and Development of 'The Pearl of Great Price,' " in *Studies in Scripture, Vol. 2: The Pearl of Great Price,* ed. Robert L. Millet and Kent P. Jackson (Sandy, Utah: Randall Book Co., 1985), pp. 11–23.

creation of the earth; the fall of Adam and Eve; the rise of the kingdom of Satan and the proliferation of evil secret societies; a lengthy section (over 100 verses) on the call, ministry, and ultimate translation of Enoch; and a brief account of Noah and his sons before the deluge.

2. "The Book of Abraham." In the summer of 1835 Joseph Smith and a number of Latter-day Saints purchased a collection of Egyptian antiquities, an important part of which were two papyrus scrolls. Joseph Smith translated these documents and published the results as the "Book of Abraham" in March of 1842, an extra-biblical account of the struggles and successes of the patriarch Abraham. There is also an account of the pre-mortal life of man, as well as the creation of man and all forms of life.[77]

3. "Joseph-Smith-Matthew." This is Joseph Smith's translation of Matthew 23:39–24:55. Joseph Smith alters the text somewhat, making a distinction between the more immediate prophecies (destruction at the hands of the Romans in 70 C.E.) and the signs incident to Christ's Second Coming in glory.

4. "Joseph Smith-History." This section of the "Pearl of Great Price" is an excerpt from the Prophet's 1838 history of the Church, and details of the particulars concerning the origins and growth of the movement from 1820–1838.

5. "The Articles of Faith." The Articles of Faith are thirteen simple statements of religious belief by Joseph Smith and his followers, articles intended to be neither creedal nor comprehensive. They were a part of a letter written by Joseph Smith to John Wentworth, editor of the *Chicago Democrat*.

---

[77]Again with the Book of Abraham we come face to face with the concept of "translation." Joseph Smith claimed to have translated the papyrus scrolls from Egyptian into English by the gift and power of God. A number of years after the death of the Mormon Prophet-Leader, the scrolls were sold by his widow and their whereabouts were unknown for some time. It was supposed by many Latter-day Saints that the antiquities had made their way to a museum in Chicago and had thus been destroyed by the Chicago fire of 1871. In 1967 Dr. Aziz Atiya, former director of the University of Utah's Middle East Center, found eleven fragments of papyrus while browsing in New York's Metropolitan Museum of Art. Atiya, not a Mormon himself but nevertheless familiar with the "Pearl of Great Price," recognized immediately one of the original illustrations from the Book of Abraham. Arrangements were thereafter made to have the fragments transferred to the LDS Church. Scholars immediately began to translate the fragments and found them to be portions of Egyptian funerary texts, parts of a "book of breathings," seemingly having little if anything to do with the life and ministry of the patriarch Abraham. Debate ensued and has continued to the present regarding the authenticity and origin of the material now had by the Mormons as the Book of Abraham.

Joseph Smith, the Scriptures, and Worship

"The sacred writings of the Latter-day Saints," observes one scholar, "perform a *practical* function within the faith; they are not used in any kind of ritual situation. They are not used in chanting, reciting, or praying, or in any similar rite. They contain no saving powers nor powers to bless; nor is reading them a sacramental act. In Latter-day Saint theology the reading of scripture functions as a means to achieving an important end—education in the principles of the faith so that one can be in harmony with the will of God."[78] For Joseph Smith scripture delivered an invitation to witness "God's own handwriting," and he felt that "he who reads it oftenest will like it the best, and he who is acquainted with it, will know the hand [of God] wherever he can see it."[79]

For the Mormon Prophet, the scriptures were to be pondered and meditated upon. Joseph Smith himself provided a pattern for pondering in the description of his early (1820) experience with the biblical passage in James: "I reflected upon it again and again, knowing that if any person needed wisdom from God, I did, for how to act I did not know and unless I could get more wisdom than I then had I would never know."[80] Both repeated reflection (meditation) upon the scripture, as well as personal application of the verses ("likening the scriptures") were here involved. For Joseph Smith the scriptures provided both timely and timeless guides for living—a universal blueprint for daily practice. "When this fact is admitted," he said in 1834, "that the immediate will of heaven is contained in Scripture, are we not bound as rational creatures to live in accordance to all its precepts?"[81]

Finally, searching and pondering the scriptures could lead one to have his own personal experience with Deity—to come to hear the voice of God. In a revelation dictated by Joseph Smith in June of 1829, God spoke in regard to the scriptures: "These words are not of men nor of man; wherefore, you shall testify that they are of me and not of man. For it is my voice which speaketh them unto you; for they are given by my Spirit unto you and by my power you can read them one to another; and save it were by my power you could not have

---

[78]Jackson, "Latter-day Saints: A Dynamic Scriptural Process", p. 79.
[79]*History of the Church,* 2:14.
[80]*Personal Writings of Joseph Smith,* p. 199.
[81]*History of the Church,* 2:11.

them; *wherefore, you can testify that you have heard my voice, and know my words.*"[82]

ZION: QUEST FOR THE CITY OF GOD

The term "Zion" first appears in the biblical narrative in conjunction with David's conquest of Jerusalem, in which it is written that David has taken "the stronghold in Zion: the same is the City of David." (2 Sam 5:6–10.) With the movement of the Ark of the Covenant to the Temple Mount, "Zion" came to be used interchangeably with the idea of the holy mountain of Yahweh. "Great is the Lord," wrote the Psalmist, "and greatly to be praised in the city of our God, in the mountain of his holiness. Beautiful for situation, the joy of the whole earth, is mount Zion." (Ps 48:1–2.) "Sons of Zion" (Ps 149:2; Joel 2:23) or "daughters of Zion" (Is 3:16; Zech 9:9) came to refer to the men and women in Jerusalem who were recipients of either God's wrath or his blessing.

Through the ultimate defeat of the powers of evil, the "city" of the Lord, the Zion of the Holy One of Israel" (Is 60:14) was to be established. Christian writers, using and extending the spiritual aspect of the Zion motif, thus contrasted the fiery and tempestuous experience of Moses and the Israelites (under the Law) at the base of Sinai with the blessed state of the righteous Christian in a future day: "But ye are come unto Mount Zion, and unto the city of the living God, the heavenly Jerusalem, and to an innumerable company of angels . . . and to Jesus, the mediator of the new covenant." (Heb 12:22–24.)

It may well have been in the Book of Mormon that Joseph Smith first employed a different usage for the word "Zion." Other than on those occasions in the record where Isaiah is cited,[83] the word Zion is used in what some would consider a most unusual way. Note the following verses from the Book of Mormon:

---

[82] *Doctrine and Covenants,* 18:34–36, italics added; see a modern commentary upon these verses by Bruce R. McConkie, late apostle of the Mormon Church, in *Ensign,* December 1985, p.59.

[83] Twenty-one complete chapters of Isaiah and excerpts from others are quoted in the Book of Mormon. The Nephite people claimed to have access to another set of records (the "plates of brass") before leaving Jerusalem, which contained essentially the Old Testament record down to the time of Jeremiah.

And blessed are they who shall seek to *bring forth my Zion* at that day, for they shall have the gift and power of the Holy Ghost.[84]

He [God] commandeth that there shall be no priest-crafts; for behold, priestcrafts are that men preach and set themselves up for a light unto the world, that they may get gain and praise of the world; but *they seek not the welfare of Zion.*

Behold, the Lord hath forbidden this thing; wherefore, the Lord God hath given a commandment that all men should have charity, which charity is love. And except that they should have charity, they were nothing. Wherefore, if they should have charity *they would not suffer the laborer in Zion to perish.*

But the laborer in Zion shall *labor for Zion;* for if they labor for money they shall perish.[85]

For behold, at that day shall he [Satan] rage in the hearts of the children of men, and stir them up to anger against that which is good.

And others will he pacify, and lull them away into carnal security, and they will say: *All is well in Zion; yea, Zion prospereth,* all is well . . . and thus the devil cheateth their souls, and leadeth them away carefully down to hell.

Therefore, *wo be unto him that is at ease in Zion.*[86]

Verily, verily, I say unto you [Christ speaking to the Nephites during his ministry among them], thus hath the Father commanded me—that I should give unto this people this land for their inheritance.

And then the words of the prophet Isaiah shall be fulfilled, which say:

Thy watchmen shall lift up the voice; with the voice together shall they sing, for they shall see eye to eye *when the Lord shall bring again Zion.*[87]

---

[84]1 Nephi 13:37, italics added.
[85]2 Nephi 26:29–31, italics added.
[86]2 Nephi 28:20–21, 24, italics added.
[87]3 Nephi 16:16–18, quoting Isaiah 52:8.

The use of the word Zion in the Book of Mormon is thus seen to be much broader that a reference to the Old Testament city of Jerusalem. Zion is to be established or "brought forth" under God's direction, and those who fight against it are to incur the displeasure of the Almighty. From other passages Zion is used to describe what appears to be a *community* or *society* of the believers. This society is one in which the citizens are to labor for "the welfare of Zion" and not for personal aggrandizement; further, the members of the community are to avoid the attitude that "all is well in Zion." (Cf. Amos 6:1) The words of Jesus in 3 Nephi 16 are instructive in the fact that a prophecy from Isaiah (52:8) is given a unique interpretation. The inheritance of the land of America by the decendants of the tribe of Joseph and the establishment of a holy people there, is seen to be a fulfillment of the prophecy that the Lord "shall bring again Zion."

In the early revelations to the Mormon Prophet a similar notion of Zion as a holy community or a society of believers is evident. Joseph Smith and Oliver Cowdery were instructed in April of 1829: "Keep my commandments, and seek to bring forth and establish *the cause of Zion.*"[88] At the time of the organization of the Church (April of 1830) a revelation stated: Joseph Smith "have I inspired to move the *cause of Zion.*"[89]

A journal entry of Joseph Smith in December of 1830 (regarding his work of Bible translation) is instructive:

> It may be well to observe here, that the Lord greatly encouraged and strengthened the faith of his little flock . . . which had embraced the fulness of the everlasting Gospel, as revealed to them in the Book of Mormon, by giving some more extended information upon the Scriptures, a translation of which had already commenced. Much conjecture and conversation frequently occurred among the Saints, concerning the books mentioned, and referred to, in various places in the Old and New Testaments, which were now nowhere to be found. The common remark was, "They are lost books"; but it seems the Apostolic Church had some of these writings, as Jude mentions or quotes the prophecy of Enoch, the seventh from Adam. To the joy of the little flock . . . did the

---

[88]*Doctrine and Covenants*, 6:6, italics added, cf. 11:6; 12:6; 14:16.
[89]Ibid., 21:7, italics added.

Lord reveal the following doings of olden times, from the prophecy of Enoch.[90]

Whereas the biblical record in Genesis 5 contains only three verses descriptive of the ministry of Enoch, the Joseph Smith translation (JST) of the corresponding parts of Genesis consists of over one hundred verses. A careful reading of the JST text reveals the following regarding Enoch:

1. At the age of sixty-five Enoch was called of God to cry repentance to a wicked people.

2. Though shy, hesitant, and slow of speech, Enoch was given divine assurance and promised great power: "Behold my spirit is upon you, wherefore all thy words will I justify; and the mountains shall flee before you, and the rivers shall turn from their course; and thou shalt abide in me; therefore walk with me." (JST, Gen 6:36.)

3. Enoch became a seer, and was given a knowledge of "things which were not visible to the natural eye." (JST, Gen 6:38.)

4. Enoch's preaching led many people to repent. The people became so righteous that "the Lord came and dwelt with his people, and they dwelt in righteousness." Further, "the fear of the Lord was upon all nations, so great was the glory of the Lord, which was upon his people." (JST, Gen 7:20–21.)

5. Enoch established an economic order to care for the poor and needy. *"And the lord called his people Zion, because they were of one heart and one mind, and dwelt in righteousness, and there was no poor among them."* The city of Enoch came to be known as *"the City of Holiness, even Zion."* (JST, Gen 7:23, 25, italics added)

6. Enoch saw in a vision a future day when the "elect" would be gathered to a "holy City," a latter-day community that "shall be called Zion, a New Jerusalem." (JST, Gen 7:70.)

7. Enoch and his city were eventually translated or taken into heaven without experiencing death. "And Enoch and all his people walked with God, and he dwelt in the midst of Zion; and it came to pass that Zion was not, for God received it up into his own bosom; and from thence went forth the saying, Zion is fled." (JST, Gen 7:77–78.)

It will be seen in what follows that Joseph Smith's "Enoch Experience" was pivotal in the quest for a Zion society—a holy city or New Jerusalem—among the Mormons. Enoch became the pattern, the scriptural prototype by which all social or economic programs were to

---

[90]*History of the Church,* 1:131–33.

be judged. From the 1830's into the twentieth century, the Latter-day Saints would be encouraged by their leaders to be "one of heart" and to seek out the poor among them. In essence:

> The vision of Enoch . . . helped define Zion's social order, which was called on occasion the "city" or "order of Enoch." Enoch's city came to be the divine model for the Mormons' earthly undertakings, the platonic essence, if you will, of Smith's subsequent commandments and revelations on the subject. According to this vision, Zion's ideal urban order would be permeated by religion. Religion, not politics, would insure domestic tranquility. Religion, not the military, would provide for a common defense. Religion, not economics, would promote the general welfare.

In short, "the vision of Enoch gave theological, cosmological, eschatological, social, and personal sanction to the quest for Zion. Strains of these ideas had been present in Mormonism prior to the vision, but the vision integrated and energized them in a powerful and unmistakable manner."[91]

For Joseph Smith, personal spirituality was of lasting value only to the degree that one could then translate godly attributes into Christian living in society. The quest for Zion was the Prophet's attempt to transform individuals who were "pure in heart"[92] into an entire commonwealth of believers. Zion had been established anciently by Enoch, and God had now called a modern Enoch to replicate ancient practices and establish a "New Jerusalem." In placing things in perspective, the Prophet remarked: "The building up of Zion is a cause that has interested the people of God in every age; it is a theme upon which prophets, priests, and kings have dwelt with particular delight; they have looked forward with joyful anticipations; they have sung and written and prophesied of this our day; but they died without the sight; we are the favored people that God has made choice of to bring about the Latter-day glory."[93]

---

[91]Steven L. Olsen, "Zion: The Structure of a Theological Revolution," *Sunstone,* Vol. 6, no. 6 (November/December 1981), p. 24.

[92]A revelation recorded on August 2, 1833 stated: "Therefore, verily, thus sayeth the Lord, Let Zion rejoice, for this is Zion—THE PURE IN HEART; therefore, let Zion rejoice, while all the wicked shall mourn." (*Doctrine and Covenants,* 97:21.)

[93]*History of the Church,* 4:609–10.

Zion and Mormon Society

The establishment of a Zion society entailed more to Joseph Smith than simply the explication of religious doctrine on Sunday mornings. Although as we have noted, religion was the basis or foundation for such a community, yet the challenge of the Church leadership was to so structure the activities of the citizens as to engender the principles of Zion within all phases of life on all days of the week. Zion was to stand as a banner, an *ensign* to the people of the earth.

> Zion as the heart of the kingdom of God was to be an ensign and a standard to the world, that all men might look to her and pattern their lives and their social arrangements after her example of truth and righteousness. An ensign is a distinguished flag or banner, used in ancient times to direct the actions of men, such as in a military campaign. As an ensign to the world in the last days, Zion was to be a rallying point of truth—a true banner of freedom, justice, union, and human dignity—to attract the attention of all men and direct them into the paths of peace and progression.
>
> As a messenger before the Lord, the society of Zion was to be a nucleus of the millennial kingdom—an opening wedge—containing the basic principles and powers through which, eventually, peace and good will could be established universally among men. The divine system was to be developed among the Saints first, and then expanded throughout the earth as the millennial kingdom of Christ was ushered in.[94]

To achieve this exalted end, the Mormon Prophet stressed that the Saints must achieve a level of personal integrity that would qualify them to be known as the "pure in heart." While striving for purity of heart, it was expected that the Latter-day Saints apply the proper standards of judgment to every facet of life, so as to insure that all programs and policies were grounded in the truth. "Behold, I, the Lord, have made my church in these last days like unto a judge sitting on a hill, or in a high place, to judge the nations. For it shall come to pass that the *inhabitants of Zion shall judge all things pertaining to Zion.*"[95]

---

[94]Hyrum L. Andrus, *Doctrines of the Kingdom* (Salt Lake City: Bookcraft Publishers, 1973), pp. 28–29.

[95]*Doctrine and Covenants,* 64:37–38, italics added.

Joseph Smith and the early Mormon leaders repeatedly emphasized that "the greatest and most important labor we have to perform is to cultivate ourselves."[96] The society of Zion was to effect a synthesis of all that was ennobling and enjoyable, and was to make available to its people all that was meant to "please the eye and gladden the heart." The members of Zion, though under strict covenantal obligations to their God and to each other, were not to be ascetics, but were to enjoy life, to find happiness and enrichment in everyday activities, and were to have "cheerful hearts and countenances."[97] It was not only the elect *people* that were to be gathered to Zion; in addition, "every accomplishment, every polished grace, every useful attainment in mathematics, music, in all science and art belong to the Saints, and they . . . rapidly collect the intelligence that is bestowed upon the nations, for *all this intelligence belongs to Zion.*"[98]

Debates were a common occurrence in the early Mormon communities and for some time were held weekly.[99] These were sponsored "for the purpose of eliciting truth, acquiring knowledge, and improving public speaking."[100] In the journal of Joseph Smith under the date December 12, 1835, is found the following entry: "In the evening attended a debate at Brother William Smith's on the following question—Was it necessary for God to reveal Himself to mankind in order for their happiness? I was on the affirmative and the last to speak on that side of the question."[101] Also very prevalent in early Mormon social life were art exhibits, lyceums, museums, and drama.[102] "There is no true enjoyment in life," stated Brigham Young, "nothing that can be a blessing to an individual or a community, but what is ordained of God to bless his people."[103]

The above statement by Brigham Young evidences the Mormon belief that no lasting enjoyment was to be had independent of God and his laws. The "spirit of Zion" was to permeate all phases of life. The following ideas in regard to music, attributed to Joseph Smith, demonstrate even more forcefully the Zion spirit that was meant to be part of every facet of life:

---

[96]Brigham Young, *Journal of Discourses,* 10:2.
[97]*Doctrine and Covenants,* 59:15–18.
[98]Brigham Young, *Journal of Discourses,* 10:224, italics added; cf. 8:279.
[99]*History of the Church,* 2:317, 330; 4:514.
[100]Ibid., 4:514.
[101]Ibid., 2:330.
[102]Ibid., 6:349–50, 471; *Times and Seasons,* Vol. 4, pp. 201–3 (the *Times and Seasons* was the official Church newspaper in Nauvoo, Illinois); *Juvenile Instructor,* Vol. 27 (June 15, 1892), p. 399.
[103]*Journal of Discourses,* 6:143.

He [Joseph] recommended the Saints to cultivate as high a state of perfection in their musical harmonies as the standard of faith which he had brought was superior to sectarian religion. To obtain this, he gave them to understand that *the refinement of singing would depend upon the attainment of the Holy Spirit. . . . When these graces and refinements and all the kindred attractions are obtained that characterized the ancient Zion of Enoch, then the Zion of the last days will become beautiful,* she will be hailed by the Saints from the four winds, who will gather to Zion with songs of everlasting joy.[104]

An axiom of religious faith among the Mormons was delivered to the members by their Prophet in 1833: "The glory of God is intelligence, or, in other words, light and truth."[105] "In knowledge there is power," Joseph taught in 1843. "God has more power than all other beings, because he has greater Knowledge, and hence he knows how to subject all other beings to him."[106] Thus it was that education assumed a prominent position among Mormon priorities from the very beginning. Schools were established for adults as well as children. For some time Joseph Smith directed a number of men in what came to be known as the "School of the Elders" or "School of the Prophets." Although theology was at the core of all that was studied, a revelation declared that this body of men should immerse itself in a varied curriculum—"things both in heaven and in the earth, and under the earth; things which have been, things which are, things which must shortly come to pass; things which are at home, things which are abroad; the wars and the perplexities of the nations, and the judgments which are on the land; and a knowledge also of countries and of kingdoms."[107] In addition, Joseph Smith and a group of his colleagues studied and taught English grammar and Biblical Hebrew.[108]

The philosophy of education in Zion placed theology at the "hub of the wheel," while the secular disciplines served as "spokes." For Joseph Smith, disciplines of study had meaning only as they extracted the same from the religion of Zion. Persons were encouraged to "seek

---

[104]Joseph Young, "Vocal Music," *History of the Organization of the Seventies* (Salt Lake City: Deseret Steam Printing Establishment, 1878), pp. 14–15.

[105]*Doctrine and Covenants,* 93:36.

[106]*Words of Joseph Smith,* p. 183.

[107]*Doctrine and Covenants,* 88:79.

[108]*History of the Church,* 2:301, 363, 376–77; 3:26.

learning, even by study and also by faith."[109] This divine directive suggested that "Zion represented a new synthesis—the combination of separate and subordinate elements of thought into a new form, a new whole—in which all known truth would be integrated into the supreme truth of Christ, and be exalted and sanctified by His divine power." Further:

> Consistent with this approach, Joseph Smith's philosophy of education suggested the need, first, for a practical program to assist the Saints to acquire divine truth by revelation through the Holy Spirit; and, second, for a program to promote learning by human reason and analysis, and to integrate that knowledge into the central core of spiritually acquired truth. On the basis that the Saints would follow this approach, the Prophet encouraged them to seek for and acquire knowledge in all fields of inquiry.[110]

Joseph the Seer taught his followers the New Testament principle that "whosoever . . . will be a friend of the world is an enemy of God." (Jas 4:4.) The people in Zion had been "called out of the world" into a fellowship separate and apart from the world. This approach to Christianity, identified by H. Richard Niebuhr as a stance of "Christ against culture," clearly defined the duty of the believer to abandon and reject the world of the rebellious and unbelieving.

> The counterpart of loyalty to Christ and the brother is the rejection of cultural society; a clear line of separation is drawn between the brotherhood of the children of God and the world. Save in two instances (1 Jn 2:2; 4:14) the word "world" evidently means for the writer of the letter (1 Jn) the whole society outside the church, in which, however, the believers live. . . . That world appears as a world under the power of evil; it is the region of darkness, into which the citizens of the kingdom of light must not enter. . . . It is a secular society, dominated by the "lust of the flesh, the lust of the eyes and the pride of life . . ."[111]

---

[109]*Doctrine and Covenants,* 88:118.

[110]Andrus, *Doctrines of the Kingdom,* p. 135.

[111]H. Richard Niebuhr, *Christ and Culture* (New York: Harper & Row, Publishers, 1951), pp. 47–48.

For the Mormons the challenge was to live *in* the world but not be *of* the world. The world and the worldly were frequently called "Babylon," and the people of Zion were directed to "go ye out from among the nations, even from Babylon, from the midst of wickedness, which is spiritual Babylon."[112] Ancient Babylon was the capital of the powerful Babylonian empire. Babylon came to represent (to Judah and Israel) all that was carnal and wicked. It followed that New Testament writers would apply the title "Babylon" to the forces of evil in the world (Rev. 17, 18). For the Saints under Joseph Smith's leadership, the proclamation was: Zion must grow and develop, while Babylon, Zion's counterpart, must eventually decay and fall. "Zion must increase in beauty, and in holiness; her borders must be enlarged; her stakes must be strengthened; yea . . . Zion must arise and put on her beautiful garments."[113] Conversely, the citizens of Babylon "seek not the Lord to establish his righteousness, but every man walketh in his own way, and after the image of his own God, whose image is in the likeness of the world, and whose substance is that of an idol, which waxeth old and shall perish in Babylon, even Babylon the great, which shall fall."[114] The two cities (not unlike St. Augustine's City of God and City of Man) were pointed in opposite directions; the Prophet taught the utter impossibility of maintaining a hold upon Babylon while concurrently standing in Zion. In the words of one nineteenth-century Church leader, one influenced a great deal by Joseph Smith, "God has commanded his people to come out of Babylon. We are trying to do it. *We are trying to establish a new order of society, not to tear down the old, but to establish a new order that will grow and increase,* and be better than the old one. *Everything connected with this people has for its design the renovation of the earth from the evils which exist at the present day.*"[115]

For the Mormons, persons of other religious persuasions were not to be shunned, nor their teachings rejected outright. Joseph Smith continued to maintain that the Church of Jesus Christ of Latter-day Saints was the "only true and living church" on earth, yet the Mormon Prophet also stressed the fact that truth was to be found in all religious sectors. "One of the grand principles of 'Mormonism' is to receive truth, let it come from whence it may," he observed in 1843.[116] Further, "We don't ask any people to throw away any good they have got;

---

[112] *Doctrine and Covenants,* 133:14.
[113] Ibid., 82:14.
[114] Ibid., 1:16.
[115] George Q. Cannon, *Journal of Discourses,* 22:367, italics added.
[116] *History of the Church,* 5:499.

we only ask them to come and get more."[117] When visited in Illinois by a Methodist minister, Joseph was extremely cordial and open. "I suppose none but Mormon preachers are allowed in Nauvoo," said the minister to the Prophet. "On the contrary," Joseph remarked, "I shall be very happy to have you address my people next Sunday, and I will assure you a most attentive congregation." "What!" the minister exclaimed, "do you mean that I may say anything I please and that you will make no reply?" "You may certainly say anything you please; but I must reserve the right of adding a word or two, if I judge best. I promise to speak of you in the most respectful manner."[118]

Zion and the Economy

As mentioned earlier, the period of the early nineteenth century is often characterized as a time of significant movements: in geography, in values, in institutions. This movement of body and mind was, however, not purposeless: many people were shaking themselves loose from their moorings and were busily in search of new ideas, of a "better way." In particular, the generation was in the throes of social revolution, a phenomenon which has been identified as a natural and inevitable result of a pluralistic way of life.[119]

A common idea of the times was that paradise or Eden or Utopia was to be had only through changing society; some were committed to the axiom that human behavior is altered only through the manipulation of the human environment. From this posture flowed the concept of a "beloved community," a model city, a pure society. Many reformers of the nineteenth century sought to restore the practices (as well as the beliefs) of New Testament Christianity. One set of scriptural passages that held special significance for those bent upon change and restoration is found in the Acts of the Apostles. Here is described a Christian community, a group of believers who "were of one heart and soul," who "had all things [in] common," and who structured society in such a way as to create a colony in which there were not "any among them that lacked." (Acts 4:32–34.) In the nineteenth century, such groups as the United Society of Believers in Christ's Second Appearing (the Shakers), led originally by Mother Ann Lee; John Humphrey Noyes and the Oneida Perfectionists; and

---

[117]Ibid., p. 259.

[118]Cited in Josiah Quincy, *Figures of the Past* (Boston: Roberts Brothers, 1883), pp. 392–93.

[119]Michael Novak, *The Spirit of Democratic Capitalism* (New York: Simon & Schuster, 1982), Chapter 9.

Jemima Wilkinson and her "New Jerusalem" community all represented novel approaches to solving family and social problems.[120]

One of the most interesting preludes to the establishment of an economic system among the Latter-day Saints was the organization of certain individuals into a group called "the family." A group was organized based on the patterns found in the New Testament, and settled upon a farm owned by Isaac Morley near Kirtland, Ohio. The situation at the Morley farm in early 1831 was a total common stock arrangement, and members of "the family" were expected to love one another, share all things, and thereby become "of one heart and one soul." As one would suppose, difficulties soon arose. John Whitmer, a Church historian commissioned by Joseph Smith, wrote of this experience: "The disciples had all things in common, and were going to destruction very fast as to temporal things for they considered from reading the scripture that what belonged to a brother, belonged to any of the brethren. Therefore they would take each others clothes and other property and use it without leave which brought on confusion and disappointment, for they did not understand the scripture."[121] "The family" was dissolved as the word of the "Restored Gospel" through Joseph Smith began to take hold in the city of Kirtland. Joseph recorded a simple statement in his journal regarding the Morley farm episode: "This plan of 'common stock,' which had existed in what was called 'the family' . . . was readily abandoned for the more perfect law of the Lord."[122]

Zion represented the fusion of the temporal and the spiritual: seemingly temporal matters had a spiritual basis and were given to achieve divine purposes; spiritual laws were kept and spiritual goals attained through the proper utilization of temporal resources. A revelation given in 1830 stated that all things were spiritual to the Almighty, and that a truly temporal law or commandment had never been given to his earthly servants.[123] Joseph Smith taught his followers further that "the order of Enoch . . . is in reality the Order of Heaven. It was revealed to Enoch when he built up his city and gathered the people together and sanctified them, so that they be-

---

[120]See Lawrence Foster, *Religion and Sexuality* (New York: Oxford University Press, 1981) for a detailed discussion of the Shakers, the Oneida community and the Mormons; see also George C. Bedell, Leo Sandon, Jr., and Charles T. Wellborn, *Religion in America* (New York: MacMillan, 1975), pp. 189–91.

[121]*An Early Latter Day Saint History: The Book of John Whitmer, Kept by John Whitmer,* ed. F. Mark McKiernan and Roger D. Launius (Independence, Mo: Herald Publishing House, 1980), p. 37.

[122]*History of the Church,* 1:146–47.

[123]*Doctrine and Covenants,* 29:34.

came so holy that they could not live among the rest of the people and the Lord took them away."[124] The early Mormons came to understand that in the Zion of Enoch the people were not only righteous—they were just and equitable. That is, the ancient city of Zion was translated, not alone because the people were "of one heart and one mind," or because they "dwelt in righteousness," but also because "there was no poor among them." They accepted the scriptural axiom that those who are not equal in earthly things could not be equal in obtaining heavenly things.[125]

On February 9, 1831, the Latter-day Saint Prophet dictated what has come to be known as a revelation embracing "the law of the Church." In this section of the present *Doctrine and Covenants* (section 42) is introduced "the Law of Consecration and Stewardship," some principles of the economic order the Saints believe were implemented by Enoch and his people. The basis of consecration and stewardship was self-denial and brotherly love, and these principles were intended to minimize and eventually eliminate inequalities and class distinctions. It was a system to be entered into by choice, as a matter of free will. One entered by *consecrating* or giving to the Lord, through the local bishop (the immediate pastor or Church officer), all personal property or holdings. In return, there was deeded back to the person an inheritance or *stewardship* which was to be managed, the nature and size of that stewardship being determined by the individual's circumstances, family, just wants, and needs.[126] It might be, therefore, that a person would, after consultation with the bishop, be issued a stewardship that consisted of exactly the same holdings as he had consecrated, depending upon the result of consultation between individual and Church leader.

Though all of the logistical details are not available to historians of Mormonism as to exactly how equality was to be maintained after the granting of stewardships had occurred, one matter was certain: in

---

[124]Brigham Young, *Journal of Discourses,* 13:2.

[125]*Doctrine and Covenants,* 78:6.

[126]Ibid., 51:3–4; 82:17. The idea of a "stewardship" was prevalent in early American thought, and had a great deal to do with the Puritan attitude toward their possessions. "In the Puritan mind the biblical idea of the stewardship was coupled with the idea of the covenant. The doctrine of stewardship held that God had given to His faithful servants a special charge to oversee not just their own material possessions, but the Lord's vineyard (in their case, New England) in its entirety. In other words, the Puritans believed themselves to be responsible for the well-being of the whole commonwealth. It comes as no surprise, then, to learn that they designed for themselves a highly regulated society. Wages and prices were set, production quotas assigned, commerce carefully managed, interest rates controlled." (Bedell et al., *Religion in America,* p. 295.)

the initial stages of this order, surplus consecration (that amount above and beyond what a man needed after his initial consecration) and surplus production (any excess beyond personal family needs resulting from proper management of the stewardship), were not to be kept by the steward; they became a part of the community *storehouse*. The storehouse was the center of economic interests in the community. Funds from the storehouse (from surplus consecration and production) were to be used for such things as care of the needy, community improvements, expansion of stewardships, and creation of new stewardships.[127]

As one might suppose, the inability of the average man to place his neighbor's interests before his own would be a practical stumbling block to the realization of an economic order whose success depended almost entirely upon selflessness and altruism. For a time it seemed as though the "law of consecration and stewardship" would be successful, that the Latter-day Saints would achieve Zion status just as Enoch had done anciently. But human weaknesses and opposition from the non-Mormon segment of the population stood in the way. The selfishness of the Saints seemed to manifest itself in a refusal to recognize and surrender one's surplus. "Go around among the Saints," one Mormon apostle of the nineteenth century said, "and there has been only now and then a man who had any surplus property [if we] let him be the judge."[128] Further: "Our own judgment! Who in the world among the Latter-day Saints would have any surplus property if it is left to his own judgment?"[129] It remains, however, for the frontier wisdom and wit of Brigham Young to describe graphically the problem of selfishness among the early Mormons:

> Some were disposed to do right with their surplus property, and once in a while you would find a man who had a cow which he considered surplus, but generally she was of the class that would kick a person's hat off, or the wolves had eaten off her teats. You would once in a while find a man who had a horse he considered surplus, but at the same time he had the ringbone, was broken-winded, spavined in both legs, and the pole evil at one end of the neck and a fistula at the other, and both knees sprung.[130]

---

[127]*Doctrine and Covenants*, 42:34–35; 83; 104:6, 77.
[128]Orson Pratt, *Journal of Discourses*, 17:110.
[129]Orson Pratt, *Journal of Discourses*, 16:157.
[130]*Journal of Discourses*, 2:307.

A number of adjustments were made in the initial system of consecration and stewardship during the years 1831–44,[131] and to a degree the Saints enjoyed some measure of success in establishing an "order of Enoch" among them. Differing approaches to achieving a cooperative community were attempted in the Great Basin during the latter part of the nineteenth century, but eventually the leaders of the Saints called for a cessation of many of the particular practices of the early law.[132] By 1844, as one historian has noted, "Joseph Smith believed that spiritual commitment and love were higher expressions of consecration than land deeds and legal stewardship agreements. In Missouri, signed documents were required as proof of inner spiritual commitment. At Nauvoo [Illinois] the verbal covenants of the faithful were sufficient. Both anticipated a total commitment of a member's resources."[133]

Zion as Covenant Society

W. D. Davies once observed in an address at Brigham Young University that "Christianty has forgotten its Jewish roots."

> Mormonism arose in a place and time when many utopian, populist, socialistic ideas were in the air. It gave these a disciplined, organized American outlet and form: what it did was re-Judaize a Christianity that had been too much Hellenized. . . . Mormonism certainly injected and I hope will continue to inject, into the American scene the realism of Judaism and thus challenged a too-Hellenized Christianity to renew its contact with its roots in Israel.[134]

Joseph Smith's hold upon ancient Israel and commitment to a "covenant theology" was strengthened in at least seven ways. First, the Latter-day Saints placed great stock in the Old Testament and felt a kinship with its characters and events. Second, the Saints' acceptance

---

[131]An excellent treatment of the different phases of the Law of Consecration and Stewardship is Lyndon W. Cook, *Joseph Smith and the Law of Consecration* (Provo, Utah: Grandin Book Co., 1985).

[132]See Leonard J. Arrington, Feramorz Y. Fox, and Dean L. May, *Building the City of God: Community and Cooperation Among the Mormons* (Salt Lake City: Deseret Book Co., 1976).

[133]Cook, *Joseph Smith and the Law of Consecration,* p. 93.

[134]"Israel, the Mormons and the Land," Paper Presentation at Brigham Young University, March 10–11, 1978, in *Reflections on Mormonism: Judaeo–Christian Parallels,* ed. Truman G. Madsen (Provo, Utah: Religious Studies Center, Brigham Young University, 1978), pp. 91–92.

of the Book of Mormon further tied them to Israel, inasmuch as the Book of Mormon is essentially a narrative and commentary upon God's dealings with another branch of the House of Israel. Third, Joseph Smith and the Mormons saw themselves as Israel wandering toward a promised land, "in the beginning of the rising up and the coming forth of my church out of the wilderness."[135] Fourth, Joseph taught his people that they were of the actual physical lineage of Jacob of old, literally modern children of Israel. "The Mormons," noted Davies, "are a continuation of what the Fathers of the Christian Church were to come to call the Old Israel. But for the Mormons there is no old Israel. They simply regard themselves as Israel in a new stage of its history."[136] Fifth, as children of Israel, the inhabitants of Zion were "covenant" people, participants in what the revelations to Joseph called the "New and Everlasting Covenant," the fulness of the gospel. Sixth, in 1833 Joseph Smith recorded a revelation which specified the need for abstinence from alcohol, tobacco, coffee, and tea.[137] This dietary and health law (accepted by the Saints then and now as of even greater spiritual value than physical) was easily likened unto the laws of health and ritual purity as practiced by ancient Israel. Finally, in Mormonism the center of all religious activity was the Temple. Like Israel of old, the ritual and religion of the holy temple helped the Saints to circumscribe all truth into a great whole, and gave meaning to all that was undertaken in a city of holiness. The temple was the navel of the earth, the center of all things, the point of intersection between the heavens and the earth.

The Prophet taught that through baptism and reception of the Holy Ghost, members entered into convenantal obligations with their God and with one another. Initiates into the faith made solemn agreements of both a horizontal and vertical nature. In regard to the former, Saints agreed to love, serve, and be sensitive to others' needs. Some of their promises to Deity consisted in keeping the commandments, maintaining personal integrity and purity, and standing as witnesses of God at all times. In return, God promised his Spirit to guide his people into all truth, until eventually they could qualify for the greatest of all divine endowments—eternal life.[138]

In summary, the attainment of Zion was for Joseph Smith and the Latter-day Saints the hope of the ages, the realization of spirituality in the community. It was a constant thrust of the Prophet. Indeed, in

---

[135]*Doctrine and Covenants,* 5:14; cf. 33:5.
[136]"Israel, the Mormons, and the Land," p. 81.
[137]*Doctrine and Covenants,* 89.
[138]See Book of Mormon, Mosiah 18:8–10.

the words of Joseph, "we ought to have the building up of Zion as our greatest object."[139]

Joseph Smith's focus was forever on the ideal, the achievement of a holy society. The realization of such an ideal is certainly more realistic when the citizens of the City of God are able to pursue life unhindered by the views and lifestyles of the unbelievers. But, as is so often the case, the ideal inevitably engages the practical and the "people of the covenant" are required to confront a pluralistic society.

The task of the early Latter-day Saints to build Zion and decry Babylon was indeed a formidable one. And there were times when the Mormon zeal for Zion seems to have exceeded their wisdom. In the early 1830's the New England-bred Mormons moved into the borders of the frontier in Independence, Missouri and announced boldly to the residents of the area that Jackson County, Missouri was the site of the center place of Zion, the future location of the "New Jerusalem." Further, the Latter-day Saints were the people of God, the area was to be given to them, and a holy commonwealth would soon eventuate. The reactions of the Missourians were predictable: the Mormons became an unpopular sect. Governor Dunklin of Missouri stated: "I am fully persuaded that the eccentricity of the religious opinions and practices of the Mormons is at the bottom of the outrages committed against them."[140] Add to this spark (religious zeal) such additional factors as the Mormons as a political threat (coming into the state in great numbers); their almost exclusive economic order; their abolitionist tendencies; and their love for the Indians, and one can see quickly that it was only a matter of time before a full-blown explosion resulted: the Latter-day Saints were eventually evicted from the state by order of the governor.[141]

The challenge of the citizens of Zion to live in the world but to avoid the "snares" of the world, the challenge to "flee from Babylon," has certainly been intensified during the century and a half of the Church's existence. In the face of what many would feel to be the secularization and fragmentation in society at large of such critical ingredients as education, the arts, and the family, the Latter-day Saints have entered upon a significant moment of truth: How much may aspects of Zion shift and still remain Zion-like? Is it possible for an ancient concept to have a contemporary image and approach to

---

[139]*History of the Church,* 3:390.

[140]Cited in *History of the Church,* 3:xlviii.

[141]See Warren E. Jennings, "Zion Is Fled: The Expulsion of the Mormons from Jackson County, Missouri," unpublished Ph.D. dissertation, University of Florida, 1962.

life? How does a Zion people interface with those outside the borders of belief to bring about good, without at the same time opening the doors to what are perceived to be the weaknesses of the world?

JOSEPH SMITH AND THE DEVOTIONAL LIFE

Spirituality is the "consciousness of victory over self, and of communion with the Infinite. Spirituality impels one to conquer difficulties and acquire more and more strength. To feel one's faculties unfolding and truth expanding the soul is one of life's sublimest experiences."[142] This statement, made by one of Joseph Smith's twentieth-century successors, aptly characterized Joseph's view of the spiritual and contemplative life. Mormons were instructed by the Prophet in his closing years that they were literally the children of God, that God was in reality an exalted man, and that man was thus of the same species as his Creator. Man was to pray to his Maker as "Our Father in heaven," and was to believe the words; the expression was more than metaphor or rhetoric—it was true.

Prayer

"Communion with the Infinite" was to be accomplished most often through personal prayer. Through sincere and pleading prayer man could come to know the will of the heavens, and could thereby live each day in accordance with that will. Joseph Smith taught and demonstrated that prayers should be simple and direct, never ostentatious or delivered for any reason other than to communicate with one's God. One member of the Church recalled: "Speaking about praying to our Father in heaven, I once heard Joseph Smith remark, 'Be plain and simple, and ask for what you want, just like you would go to a neighbor and say, I want to borrow your horse to go to the mill.' "[143] Another recollection of the Prophet demonstrates his practicality in prayer. It is as follows:

> In my early years I used to eat often at the table with Joseph the Prophet. At one time he was called to dinner. I was at play in the room with his son Joseph when he called us to him, and we stood one on each side of him. After he

---

[142]David O. McKay, *Gospel Ideals* (Salt Lake City: The Improvement Era, 1953), p. 390.
[143]Henry William Bigler, as cited in Andrus, *They Knew the Prophet*, p. 100.

had looked over the table he said, "Lord, we thank thee for this johnny cake, and ask Thee to send us something better. Amen."

The cornbread was cut and I received a piece from his hand. Before the bread was all eaten, a man came to the door and asked if the Prophet Joseph Smith was at home.

Joseph replied he was, whereupon the visitor said, "I have brought you some flour and a ham."

Joseph arose and took the gift, and blessed the man in the name of the Lord. Turning to his wife, Emma, he said, "I knew the Lord would answer my prayer."[144]

In typifying Joseph's experience with prayer on a more solemn occasion, Daniel Tyler recalled:

At the time William Smith and others rebelled against the Prophet at Kirtland, I attended meeting . . . where Joseph presided. Entering the school house a little before the meeting opened and gazing upon the man of God, I perceived sadness in his countenance and tears trickling down his cheeks. A few moments later a hymn was sung and he opened the meeting by prayer. Instead of facing the audience, however, he turned his back and bowed upon his knees, facing the wall. This, I suppose, was done to hide his sorrow and tears.

I had heard men and women pray—especially the former—from the most ignorant, both as to letters and intellect, to the most learned and eloquent. But never until then had I heard a man address his Maker as though He was present listening as a kind father would listen to the sorrows of a dutiful child. Joseph was at that time unlearned, but that prayer, which was to a considerable extent in behalf of those who accused him of having gone astray and fallen into sin, was that the Lord would forgive them and open their eyes that they might see aright. That prayer, I say, to my humble mind, partook of the learning and eloquence of heaven. There was no ostentation, no raising of the voice as by enthusiasm, but a plain conversational tone, as a man would address a present friend. It appeared to me as

---

[144]John Lyman Smith, in *The Juvenile Instructor,* Vol. 27 (15 March 1892), pp. 172–73.

though, in case the veil were taken away, I could see the Lord standing facing his humblest of all servants I had ever seen. It was the crowning of all the prayers I ever heard.[145]

Joseph Smith further explained (consistent with the New Testament) that *fasting,* when accompanied by prayer, would lead to a heightened spirituality and do much to bring down the powers of heaven. A revelation given in 1832 declared: "I give unto you a commandment that ye shall continue in prayer and fasting from this time forth."[146]

Receiving Revelation

From the time of his First Vision in the spring of 1820 until the time of his death, the Mormon Prophet-Leader contended that revelation was essential to the highest of eternal opportunities. "Salvation cannot come without revelation, it is in vain for anyone to minister without it."[147] Joseph stressed that revelation—communication from God to man—was essential in both a personal as well as an institutional sense. True enough, he would observe, the "living church" must have guidance from living oracles in order to function properly.[148] This, however, was only a part of the prerequisite. Baptized members of the Church were entitled to the gift and influences of the Holy Ghost, the member of the Godhead responsible for revealing matters of eternal import to people. "No man can receive the Holy Ghost without receiving revelations, The H. G. is a revelator," Joseph Smith said in 1843.[149]

Revelation, for the Mormons, was not independent of one's reason; in fact, both mind and heart were considered necessary in the reception and comprehension of oracles. "Behold, I will tell you in your mind and in your heart, by the Holy Ghost, which shall come upon you and which shall dwell in your heart. Now behold, this is the spirit of revelation."[150] In commenting upon this verse, one Latter-day Saint writer explained:

---

[145]Cited in Andrus, *They Knew the Prophet,* pp. 51–52.
[146]*Doctrine and Covenants,* 88:76; cf. 95:7; Book of Mormon, Omni 1:26; Alma 5:46; 17:3, 9; Helaman 3:34–35.
[147]*Words of Joseph Smith,* p. 10.
[148]*Doctrine and Covenants,* 1:30; 90:3–5.
[149]*Words of Joseph Smith,* p. 256.
[150]*Doctrine and Covenants,* 8:2–3.

We observe that neither [Oliver Cowdery] nor Joseph was to experience any suspension of their natural faculties in the process of obtaining revelation. Quite to the contrary, their hearts and minds were to be the very media through which the revelation came. Prophets are not hollow shells through which the voice of the Lord echoes, nor are they mechanical recording devices; prophets are men of passion, feeling, intellect. One does not suspend agency, mind, or spirit in the service of God. It is . . . with heart, might, mind and strength that we have been asked to serve, and in nothing is this more apparent than the receiving of revelation. There is no mindless worship or service in the kingdom of heaven.[151]

Joseph Smith taught that one of the greatest revelations a man or woman could receive was the peaceful assurance that the tests in mortality had been passed, that the Lord was pleased with one's performance in life, and that eternal life—the glory and life associated with the highest heaven hereafter—was a reality. To receive such an assurance was to receive the promise of salvation, the consummation of a process called "making one's calling and election sure." (Cf. 2 Pet 1.) One who had received this guarantee was also entitled, upon continued faithfulness, to an additional spiritual benefit, that which Jesus called "another Comforter" in the 14th chapter of John. "This is the sum & substance of the whole matter, that when any person obtains this last Comforter he will have the personage of Jesus Christ to attend him or appear unto him from time to time & even he will manifest the Father unto him & they will take up their abode with him, & the visions of the heavens will be opened unto him & the Lord will teach him face to face & he may have a perfect knowledge of the mysteries of the kingdom of God."[152] In sum, Joseph Smith believed that man is a child of God and, when worthy, is able to communicate with his exalted Father; it is likewise not out of the ordinary for God to speak to man, whether through feelings, thoughts, or open vision.[153]

A final statement from Joseph indicates his feelings about the matter of spirituality as a process, an arduous journey from the finite to the infinite, but a journey whose sublime by-products are worth the struggle.

---

[151]Joseph F. McConkie, "The Principle of Revelation," in Millet and Jackson, *Studies in Scripture, Vol. 1: The Doctrine and Covenants*, p. 83.

[152]*Words of Joseph Smith*, p. 5; cf. *Doctrine and Covenants*, 130:3.

[153]See *Doctrine and Covenants*, 6:14–24; 9:7–9; 76; 110; *Words of Joseph Smith*, pp. 5–6.

We consider that God has created man with a mind capable of instruction, and a faculty which may be enlarged in proportion to the heed and diligence given to the light communicated from heaven to the intellect, and that the nearer man approaches perfection, the clearer are his views, and the greater his enjoyments, till he has overcome the evils of his life and lost every desire for sin; and like the ancients, arrives at that point of faith where he is wrapped in the power and glory of his Maker, and is caught up to dwell with Him. But we consider that this is a station to which no man ever arrived in a moment. . . .[154]

THE CONCLUSION OF A MINISTRY

Few great religious innovators are completely understood. Frequently their existence is a lonely one. In spite of what Joseph the Prophet was able to make known to his people, he felt the desire to reveal so much more, often things which he sensed the people were not able to grasp. And some things which he did reveal proved to be extremely explosive and divisive in the Church.

It is traditionally believed among the Latter-day Saints that Joseph Smith first learned of the concept of plural marriage as early as 1831, while engaged in his work of Bible translation. While studying the lives of the ancient patriarchs and of such personalities as David and Solomon, Joseph noticed the frequency with which these men (acknowledged in the biblical account as worthy and noble) had taken more than one wife. His questions regarding the propriety and legality of such things resulted in a revelation concerning eternal and plural marriage, an oracle finally committed to writing in July of 1843.[155]

Joseph Smith shared many of the details of the revelation with intimate associates, particularly when he felt one could be trusted to value and preserve what he believed to be a sacred matter. Between 1831 and 1843 a number of the leaders of the Church were instructed

---

[154]*History of the Church,* 2:8.

[155]Works dealing with Mormon polygamy include Lawrence Foster, *Religion and Sexuality;* Danel Bachman, "A Study of the Mormon Practice of Plural Marriage Before the Death of Joseph Smith," M.A. Thesis, Purdue University, 1975; Linda King Newell and Valeen Tippetts Avery, *Mormon Enigma* (New York: Doubleday, 1984); Richard S. Van Wagoner, *Mormon Polygamy: A History* (Salt Lake City: Signature Books, 1986).

concerning the eternal marriage covenant (including plurality of wives) and were told that eventually many of the faithful would be called upon to comply with what Joseph declared to be the will of God. As one might expect, the practice of polygamy was not easily received, even by those who were otherwise counted as faithful. John Taylor, who became the third president of the Church, explained that "when this system was first introduced among this people, it was one of the greatest crosses that was ever taken up by any set of men since the world stood."[156] Helen Mar Whitney, who became one of Joseph's plural wives, recalled that Joseph "said that the practice of this principle would be the hardest trial the Saints would ever have to test their faith."[157]

Joseph Smith must have experienced the pangs of loneliness and frustration to a degree that few have known, for he felt as though he were being asked to stand between the law of God on one hand and the law of the land and accepted moral precepts and societal standards on the other. He believed and taught that God had commanded that plural marriage be practiced as an integral part of the "restoration of all things," a key element of the modern renewal and receipt of the "ancient order of things."

Other than the challenges associated with practicing plural marriage (which must have been immense), the Nauvoo, Illinois, era of Mormon history (1839–46) was a time of renewal and, for Joseph Smith, a time of spiritual refreshment. He was able to involve himself in civic affairs and to be a part of the lives of the people—to work as city planner, military leader, mayor, Church President, U.S. presidential candidate, and public speaker and orator. In Nauvoo the Mormon Prophet began to reveal what later generations have come to know as deeper doctrines, many of the more peculiarly LDS teachings. In Nauvoo he introduced the concept of salvation for the dead, the idea that members of the faith could receive the required sacraments or ordinances of the Church on behalf of dead friends or relatives; the importance of temples as holy sanctuaries wherein ordinances could be performed whereby parents and children could be "sealed" (by proper authority) as family units for eternity; and the doctrine of "eternal progression," the belief that man could progress, through faithful obedience, to the point of godhood.

In Nauvoo, Illinois, things erupted when certain persons who had been especially close to Joseph rebelled at his teachings and practices

---

[156]*Journal of Discourses,* 11:221.
[157]*Woman's Exponent 10* (November 1, 1881):83.

and denounced him as a fallen prophet. On June 7, 1844, a dissident newspaper entitled *Nauvoo Expositor* was released, an organ intent upon making public the views of those who felt a need for reformation in the Church of Jesus Christ of Latter-day Saints. Two central issues—areas of attack—were plural marriage and the Prophet's teachings concerning the nature of God: that the Almighty was an exalted man, was of the same species with mortal man, and that man could eventually become even as God Himself. "We are earnestly seeking to explode the vicious principles of Joseph Smith," the paper read, "and those who practice the same abominations and whoredoms." Further, "it is absurd for men to assert that all is well, while wicked and corrupt men are seeking our destruction, by a perversion of sacred things; for all is not well, while whoredoms and all manner of abominations are practiced under the cloak of religion." Regarding the doctrinal teachings of Joseph Smith: "Among the many items of false doctrine that are taught in the Church, is the doctrine of many Gods, one of the most direful in its effects that has characterized the world for many centuries. We know not what to call it other than blasphemy, for it is most unquestionably, speaking of God in an impious and irreverent manner."[158]

The Mormon Prophet ordered the press destroyed as a "public nuisance," and was jailed within a matter of days for what his enemies labeled as treasonous actions (impeding the freedom of the press). Joseph Smith, Jr., was murdered with his brother, Hyrum, in Carthage jail on Thursday, June 27, 1844, by a mob of between 150–200 persons. He was thirty-eight years old and at what many felt to be the zenith of his prophetic ministry.

It is often the case that important men and women live and die and they and their generation do not know just how great an impact has been made by their presence. Josiah Quincy, son of the President of Harvard University, and later himself the mayor of Boston, visited the Prophet Joseph Smith in Nauvoo, Illinois, in May of 1844. His retrospective impressions of that brief encounter are worthy of reflection:

> It is by no means improbable that some future textbook, for the use of generations yet unborn, will contain a question something like this: What historical American of the nineteenth century has exerted the most powerful influence upon the destinies of his countrymen? And it is by no means impossible that the answer to that interrogatory may

---

[158]*Nauvoo Expositor*, Vol. 1, No. 1 (June 7, 1844).

be thus written: *Joseph Smith, the Mormon Prophet.* And the reply, absurd as it doubtless seems to most men now living, may be an obvious commonplace to their descendants. . . . The man who established a religion in this age of free debate, who was and is to-day accepted by hundreds of thousands as a direct emissary from the Most High,—such a rare human being is not to be disposed of by pelting his memory with unsavory epithets. Fanatic, imposter, charlatan, he may have been; but these hard names furnish no solution to the problem he presents to us. Fanatics and impostors are living and dying every day, and their memory is buried with them; but the wonderful influence which this founder of a religion exerted and still exerts throws him into relief before us, not as a rogue to be criminated, but as a phenomenon to be explained.[159]

From within the fold came this tribute in 1837 to the Mormon leader, a statement by one who knew him well: "There is not so great a man as Joseph standing in this generation. The gentiles [non-Mormons] look upon him as he is like a bed of gold concealed from human view. They know not his principles, his spirit, his wisdom, his virtues, his philanthropy, nor his calling. His mind, like Enoch's, expands as eternity, and only God can comprehend his soul."[160]

Joseph Smith laid the foundation for what has become a world-wide movement. In a proclamation to the church membership dated January 1, 1845, Parley P. Pratt, one of the Mormon apostles, wrote of the impact of the church's founder:

He has organized the kingdom of God.—We will extend its dominion.

He has restored the fulness of the gospel.—We will spread it abroad.

He has laid the foundation of Nauvoo.—We will build it up.

He has laid the foundation of the Temple.—We will bring up the topstone with shouting.

He has kindled a fire.—We will fan the flame.

He has kindled up the dawn of a day of glory.—We will bring it to its meridian splendor.

---

[159]*Figures of the Past,* pp. 376–77.
[160]Wilford Woodruff, *Journal History,* entry for April 9, 1837.

He was a 'little one,' and became a thousand. We are a small one, and will become a strong nation.

In short, he quarried the stone from the mountain; we will cause it to become a great mountain and fill the whole earth.[161]

---

[161]*Millennial Star,* Vol. 5, pp. 151–52; cf. Daniel 2:35.

II.

PERSONAL REFLECTIONS

JOSEPH SMITH TELLS HIS OWN STORY (1838)

The text that follows is from the most complete history of Joseph Smith and the beginnings of Mormonism, a work begun in 1838. It was prepared to "set the record straight" or, in the words of Joseph, "to disabuse the public mind" of what the Saints perceived to be scandalous or at best inaccurate accounts of the movement. An edited version of this excerpt of the history has been formally canonized by the Latter-day Saints as "Joseph Smith-History" and is now a part of the "Pearl of Great Price." This text is from Personal Writings of Joseph Smith, *pp. 196–210.*

Owing to the many reports which have been put in circulation by evil disposed and designing persons in relation to the rise and progress of the Church of Jesus Christ of Latter day Saints, all of which have been designed by the authors thereof to militate against its character as a church, and its progress in the world; I have been induced to write this history so as to disabuse the publick mind, and put all enquirers after truth into possession of the facts as they have transpired in relation both to myself and the Church as far as I have such facts in possession.

In this history I will present the various events in relation to this Church in truth and righteousness as they have transpired, or as they at present exist, being now the eighth year since the organization of said Church.[1] I was born in the year of our Lord One thousand Eight hundred and five, on the twenty third day of December, in the town of Sharon, Windsor County, State of Vermont. My father Joseph

Smith Senior left the State of Vermont and moved to Palmyra, Ontario, (now Wayne) County, in the State of New York when I was in my tenth year. or thereabout.

In about four years after my father's arrival at Palmyra, he moved with his family into Manchester in the same County of Ontario. His family consisting of eleven souls, namely, My Father Joseph Smith, My Mother Lucy Smith whose name previous to her marriage was Mack, daughter of Solomon Mack, My brothers Alvin (who died Nov. 19th: 1823 in the 25 year of his age. ~~is now dead~~) Hyrum, Myself, Samuel-Harrison, William, Don Carloss, and my Sisters Soph[r]onia, Catherine, and Lucy. Sometime in the second year after our removal to Manchester, there was in the place where we lived an unusual excitement on the subject of religion. It commenced with the Methodists, but soon became general among all the sects in that region of country, indeed the whole district of Country seemed affected by it and great multitudes united themselves to the different religious parties, which created no small stir and division among the people, Some crying, "Lo here" and some Lo there. Some were contending for the Methodist faith, Some for the Presbyterian, and some for the Baptist; for notwithstanding the great love which the converts to these different faiths expressed at the time of their conversion, and the great Zeal manifested by the respective Clergy who were active in getting up and promoting this extraordinary scene of religious feeling in order to have everybody converted as they were pleased to call it, let them join what sect they please[d;] yet when the Converts began to file off some to one party and some to another, it was so that the seemingly good feelings of both the Priests and the Converts were ~~mere pretense~~ more pretended than real, for a scene of great confusion and bad feeling ensued; Priest contending against priest, and convert against convert so that all their good feelings one for another (if they ever had any) were entirely lost in a strife of words and a contest about opinions.

I was at this time in my fifteenth year. My Fathers family was proselyted to the Presbyterian faith and four of them joined that Church, Namely, My Mother Lucy, My Brothers Hyrum, Samuel Harrison, and my Sistesr Soph[r]onia.

During this time of great excitement my mind was called up to serious reflection and great uneasiness, but though my feelings were deep and often pungent, still I kept myself aloof from all these parties though I attended their several meetings as often as occasion would permit. But in process of time my mind became somewhat partial to the Methodist sect, and I felt some desire to be united with them, but

so great was the confusion and strife amongst the different denominations that it was impossible for a person young as I was and so unac-
quainted with men and things to come to any certain conclusion who
was right and who was wrong. My mind at different times was greatly
excited for the cry and tumult were so great and incessant. The Presbyterians were most decided against the Baptists and Methodists, and
used all their powers of either reason or sophistry to prove their
errors, or at least to make the people think they were in error. On the
other hand the Baptists and Methodists in their turn were equally
Zealous in endeavoring to establish their own tenets and disprove all
others.

In the midst of this war of words, and tumult of opinions, I often
said to myself, what is to be done? Who of all these parties are right?
Or are they all wrong together? And if any one of them be right which
is it? And how shall I know it?

While I was laboring under the extreme difficulties caused by the
contests of these parties of religionists, I was one day reading the
Epistle of James, First Chapter and fifth verse which reads, "If any of
you lack wisdom, let him ask of God, that giveth to all men liberally
and upbraideth not, and it shall be given him." Never did any passage
of scripture come with more power to the heart of man that this did at
this time to mine. It seemed to enter with great force into every
feeling of my heart. I reflected on it again and again, knowing that if
any person needed wisdom from God, I did, for how to act I did not
know and unless I could get more wisdom than I then had would
never know, for the teachers of religion of the different sects understood the same passage of scripture so differently as to destroy all
confidence in settling the question by an appeal to the Bible. At
length I came to the conclusion that I must either remain in darkness
and confusion or else I must do as James directs, that is, Ask of God.
I at last came to the determination to ask of God, concluding that if
he gave wisdom to them that lacked wisdom, and would give liberally
and not upbraid, I might venture. So, in accoradance with this, my
determination to ask of God, I retired to the woods to make the
attempt. It was on the morning of a beautiful clear day early in the
spring of Eighteen hundred and twenty. It was the first time in my life
that I had made such an attempt, for amidst all my anxieties I had
never as yet made the attempt to pray vocally.

After I had retired into the place where I had previously designed to go, having looked around me and finding myself alone, I
kneeled down and began to offer up the desires of my heart to God, I
had scarcely done so, when immediatley I was seized upon by some

power which entirely overcame me and had such astonishing influence over me as to bind my tongue so that I could not speak. Thick darkness gathered around me and it seemed to me for a time as if I were doomed to sudden destruction. But exerting all my powers to call upon God to deliver me out of the power of this enemy which had seized upon me, and at the very moment when I was ready to sink into despair and abandon myself to destruction, not an imaginary ruin but to the power of some actual being from the unseen world who had such a marvelous power as I had never before felt in any being. Just at this moment of great alarm I saw a pillar of light exactly over my head above the brightness of the sun, which descended ~~gracefully~~ gradually untill it fell upon me. It no sooner appeared than I found myself delivered from the enemy which held me bound. When the light rested upon me I saw two personages (whose brightness and glory defy all description) standing above me in the air. One of them spake unto me calling me by name and said (pointing to the other) "This is my beloved Son, Hear him." My object in going to enquire of the Lord was to know which of all the sects was right, that I might know which to join. No sooner therefore did I get possession of myself so as to be able to speak, than I asked the personages who stood above me in the light, which of all the sects was right, (for at this time it had never entered into my heart that all were wrong) and which I should join. I was answered that I must join none of them, for they were all wrong, and the Personage who addressed me said that all their Creeds were an abomination in his sight, that those professors were all corrupt, that "they draw near to me with their lips but their hearts are far from me, They teach for doctrines the commandments of men, having a form of Godliness but they deny the power thereof." He again forbade me to join with any of them and many other things did he say unto me which I cannot write at this time. When I came to myself again I found myself lying on my back looking up into Heaven. Some few days later after I had this vision I happened to be in the company with one of the Methodist Preachers who was very active in the before mentioned religious excitement and conversing with him on the subject of religion I took occasion to give him an account of the vision which I had had. I was greatly surprised at his behaviour, he treated my communication not only lightly but with great contempt, saying it was all of the Devil, that there was no such things as visions or revelations in these days, that all such things had ceased with the apostles and that there never would be any more of them. I soon found however that my telling the story had excited a great deal of prejudice against me among the professors of religion and was the cause of great persecution which continued to increase and though I was an obscure boy only between fourteen and fifteen years of age or thereabouts, and my circumstances in life such as to make a boy of no consequence in the world, yet men of high standing would take notice sufficiently to excite the public mind against me and create a hot persecution, and this was common among all the sects: all united to persecute me. It has often caused me serious reflection both then and since, how very strange it was that an obscure boy of a little over fourteen years of age and one too who was doomed to the necessity of obtaining a scanty maintainance by his daily labor should be thought a character of sufficient importance to attract the attention of the great ones of the most popular sects of the day so as to create in them a spirit of the bitterest persecution and reviling. But strange or not, so it was, and was often the cause of great sorrow to myself. However it was nevertheless a fact, that I had had a vision. I have thought since that I felt much like as Paul did when he made his defence before King Aggrippa and related the account of the vision he had when he saw a light and heard a voice, but still there were but few who beleived him, some said he was dishonest, others said he was mad, and he was ridiculed and reviled, But all this did not destroy the reality of his vision. He had seen a vision he knew he had, and all the persecution under Heaven could not make it otherwise, and though they should persecute him unto death yet he knew and would know to his latest breath that he had both seen a light and heard a voice speaking unto him and all the world could not make him think or believe otherwise. So it was with me, I had actualy seen a light and in the midst of that light I saw two personages, and they did in reality speak unto me, or one of them did, And though I was hated and persecuted for saying that I had seen a vision, yet it was true and while they were persecuting me reviling me and speaking all manner of evil against me falsely for so saying, I was led to say in my heart, why persecute me for telling the truth? I have actually seen a vision, "and who am I that I can withstand God" or why does the world think to make me deny what I have actually seen, for I had seen a vision, I knew it, and I knew that God knew it, and I could not deny it, neither dare I do it, at least I knew that by so doing, I would offend God and come under comdemnation. I had now got my mind satisfied so far as the sectarian world was concerned, that it was not my duty to join with any of them, but continue as I was untill further directed, for I had found the testimony of James to be true, that a man who lacked wisdom might ask of God, and obtain and not be upbraided. I continued to pursue my common avocations in life untill the twenty first of

September, One thousand Eight hundred and twenty three, all the time suffering severe persecution at the hand of all classes of men, both religious and irreligious because I continued to affirm that I had seen a vision. During the space of time which intervened between the time I had the vision and the year Eighteen hundred and twenty three, (having been forbidden to join any of the religious sects of the day and being of very tender years and persecuted by those who ought to have been my friends, and to have treated me kindly and if they supposeed me to be deluded to have endeavored in a proper and affectionate manner to have reclaimed me) I was left to ~~all kinds of~~ temptations, and mingling with all kinds of society I frequently fell into many foolish errors and displayed the weakness of youth and the corruption foibles of human nature which I am sorry to say led me into divers temptations to the ~~gratification of many appetites~~ offensive in the sight of God. In consequence of these things I often felt condemned for my weakness and imperfections; when on the evening of the above mentioned twenty first of september, after I had retired to my bed for the night I betook myself to prayer and supplication to Almighty God for forgiveness of all my sins and follies, and also for a manifestation to me that I might know of my state and standing before him. For I had full confidence in obtaining a divine manifestation as I had previously had one. While I was thus in the act of calling upon God, I discovered a light appearing in the room which continued to increase untill the room was lighter than at noonday ~~and~~ when immediately a personage appeared at my bedside standing in the air for his feet did not touch the floor. He had on a loose robe of most exquisite whiteness. It was a whiteness beyond any thing earthly I had ever seen, nor do I believe that any earthly thing could be made to appear so exceedingly white and brilliant, His hands were naked and his arms also a little above the wrists. So also were his feet naked as were his legs a little above the ankles. His head and neck were also bare. I could discover that he had no other clothing on but this robe, as it was open so that I could see into his bosom. Not only was his robe exceedingly white but his whole person was glorious beyond description, and his countenance truly like lightening. The room was exceedingly light, but not so very bright as immediately around his person. When I first looked upon him I was afraid, but the fear soon left me. He called me by name and said unto me that he was a messenger sent from the presence of God to me and that his name was Nephi.[2] That God had a work for me to do, and that my name should be had for good and evil among all nations kindreds and tongues. or that it should be both good and evil spoken of among all people. He said there was a book deposited written upon gold plates, giving an account of the former inhabitants of this continent and the source from whence they sprang. He also said that the fullness of the everlasting Gospel was contained in it as delivered by the Saviour to the ancient inhabitants. Also that there were two stones in silver bows and these (stones fastened to a breast plate) which constituted what is called the Urim & Thummin deposited with the plates, and the possession and use of these stones that was what constituted seers in ancient or former times and that God had prepared them for the purpose of translating the book. After telling me these things he commenced quoting the prophecies of the old testament, he first quoted part of the third chapter of Malachi and he quoted also the fourth or last chapter of the same prophecy though with a little variation from the way it reads in our Bibles. Instead of quoting the first verse as reads in our books he quoted it thus, "For behold the day cometh that shall burn as an oven, and all the proud yea and all that do wickedly shall burn as stubble, for they day[3] that cometh shall burn them saith the Lord of hosts, that it shall leave them neither root nor branch." And again he quoted the fifth verse thus, "Behold I will reveal unto you the Priesthood by the hand of Elijah the prophet before the coming of the great and dreadful day of the Lord." He also quoted the next verse differently. "And he shall plant in the hearts of the children the promises made to the fathers, and the hearts of the children shall turn to their fathers, if it were not so the whole earth would be utterly wasted at his coming."[4] In addition to these he quoted the Eleventh Chapter of Isaiah saying that it was about to be fulfilled. He quoted also the third chapter of Acts, twenty second and twenty third verses precisely as they stand in our new testament. He said that that prophet was Christ, but the day had not yet come when "they who would not hear his voice should be cut off from among the people" but soon would come.

He also quoted the second chapter of Joel from the twenty eighth to the last verse. He also said that this was not yet fulfilled but was soon to be. And he further stated the fullness of the gentiles was soon to come in.[5] He quoted many other passages of scripture and offered many explanations which cannot be mentioned here. Again he told me that when I got those plates of which he had spoken (for the time that they should be obtained was not yet fulfilled) I should not show them to any person, neither the breastplate with the Urim and Thummin only to those to whom I should be commanded to show them. If I did I should be destroyed. While he was conversing with me about the plates the vision was opened to my mind that I could see the place where the plates were deposited and that so clearly and distinctly that I knew the place again when I visited it.

After this ~~conversation~~ communication I saw the light in the room begin to gather immediately around the person of him who had been speaking to me, and it continued to do so untill the room was again left dark except just around him, when instantly I saw as it were a conduit open right up into heaven, and he ascended up till he entirely disappeared and the room was left as it had been before this heavenly light had made its appearance.

I lay musing on the singularity of the scene and marvelling greatly at what had been told me by this extraordinary messenger, when in the midst of my meditation I suddenly discovered that my room was again beginning to get lighted, and in an instant as it were, the same heavenly messenger was again by my bedside. He commenced and again related the very same things which he had done at his first visit without the least variation which having done, he informed me of great judgements which were coming upon the earth, with great desolations by famine, sword, and pestilence, and that these grievous judgments would come on the earth in this generation: Having related these things he again ascended as he had done before.

By this time so deep were the impressions made on my mind that sleep had fled from my eyes and I lay overwhelmed in astonishment at what I had both seen and heard; But what was my surprise when again I beheld the same messenger at my bed side, and heard him rehearse or repeat over again to me the same things as before and added a caution to me, telling me that Satan would try to tempt me (in consequence of the indigent circumstances of my father's family) to get the plates for the purpose of getting rich, This he forbid me, saying that I must have ~~mo~~ no other object in view in getting the plates but to glorify God, and must not be influenced by any other motive but that of building his kingdom, otherwise I could not get them. After this third visit he again ascended up into heaven as before and I was again left to ponder on the strangeness of what I had just experienced, when almost immediately after the heavenly messenger had ascended from me the third time, the cock crew, and I found that day was approaching so that our interviews must have occupied the whole of that night. I shortly arose from my bed, and as usual went to the necessary labors of the day, but in attempting to labor as at other times, I found my strength so exhausted as rendered me entirely unable. My father who was laboring along with me discovered something to be wrong with me and told me to go home. I started with the intention of going to the house, but in attempting to cross the fence out of the field where we were, my strength entirely failed me and I fell helpless on the ground and for a time was quite unconscious of any thing. The first thing I can recollect was a voice speaking unto me calling me by name. I looked and beheld the same messenger standing over my head surrounded by light as before. He then again related unto me all that he had related to me the previous night, and commanded me to go to my father and tell him of the vision and commandments which I had received.

I obeyed. I returned back to my father in the field and rehearsed the whole matter to him. He replyed to me, that it was of God, and to go and do as commanded by the messenger. I left the field and went to the place where the messenger had told me the plates were deposited, and owing to the distinctness of the vision which I had had concerning it, I knew the place the instant I arrived there. Under a ~~stound~~ stone of considerable size, lay the plates deposited in a stone box, This stone was thick and rounding in the middle on the upper side, and thinner towards the edges, so that the middle part of it was visible above the ground, but the edge all round was covered with earth. Having removed the earth ~~off the edge of the stone~~, and obtained a lever which I got fixed under the edge of the stone, and with a little exertion raised it up. I looked in and there indeed did I behold the plates, the Urim and Thummin and the Breastplate as stated by the messenger The box in which they lay was formed by laying stones together in some kind of cement, in the bottom of the box were laid two stones crossways of the box, and on these stones lay the plates and the other things with them. I made an attempt to take them out but was forbidden by the messenger and was again informed that the time for bringing them forth had not yet arrived, neither would untill four years from that time, but he told me that I should come to that place precisely in one year from that time, and that he would there meet with me, and that I should continue to do so untill the time should come for obtaining the plates. Accordingly as I had been commanded I went at the end of each year, and at each time I found the same messenger there and received instruction and intelligence from him at each of our interviews respecting what the Lord was going to do, and how and in what manner his kingdom was to be conducted in the last days. As my father's worldly circumstances were very, limited we were under the necessity of laboring with our hands, hiring by days works and otherwise as we could get opportunity, sometimes we were at home and some times abroad and by continued labor were enabled to get a comfortable maintenance.

In the year Eighteen hundred and twenty four my fathers family met with a great affliction by the death of my eldest brother Alvin.[6] In the month of October Eighteen hundred and twenty five I hired with an old Gentleman by the name of Josiah Stoal who lived in Chenango County, State of New York. He had heard something of a silver mine having been opened by the Spaniards in Harmony, Susquahana County, State of Pensylvania, and had previous to my hiring with him been digging in order if possible to discover the mine. After I went to live with him he took me among the rest of his hands to dig for the silver mine, at which I continued to work for nearly a month without success in our undertaking, and finally I prevailed with the old gentleman to cease digging after it. Hence arose the very prevalent story of my having been a money digger.[7]

During the time that I was thus employed I was put to board with a Mr. Isaac Hale of that place, Twas there that I first saw my wife, (his daughter) Emma Hale. On the eighteenth of January Eighteen hundred and twenty seven we were married while yet I was employed in the service of Mr. Stoal. Owing to my still continuing to assert that I had seen a vision, persecution still followed me, and my wife's father's family was so much opposed to our being married, ~~in so much that he would no suffer us to be married at his house~~, I was therefore under the necessity of taking her elsewhere, so we went and were married at the house of Mr. Squire Tarbill in the South Bainbridge. Chenango County, New York. Immediately after my marriage I left Mr. Stoals, and went to my father's and farmed with him that season.

At length the time arrived for obtaining the plates, the Urim and Thummin and the breastplate. On the twenty second day of September, One thousand Eight hundred and twenty seven, having went as usual at the end of another year to the place where they were deposited, the same heavenly messenger delivered them up to me with this charge that I should be responsible for them. That if I should let them go carelessly or through any neglect of mine I should be cut off, but that if I would use all my endeavors to preserve them untill he (the messenger) should call for them, they should be protected.

I soon found out the reason why I had received such strict charges to keep them safe and why it was that the messenger had said that when I had done what was required at my hand, he would call for them, for no sooner was it known that I had them than the most strenious exertions were used to get them from me. Every stratagem that could be ~~resorted~~ invented was resorted to for that purpose. The persecution became more bitter and severe than before, and multitudes were on the alert continualy to get them from me if possible but by the wisdom of God they remained safe in my hands untill I had accomplished by them what was required at my hand, when according to arrangement the messenger called for them, I delivered them up to him and he has them in his charge untill this day, being the Second day of May, One thousand Eight hundred and thirty eight.

The excitement however still continued, and rumour with her thousand tongues was all the time employed in circulating tales about my father's family and about myself. If I were to relate a thousandth part of them it would fill up volumes. The persecution however became so intolerable that I was under the necessity of leaving Manchester and going with my wife to Susquahanah County in the State of Pensyllvania. While preparing to start (being very poor and the persecution so heavy upon us that there was no probability that we would ever be otherwise) in the midst of our afflictions we found a friend in a Gentleman by the name of Martin Harris,[8] who came to us and gave me fifty dollars to assist us in our affliction, Mr Harris was a resident of Palmyra township Wayne County in the State of New York and a farmer of respectability. By this timely aid was I enabled to reach the place of my destination in Pensylvania, and immediately after my arrival there I commenced copying the characters of all the plates. I copied a considerable number of them and by means of the Urim and Thummin I translated some of them which I did between the time I arrived at the house of my wife's father in the month of December, and the February following. Sometime in this month of February the aforementioned Mr Martin Harris came to our place, got the characters which I had drawn off of the plates and started with them to the City of New York. For what took place relative to him and the characters I refer to his own account which was as follows. "I went to the City of New York and presented the Characters which had been translated, with the translation thereof, to Professor Charles Anthony a gentleman celebrated for his literary attainments.[9] Professor Anthony stated that the translation was correct, more so than any he had before seen translated from the Egyptian.[10]

"I then shewed him those which were not yet translated, and he said they were Egyptian, Chaldeak, Assyriac, and Arabac, and he said that they were true characters. He gave me a certificate certifying to the people of Palmyra that they were true characters and that the translation of such of them as had been translated was also correct.

"I took the Certificate and put it into my pocket, and was just leaving the house, when Mr Anthony called me back and asked me how the young man found out that there were gold plates in the place where he found them, I answered that an Angel of God had revealed it unto him. He then said unto me, let me see that certificate, I accordingly took it out of my pocket and gave it to him when he took it and tore it to pieces, saying there was no such thing now as ministering of angels, and that if I would bring the plates to him, he would translate them. I informed him that part of the plates were sealed, and that I was forbidden to bring them. he replied 'I cannot read a sealed book.' I left him and went to Dr Mitchel[11] who sanctioned what Professor Anthony had said respecting both the Characters and the translation."

Mr Harris having returned from this tour he left me and went home to Palmyra, arranged his affairs, and returned again to my house about the twelfth of April, Eighteen hundred and twenty eight, and commenced writing for me while I translated from the plates, which we continued untill the fourteenth of June following, by which time he had written one hundred and sixteen pages of manuscript of foolscap paper. Some time after Mr Harris had began to write for me, he began to tease me to give him liberty to carry the writings home and shew them, and desired of me that I would enquire of the Lord through the Urim and Thummin if he might not do so. I did enquire, and the answer was that he must not do so. However he was not satisfied with this answer, and desired that I should enquire again. I did so, and the answer was as before. Still he could not be contented but insisted that I should enquire once more. After much solicitation I again enquired of the Lord, and permission was granted him to have the writings on certain conditions, which were, that he shew them only to his brother. Preserved Harris, his own wife, his father and his mother, and a Mrs Cobb a sister to his wife. In accordance with this last answer I required of him that he should bind himself in a covenant to me in the most solemn manner that he would not do otherwise than had been directed. He did so. He bound himself as I required of him, took the writings and went his way.

Notwithstanding however the great restrictions which he had been laid under, and the solemnity of the covenant which he had made with me, he did shew them to others and by stratagem they got away from him, and they never have been recovered nor obtained back again untill this day. In the mean time while Martin Harris was gone with the writings, I went to visit my father's family at Manchester. I continued there for a short season and then returned to my place in Pensylvania. Immediately after my return home I was walking out a little distance, when Behold the former heavenly messenger appeared and handed to me the Urim and Thummin again (for it had been taken from me in consequence of my having wearied the Lord in asking for the privilege of letting Martin Harris take the writings which he lost by transgression). . . .

Notes

1. The Church was organized in Fayette, New York on April 6, 1830.
2. This appears to be a clerical error and should read Moroni. In the numerous other times that Joseph told the story and those places wherein the angel associated with the coming forth of the Book of Mormon is mentioned, Moroni is always identified by name.
3. Later scribes or historians seem to have put the words "they day" together to form "they," the word found in the present (1981) edition of the "Pearl of Great Price."
4. Moroni's altered version of Malachi 4:5–6 is now section two of the *Doctrine and Covenants*.
5. The "times of the Gentiles" represents that era in the latter days when the gospel is taken to the Gentiles on a preferential basis (as contrasted with the order of things in first-century Christianity). The "fulness of the Gentiles" is that time when the Gentile nations come to reject the gospel and the order of presentation therefore reversed—the message will then go to Israel.
6. The correct date of Alvin's death was November 19, 1823.
7. See Bruce A. Van Orden, "Joseph Smith's Developmental Years, 1823–29," in *Studies in Scripture, Vol. 2: The Pearl of Great Price,* ed. Robert L. Millet and Kent P. Jackson (Sandy, Utah: Randall Book Co., 1985), pp. 367–87.
8. Martin Harris (1783–1875) became one of the three witnesses to the authenticity of the golden plates. He also mortgaged a part of his property to pay for the first printing of the Book of Mormon.
9. Charles Anthon (1787–1867) was a professor of Classical Studies at Columbia University from 1820 until his death. For a detailed discussion of the Anthon episode, see Stanley B. Kimball, "The Anthon Transcript: People, Primary Sources, and Problems," *Brigham Young University Studies,* Vol. 10, No. 3 (Spring 1970), pp. 325–52.
10. This incident took place in February of 1828. One wonders how much Anthon would have known about Egyptian, particularly since Champollion's work was but six years old by this time.
11. Samuel L. Mitchell (1776–1831) was a vice-president of Rutgers Medical College in New York during the years 1826–1830. His early studies were in the classics. See Kimball, "The Anthon Transcript," pp. 332–34.

III.

LETTERS

1. THE THROES OF LONELINESS:
COMFORT IN GOD (1832)

As early as 1831 the Church was strongly established in both Ohio and Missouri. Inasmuch as the Prophet lived in Kirtland, Ohio, it was frequently necessary to travel to Missouri to attend to Church business there. In May of 1832 Joseph and some of his travelling companions (leaders of the Church) began their return to Ohio by stagecoach. While in Indiana, one of the Church leaders, Newel K. Whitney, was badly injured as he attempted to leap from a runaway coach. Joseph remained behind with Whitney while his broken leg mended; the other leaders of the Church continued their journey to Ohio. Joseph wrote the following letter to his wife, Emma, in the month of June. It is from Personal Writings of Joseph Smith, *pp. 238–39.*

June 6th Greenville Floid Co. ~~1823~~
1832

Dear Wife,

I would inform you that Brother Martin[1] has arrived here and braught the pleasing news that our Familys were well when he left there which Greately Cheared our hearts and revived our Spirits we thank our hevenly Father for his Goodness ~~uto~~ unto us and all of you you Martin arrived on Satterday the Same week he left Chagrin[2] haveing a prosperous time we are all in good health Brother Whitenys leg is gaining and he thinks he Shall be able to perform his Journey so as to get home about as Soon as the 20th my Situation is a very unpleasant one[3] although I will endeavor to be Contented the Lord assisting me I have visited a grove which is Just back of the town almost every day where I can be Secluded from the eyes of any mortal and there give vent to all the feelings of my heart in meaditation and prayr I have

70

Called to mind all the past moments of my life and am left to morn w and Shed tears of sorrow for my folly in Sufering the adversary of my Soul to have so much power over me as he has had in times past but God is merciful and has fo[r]given my Sins and I r[e]joice that he Sendeth forth the Comferter unto as many as believe and humbleeth themselves before him I was grieved to hear that Hiram had lost his little Child[4] I think we Can in Some degree Simpathise with him[5] but we all must be reconciled to our lots and say the will of the Lord be done Sister Whitney wrote a letter to her husband which which was very chearing but and being unwell at that time and filled with much anxiety it would have been very Consoling to me to have received a few lines from you but as you did not take the trouble I will try to be contented with my lot knowing that God is my friend in him I shall find comfort I have given myf life into his hands I am prepared to go at his Call I desire to be with Christ I Count not my life dear to me only to do his will I am not pleased to hear that William McLelin has come back and disobayed the voice of him who is altogether Lovely for a woman[6] I am astonished at Sister Emaline yet I cannot belive she is not a worthy sister I hope She he will find him true and kind to her but have no reason to expect it his Conduct merits the disapprobation of every true follower of Christ but this is a painful subject I hope you will excuse my warmth of feeling in mentioning this sub subject and also my inability in conveying my ideas in writing I am happy to find that you are still in the faith of Christ and at Father Smiths I hope you will Comfort Father and Mother in their trials and Hiram and Jerutia Jerusha and the rest of the Family tell Sophronia I remember her and Kalvin in my prayers my respects to the rest I Should Like [to] See little Julia and once more take her on my knees and converse with you on all the subjects which concerns us things I cannot is not prudent for me to write I omit all the important things which could I See you I could make you acquainted with tell Brother Williams that I and Brother Whitney will arrange the business of that farm when we Come give my respects to all the Brotheren Br-Whitney['s] Family tell them he is Chearfull and patient and a true Brother to me I subscribe myself your Husband the Lord bless you peace be with [you] so Farewell until I return

Joseph Smith Jr—

(martin will come with us)
Greenville Ind
June 7th 1834

Mrs. Emma Smith
Kirtland Geauga Co.
Ohio

Notes

1. Martin Harris.
2. Later known as Willoughby, Ohio.
3. Joseph somehow consumed poison while there. His continued vomiting led to a dislocation of his jaw; in addition, the sickness caused "much of the hair to become loosened from [his] head." (*History of the Church,* 1:271.)
4. Hyrum Smith (1800–1844), Joseph's older brother, lost his infant daughter, Mary, in death. She was born June 27, 1829, and died May 29, 1832.
5. Joseph and Emma lost many children themselves before the children reached maturity.
6. William E. McLellin (1806–1883) was called on a preaching mission in January of 1832. In April, McLellin decided to forsake his mission, return home, and find a woman to marry. He returned and married Emeline Miller.

2. IMPRESSIONS OF NEW YORK CITY (1832)

While visiting New York City with Newel K. Whitney to transact Church business, as well as "preach repentance" to the people of the Northeast, Joseph Smith wrote the following letter to his wife, Emma, from his room in the Pearl Street House in Manhatten. The text is in Personal Writings of Joseph Smith, *pp. 252–54.*

Oct 13 1832
P Pearl Street House NY
My Dear Wife
     This day I have been walking through the most splendid part of the City of n New Y[1]——the buildings are truly great and wonderful to the astonishing of to eve[r]y beholder and the language of my heart is like this can the great God of all the Earth maker of all thing[s] magnificent and splendid be displeased with man for all these great inventions saught out by them my answer is no it can not be seeing these works ~~are~~ are calculated to mak[e] men comfortable wise and happy therefore not for the works can the Lord be displeased only against man in the anger of the Lord Kindled because they Give him not the Glory therefore their iniquities shall be visited upon their heads and their works shall be burned up with unquenchable fire the inequity of the people is printed in every countinance and nothing but

the dress of the people makes them look fair and butiful all is defor-
mity there is something in every countinance that is disagrealbe with
few exceptions Oh how long Oh Lord Shall this order of things exist
and darkness cover the Earth and gross darkness cover the people
after beholding all that I had any desire to behold I returned to my
room to meditate and calm my mind and behold the thaughts of home
and Emma and Julia rushes upon my mind like a flood and I could
wish for [a] moment to be with them my breast is filld with all the
feelings and tenderness of a parent and a Husband and could I be with
you I would tell you many things yet when I reflect upon this great
city like Ninevah not desearning their right hand from their left yea
more then two hundred thousand souls my bowels is filled with compassion towards them and I am determined to lift up my voice in this
City and leave the Event with God who holdeth all things in his hands
and will not suffer an hair of our heads unnoticed to fall to the ground
there is but few Cases of the cholra in this City[2] now and if you should
see the people you would not ~~that~~ know that they ~~people~~ had ever
heard of the cholera I hope you will excuse me for writing this letter
so soon after w[r]iting for I feel as if I wanted to ~~say you~~ say something to you to comfort you in your beculiar triel and present affliction[3] I hope God will give you strength that you may not faint I pray
God to soften the hearts of those arou[n]d you to be kind to you and
take the burden of[f] your shoulders as much a posable and not afflict
you I feel for you for I know you[r] state and that others do not but
you must cumfort yourself knowing that God is your friend in heaven
and that you hav[e] one true and living friend on Earth your Husband
Joseph Smith Jr

PS while Brother Whitney [is] Selecting goods I have nothing to [do]
but to sit in my room and pray for him that he may have strength to
indure his labours for truly it is [a] tedious Job to stand on the feet all
day to select goods its wants good Judgement and a long acquaintence
with goods to git good ones and a man must be his own Judge for no
one will Judge for him and it is much pepleccity [perplexity] of mind I
prefer reading and praying and holding comuneion with the holy
spirit and writing to you then walking the streets and beholding the
distraction of man I have had some conversation with few which gave
satisfaction and one very butiful young gentlemen from Jersy whose
countinance was very sollam he came and set by my side and began to
converce with me about the Cholra and I learned he had been seased
with it and came very near die[i]ng with it he said the Lord had spared
him for some wise pu[r]pose I took advantage of this and opened a

long discours with him he received my teaching ~~with~~ appearan[t]ly
with much pleasure and becam[e] very strongly attacth to me we talkd
till late at night and concluded to omit conversation till the next day
but having some business to do he was detained untill the boat was
ready to go out and must leave he came to me and bid me Farewell,
and we parted with much reluctance Brother Whitney is received with
great kindness by all his old acquaintance[s] he is faithful in prayer
and fervant in spirit and we take great comfort together there is about
one hundred boarders and sometimes more in this house every day
from one to two from all parts of the world I think you would hav[e]
laughed right harty if you could [have] been whe[r]e you could see the
waiters to day noon [as they] waited on the table both Black and
white and molato runing bowing and maneuvering but I must con-
clude I remain your affectionate Husband until Death

Joseph Smith Junior

Emma Smith
Kirtland Geauga Co.
Ohio

Notes

1. The population of New York City in 1832 was approximately
   200,000.
2. A cholera epidemic in New York City in 1832 left over 1,500
   dead.
3. Emma was pregnant at the time.

3. LETTER TO AN EDITOR (1833)

*On Christmas day, 1832, Joseph Smith dictated a revelation,
what he called a "Prophecy on War." This prophecy stressed that the
chastening hand of God was about to be manifest because of the
unbelief of the people of America, and that wars would soon begin to
be poured out upon all nations, beginning with the rebellion in South
Carolina (the "Nullification Crisis" of 1832). Joseph wrote the following letter to N. C. Saxton, editor of a paper in Rochester, New York,
and explained that the nation's only recourse was to repent and receive the "New Covenant" made available through the Latter-day
Saints. From* Personal Writings of Joseph Smith, *pp. 270–74.*

Kirtland 4th Jany. 1833-

Mr. Editor Sir,

Considering the Liberal prisciples upon which your interesting and valuable paper is published and myself being a subscriber and feeling a deep intrist in the cause of Zion and in the happiness of my brethren of mankind I cheerfully take up my pen to contribute my mite at this every [very] interesting and important period.

For some length of time I have been carfully viewing the state of things as now appear throug[h]out our christian Land and have looked at it with feelings of the most painful anxiety while upon the one hand beholding the manifeste withdrawal of Gods holy Spirit and the vail of stupidity which seems to be drawn over the hearts of the people and upon the other hand beholding the Judgements of God that have swept and are still sweeping hundreds and thousands of our race (and I fear unprepared) down to the shades of death with this solemn and alarming fact before me I am led to exclaim ["] O that my head were waters and mine ey[e]s a fountain of tears that I might weep day and night &c." I think that it is high time for a christian world to awake out of sleep and cry mightely to that God day and night whose anger we have Justly incured. Are not these things a sufficient stimulant to arouse the faculties and call forth the energies of evvry man woman and child that poseses feeling of sympathy for his fellow[s] or that is in any degree endeared to the buding cause of our glorious Lord; I leave an inteligent community to answer this important question with a confession that this is what has caused me to overlook my own inability and expose my weakness to a learned world but trusting in that God who has said these things are hid from the wise and prudent and reve[a]lled unto babes I step forth into the field to tell you what the Lord is doing and what you must do to enjoy the smiles of your saviour in these last day[s]—The time has at last come arrived when the God of Abraham of Isaac and of Jacob has set his hand again the seccond time to recover the remnants of his people[1] which have been left from Assyria, and from Egypt and from Pathros &.c. and from the Islands of the sea with them to bring in the fulness of the Gentiles and establish that covenant with them which was promised when their sins should be taken away. See Romans 11. 25, 26, & 27 and also Jeremiah 31. 32, & 33, This covenant has never been established with the house of Israel nor with the house of Judah for it requires two parties to make a covenant and those two parties must be agreed or no covenant can be made. Christ in the days of his flesh proposed to make a covenant with them but they rejected him and his proposals and in consequence thereof they were broken off and no covenant was made with them at that time but their unbelief has not rendered the promise of God of none effect; no, for there was another day limited in David which was the day of his power and then his people *Isreal,* should be a willing people and he would write his laws in their hearts and print them in their thoughts their sins and eniquities he would remember no more, Thus after this chosen family had rejected Christ and his proposals the heralds of salvation said to them "lo we turn unto the gentiles," and the gentiles received the covenant and were grafted in from whence the chosen family were broken off but the Gentiles have not continued in the goodness of God but have departed from the faith that was once delivered to the saints and have broken the ~~everlasting~~ covenenant in which their fathers were established see Isaiah 24th 5th and have become high minded and have not feared therefore but few of them will be gathered with the *chosen family* Has not the pride highmindedness and unbelief of the Gentiles provoked the holy one of Israel to withdraw his holy spirit from them and send forth his Judgements to scourge them for their wickedness; this is certainly the case, Christ said to his desciples Mark 16, 17 & 18 that these signs should follow them that believe; In my name shall they cast out Devils they shall speak with new tongues they shall take up serpants and if they drink any deadly thing it shall not hurt them they shall lay hands on the sick and they shall recover, and also in connection with this read 1 Corinthians 12 Chapt, By the foregoing testamonies or through the glass of the foregoing testamonies we may look at the Christian world and see the apostacy there has been from the Apostolic platform, and who can look at this, and and not exclaim in the language of Isaiah, ["]the earth is defiled under the inhabitants thereof because they have transgressed the Laws, changed the ordinances and broken the everlasting covenant."[2]

The plain fact is this, the power of God begins to fall upon the Nations, and the light of the latter day glory begins to break forth through the dark atmosphere of sectarian wickedness and their iniquity rools [rolls] up into view and the Nations of the Gentiles are like the waves of the sea casting up mire and dirt or all in commotion and they hastily are preparing to act the part allotted them when the Lord rebukes the nations, when he shall rule them with a rod of iron & break them in peaces like a potters vessel, The Lord has declared to his servants some Eighteen months since that he was then withdrawing his spirit from the earth,[3] and we can see that such is the fact for not only the churchs arc dwindling away, but there are no conversions, or but very few, and this is not all, the governments of the earth are thrown into confusion & division, and distruction to the eye of the spiritual beholder seemes to be written by the finger of an invisable hand in Large capitals upon almost evry thing we behold --------------

And now what remains to be done under circumstances like these, I will proced to tell you what the Lord requires of all people high and low, rich and poor, male and female, ministers & people professors of religion, and nonproffessors in order that they may enjoy the holy spirit of God to a fulness, and escape the Judgments of God, which are almost ready to burst upon the nations of the earth— Repent of all your sins and be baptized in water for the remission of them, in the name of the father, and of the son, and of the Holy Ghost, and receive the ordinance of the laying on of the hands of him who is ordained and sealed unto this power, that ye may receive the holy spirit of God, and this according to the holy scriptures, and of the Book of Mormon; and the only way that man can enter into the Celestial kingdom.[4] These are the requesitions of the new Covenant or first principles of of the Gospel of Christ; then add to you[r] faith virtue and to virtue knowledge and to knowledge temperance, and to temperance patience, and to patience, brotherly kindness and to brotherly kindness charity (or Love) and if these things be in you and abound, they make you to be neither baran nor unfruitful in the knowledge of our Lord Jesus Christ---

The Book of Mormon is a record of the forefathers of our western Tribes of Indians, having been found through the ministration of an holy Angel translated into our own Language by the gift and power of God, after having been hid up in the earth for the last fourteen hundred years containing the word of God, which was delivered unto them, By it we learn that our western tribes of Indians are desendants from that Joseph that was sold into Egypt, and that the land of America is a promised land unto them, and unto it all the tribes of Israel will come. with as many of the gentiles as shall comply with the requesitions of the new co[v]enant. But the tribe of Judah[5] will return to old Jerusalem. The City, of Zion, spoken of by David in the 102 Psalm will be built upon the Land of America and the ransomed of the Lord shall return and come to it with songs and everlasting joy upon their heads, and then they will be delivered from the overflowing scourge that shall pass through the Land But Judah shall obtain deliverance at Jerusalem see Joel 2. 32. Isaiah 26, 20 & 21, Jer. 31, 12, Psalm 50. 5, Ezekiel 34, 11. 12 & 13, These are testamonies that the good Shepherd will put forth his own sheep and Lead them out from all nations where they have been scattered in a cloudy and dark day, to Zion and to Jerusalem beside many more testamonies which might be brought—And now I am prepared to say by the authority of Jesus Christ, that not many years shall pass away before the United States shall present such a scene of *bloodshed* as has not a parallel in the hystory of our nation pestalence hail famine and earthquake will sweep the wicked off this generation from off the face of this Land to open and prepare the way for the return of the lost tribes of Israel from the north country—The people of the Lord, those who have complied with the requisitions of the new covenant have already commenced gathering togethe[r] to Zion which is in the State of Missouri.[6] Therefore I declare unto you the warning which the Lord has commanded me to declare unto this generation, rem[em]bering that the eyes of my maker are upon me and that to him I am accountable for evry word I say wishing nothing worse to my fellow men then their eternal salvation therefore fear God, and give glory to him for the hour of his Judgement is come,[7] Repent ye Repent, ye and imbrace the everlasting Covenant and flee to Zion before the overflowing scourge overtake you, For there are those now living upon the earth whose eyes shall not be closed in death until they see all these things which I have spoken fulfilled Rem[em]ber these things, call upon the Lord while he is near and seek him while he may be found is the exhortation of your unworthy servant

Joseph Smith Jr

To N. E. Sexton Rochester N.Y.

Notes

1. Joseph Smith felt that bringing people into the Church through conversion represented the "gathering of Israel" predicted by the ancient prophets.
2. See Isaiah 24:5–6.
3. *Doctrine and Covenants,* 63:32.
4. The Celestial Kingdom is the highest of the heavens. See Section Five entitled "Revelations," and specifically note "Three Degrees of Glory: Many Mansions of the Father."
5. That is, the Jews.
6. Independence (Jackson County) Missouri became known as the site of the New Jerusalem.
7. Revelation 14:7.

4. LETTER TO UNCLE SILAS SMITH:
GOD SPEAKS AGAIN (1833)

All but one of Joseph Smith, Sr.'s, family came to believe the claim of young Joseph and eventually joined the Church of Jesus Christ of Latter-day Saints. Two years before Joseph's Uncle Silas (1779–1839) was baptized, Joseph, Jr., wrote him the following letter. It is essentially a defense of the proposition that God has spoken again in modern times, and a statement of the logic associated with the claim that current revelation is needed. From Personal Writings of Joseph Smith, *pp. 297–301.*

Kirtland Mills Ohio sept 26 [1833]

Respected Uncle Silas

It is with feeings of deep interest for the wellfare of mankind which fills my mind on the reflection that all were formed by the hand of him who will call the same to give an impartial account of all their works on that great day to which you and myself in common with them are bound, that I take up my pen and seat myself in an attitude to address a few though imperfect lines to you for your perusal.

I have no doubt but that you will agree with me that men will be held accountable for the things which they have and not for the things they have not or that all the light and intelligence communicated to them from ther benifficen[t] creator whether it is much or little by the same they in justice will be judged, and that they are required to yield obedience and improve upon that and that only which is given for man is not to live by bread alone but by every word that proceeds out of the mouth of God.[1]

Seeing that the Lord has never given the world to understand by anything heretofore revealed that he had ceased forever to speak to his creatures when saught unto in a proper manner why should it be thought a thing incredible that he should be pleased to speak again in these last days for their salvation Perhaps you may be surprized at this assertion that I should say for the salvation of his creatures in these last days since we have already in our possession a vast volume of his word which he has previously given—But you will admit that the word spoken to Noah was not sufficient for Abraham or it was not required of Abraham to leave the land of his nativity and seek an Inheritance in a strange ~~land~~ Country upon the word spoken to Noah but for himself he obtained promises at the hand of the Lord and walked in that perfection that he was called the friend of God Isaac the promised seed was not required to rest his hope upon the promises made to his father Abraham but was privileged with the assurance of his approbation in the sight of Heaven by the direct voice of the Lord to him If one man can live upon the revelations given to another might not I with propriety ask why the necessity then of the Lord speaking to Isaac as he did as is recorded in the 26th chapter of Genesis for the Lord there repeats or rather promises again to perform the oath which he had previously sworn unto Abraham and why this repet[it]ion to Isaac Why was not the first promise as sure for Isaac as it was for Abraham. Was not Isaac Abraham's son And could he not place implicit confidence in the word of his father as being a man of God.

Perhaps you might say that he was a very peculiar man and different from men in these last days consequently the Lord favored him with blessings peculiar and different as he was different from men in this age I admit that he was a peculiar man and was not only peculiarly blessed but greatly blessed. But all the peculiarity that I can now discover in the man or all the difference between him and men in this age is that he was more holy and more perfect before God and came to him with a purer heart and more faith than men in this day.

The same might be said on the subject of Jacobs history Why was it that the Lord spake to him concerning the same promise after he had made it once to Abraham and renewed it to Isaac why could not Jacob rest contented upon the word spoken to his fathers When the time of the promise drew nigh for the deliverance of the children of Israel from the land of Egypt why was it necessary that the Lord should begin to speak to them The promise or word to Abraham was that his seed should serve in bondage and be afflicted four hundred years and after that they should come out with great substance Why did they not rely upon this promise and when they had remained in Egypt in bondage four hundred [years] come out without waiting for further revelation but act entirely upon the promise given to Abraham that they should come out.

Paul said to his Hebrew brethren that God b[e]ing more abundantly willing to show unto the heirs of his promises the immutability of his council ["] confirmed it by an oath." He also extorts them who throug[h] faith and patience inherit the promises.

["]Notwithstanding we (said Paul) have fled for refuge to lay hold of the hope set before us which hope we have as an anchor to the soul both sure and steadfast and which entereth into that within the vail."[2] Yet he was careful to press upon them the necessity of continuing on untill they as well as those who inherited the promises might have the assurance of their salvation confirmed to them by an oath from the mouth of him who ~~cannot~~ could not lie for that seemed to be the example anciently and Paul holds it out to his brethren as an object attainable in his day and why not I admit that by reading the scriptures of truth saints in the days of Paul could learn beyond the power of contradiction that Abraham Isaac and Jacob had the promise of eternal life confirmed to them by an oath of the Lord but that promise or oath was no assurance to them of their salvation but they could by walking in the footsteps and continuing in the faith of their fathers obtain for themselves an oath for confirmation that they were meet to be partake[r]s of the inheritance with the saints in light.[3]

If the saints in the days of the Apostles were privileged to take the saints for example and lay hold of the same promises and attain to the same exalted priviledges of knowing that their names were writen in the Lambs book of life and that they were sealed there as a perpetual memorial before the face of the most high will not the same faithfulness the same purity of heart and the same faith bring the same assurance of eternal life and that in the same manner to the children of men now in this age of the world

I have no doubt but that the holy prophets and apostles and saints in the ancient days were saved in the Kingdom of God. Neither do I doubt but that they held converse and communion with them while in the flesh as Paul said to the corinthian brethren that the Lord Jesus showed himself to above 500 saints at one time after his resurre[c]tion.[4] Job said that he knew that his Redeemer lived and that he should see him in the flesh in the latter days.[5] I may believe that Enoch walked with God I may believe that Abraham communed with God and conversed with angels. I may believe that Isaac obtained a renewal of the covenant made to Abraham by the direct voice of the Lord. I may believe that Jacob conversed with holy angels and heard the word of his Maker. that he wrestled with the angel until he prevailed and obtained a blessing I may believe that Elijah was taken to Heaven in a chariot of fire with fiery horses I may believe that the saints saw the Lord and conversed with him face to face after his resurrection I may believe that the Hebrew Church came to Mount Zion and unto the city of the living God the *Heave[n]ly* Jerusalem and to an innumerable company of angels. I may believe that they looked into Eternity and saw the Judge of all, and Jesus the Mediator of the new covenant; but will all this purchase an assurance for me, or waft me to the regions of Eternal day with my garments spotless, pure, and white? Or, must I not rather obtain for myself, by my own faith and diligence, in keeping the commandments of the Lord, an assurance of salvation for myself And have I not an equal priviledge with the ancient saints? and will not the Lord hear my prayers, and listen to my cries, as soon [as] he ever did to their's if I come to him in the manner they did or is he a respector of persons?

I must now close this subject for the want of time; and I may say with propriety at the beginning; we would be pleased to see you in Kirtland and more pleased to have you embrace the New Covenant. I remain

Yours affectionately
Josep[h] Smith Jr

Notes

1. Deuteronomy 8:3; Matthew 4:4.
2. Hebrews 6:17–18.
3. Colossians 1:12.
4. 1 Corinthians 15:6.
5. Job 19:25–26.

5. IN RESPONSE TO ALEXANDER CAMPBELL (1834)

As noted in the Introduction, Alexander Campbell was a contemporary of Joseph Smith. Campbell lost a number of his followers to the Mormon movement. Sidney Rigdon, once affiliated closely with Campbell, became a counselor to Smith in the presidency of the Church. Campbell opposed the Latter-day Saints and published a number of anti-Mormon materials. He was one of the first persons to propose that the Book of Mormon was simply Joseph Smith's written response to many of the social, economic, political and religious questions of the nineteenth century. This letter was written to Oliver Cowdery, early convert and "second elder" of the Church, for inclusion in The Evening and Morning Star, *a Church periodical. In* Personal Writings of Joseph Smith, *pp. 333–34.*

Kirtland, Ohio, September 24, 1834

DEAR BROTHER,———

I have, of late, been perusing Mr. A. Campbell's "Millennial Harbinger." I never have rejoiced to see men of corrupt hearts step forward and assume the authority and pretend to teach the ways of God—this is, and always has been a matter of grief; therefore I cannot but be thankful, that I have been instrumental in the providence of our heavenly Father in drawing forth, before the eyes of the world, the *spirits* by which certain ones, who profess to be "Reformers, and Restorers of ancient principles," are actuated! I have always had the satisfaction of seeing the truth triumph over error, and darkness give way before light, when such men were *provoked* to expose the corruption of their own hearts, by crying delusion, deception, and false prophets, accusing the innocent, and condemning the guiltless, and exalting themselves to the stations of gods, to lead blind-fold, men to perdition!

I have never been blessed, (if it may be called such,) with a personal acquaintance with Mr. Campbell, neither a personal interview, but the GREAT MAN, not infrequently condescends to notice an individual of as obscure birth as myself, if I am at liberty to interpret the language of his "Harbinger," where he says, "Joe Smith! Joe Smith! imposture! imposture!" I have noticed a strange thing! I will inform you of my meaning, though I presume you have seen the same ere this. Mr. Campbell was very lavish of his expositions of the falsity and incorrectness of the book of Mormon, some time since, but of late, since the publication of the Evening and the Morning Star, has said little or nothing, except some of his back-handed *cants.* He did, to be sure, about the time the church of Christ was established in Ohio, come out with a lengthy article, in which he undertook to prove that it was incorrect and contrary to the former revelations of the Lord. Perhaps, he is of the opinion that he so completely overthrew the foundation on which it was based, that all that is now wanting to effect an utter downfall of those who have embraced its principles is, to continue to *bark* and *howl,* and cry, Joe Smith! false prophet! and ridicule every man who may be disposed to examine the evidences which God has given to the world of its truth!

I have never written Mr. Campbell, nor received a communication from him but a public notice in his paper:—If you will give this short note a place in the Star you will do me a kindness, as I take this course to inform the gentleman, that while he is breathing out scurrility he is effectually showing the honest, the motives and principles by which he is governed, and often causes men to investigate and embrace the book of Mormon, who might otherwise have never perused it. I am satisfied, therefore he should continue his scurrility; indeed, I am more than gratified, because his cry of Joe Smith! Joe Smith! false prophet! false prophet! must manifest to all men the spirit he is of, and serves to open the eyes of the people.

I wish to inform him further, that as he has, for a length of time, smitten me upon one cheek, I have offered no resistance, I have turned the other also, to obey the commandment of our Savior;[1] and am content to sit awhile longer in silence and see the great work of God roll on, amid the opposition of this world in the face of every scandal and falsehood which may be invented and put in circulation.

I am your brother in the testimony of the book of Mormon, and shall ever remain.

JOSEPH SMITH jr.

TO OLIVER COWDERY.

Notes

1. Matthew 5:39.

6. LETTERS FROM LIBERTY JAIL:
A RAY OF LIGHT IN THE DARKNESS (1839)

Some of the most poignant correspondence of Joseph Smith's prophetic ministry is to be found in his communication with the Saints while he was a prisoner in the jail at Liberty, Missouri. Under what were considered at the time to be hellish living conditions, he mixed specific administrative instructions for the members of the Church (at that point beginning to settle in Illinois) with profound poetic insight into the meaning of suffering and the vision of eventual deliverance and peace. These instructions were written on March 20, 1839, and are now found in Personal Writings of Joseph Smith, *pp. 389–407. Orson Pratt, Mormon Apostle, later edited the correspondence and placed portions of it into the 1878 edition of the* Doctrine and Covenants. *The edited portions are now known to the modern Church as sections 121, 122, and 123 of the Doctrine and Covenants.*

Liberty Jail Clay County Mo

March 20th 1839

To the church of Latterday saints at Quincy Illinois and scattered abroad and to Bishop Partridge[1] in particular. your humble servant Joseph Smith Jr prisoner for the Lord Jesus Christ's sake and for the saints taken and held by the power of mobocracy under the exterminating reign of his excelancy the Governor Lilburn W. Boggs in company with his fellow prisoners and beloved Brethren Caleb Baldwin Lymon Wight Hyram Smith and Alexander McRae send unto you all greeting.[2] May the grace of God and the father and of our Lord and savior Jesus Christ rest upon you all and abide with you for ever. May knoledge be multiplied unto you by the meorcy of God. And may faith and virtue and knoledge and temperance and pationce and Godliness and Brotherly kindness and charity be in you and abound that you may not be baron in anything nor unfrutefull.[3] Forasmuch as we know that the most of you are well acquainted with the rongs and the high toned injustice and cruelty that is practiced upon us whereas we have been taken prisoners charged falsly with evry kind of evil and thrown into prison inclosed with strong walls surrounded with a strong guard who continually watch day and knight as indefatigable as the devil is in tempting and laying snayers for the people of God. Therefore dearly and beloved Brethren we are the more ready and willing to lay ~~clam~~ claim to your fellowship and love. For our curcumstances are calculated to awaken our spirits to a sacred remembrance of evry thing and we think that yours are also and that nothing therefore can seperate us from the love of God.[4] and fellowship one with another and that evry species of wickedness and cruelty practised upon us will only tend to bind our harts together and seal them together in love we have no need to say to you that we are held in bonds without cause neither is it needful that you say unto us we are driven from our homes and smitten without cause we mutually understand that if the inhabitance of the state of Missouri had let the saints alone and had been as desirable of peace as they ware there would have been nothing but peace and quiatude in this state unto this day we should not have been in this hell surrounded with demonds if not those who are damned, they are those who shall be damned and where we are compeled to hear nothing but blasphemos oaths and witness a scen of blasphemy and drunkeness and hypocracy and debaucheries of evry description. And again the cries of orphans and widdows would not have assended up to God. the blood of inocent women and children yea and of men would not have cried to God against them it would not have stained the soyl of Missouri. but oh! the unrelenting hand the inhumanity and murderous disposition of this people it shocks all nature it beggers and defies all discription. it is a tail of wo a lamentable tail yea a sorrifull tail too much to tell too much for contemplation too much to think of for a moment to much for human beings it cannot be found among the hethans it cannot be found among the nations where Kings and tyrants are inthroned it cannot be found among the savages of the wilderness yea and I think it cannot be found among the wild and ferocious beasts of the forist that a man should be mangled for sport women be ~~violated~~ robed of all that they have their last morsel for subsistance and then be violated to gratify the hell[i]sh desires of the mob and finally left to perish with their helpless ofspring clinging around their necks but this is not all after a man is dead he must be dug up from his grave and mangled to peaces for no other purpose than to gratify their splean against the religeon of god. They practise these things upon the saints who have done them no rong who are inocent and virtuous who loved the Lord their god and were willing to forsaik all things for ~~his~~ Christ sake these things are awfull to relait but they are verily true it must needs bee that offences come, but WO! to them by whom they come. O God where art thou and where is the pavilion that covereth thy hiding place how long shall thy hand be stayed and thine eye yea thy pure eye behold ~~from~~ from the etearnal heavens the rongs of thy people and of thy servants and thine ear be penetrated with their c[r]yes yea o Lord how long shall they suffer these rongs and unlawful oppressions before thine hart shall be softened towards them and thy bowels be moved with compassion to-words them. O Lord God almity maker of heaven earth and seas and of all things that in them is and who controleth and subjecteth the devil and the dark and benig[h]ted dominion of shayole.[5] Streach forth thy hand let thine eye pierce let thy pavilion be taken up let thy hiding place no longer be covered let thine ear be inclined let thy hart be softened and thy bowels moved with compassion toward us let thine anger be kindle[d] against our enemis and in the fury of thine hart with thy sword avenge us of our rongs remember thy suffering saint[s] oh our God and thy servants will rejoyce in thy name for ever. Dearly and beloved Breth-r[en] we see that peralas times have come as was testified of we may look then with most purfect asshurance for the roling in of all those things that have been written and with more confidence than ever before lift up our eyes to the luminary of day and say in our harts soon thou will vail thy blushing face he that said let there be light, and there was light hath spoken this word, and again thou moon thou dimmer light thou luminary of night shall ~~truru~~ turn to blood[6] we see that evry thing is fulfilling and the time shall soon come when the son of man shall desend in the clouds of heaven. our harts do not shrink neither are our spirits altogether broken at the grievious yoak which is put upon us. We know that God will have our oppressors in derision that he ~~laf~~ will laugh at their calamity and mock when their fear comith oh that we could be with you Brethren and unbosome our feeling to you we would tell [you] that we should have been at liber-ated the time Elder Rigdon was on the writ of habeas corpus had not our own lawyers interpreted the law contrary to what it reads against us which prevented us from introducing our evidence before the mock court, they have done us much harm from the begining they have of late acknoledged that the law was misconstrewed and tantalised our feelings with it and have intirally forsaken us and have forfeited their oaths and their bonds and we have a come back on them for they are co-workers with the mob. As nigh as we can learn the publick mind has been for a long time turning in our favor and the majority is now friendly and the lawyers can no longer browbeat us by saying that this or that is a matter of publick oppiniion for publick oppinion is not willing to brook it for it is beginning to look with feelings of indignation against our oppresors and to say that the mormons were not in the fault in the least we think that truth and honor and virtue and inocence will eventually come out tryumphant we should have taken a habeas corpus before the high Judge and escaped the mob in a summary way but unfortuantely for us the timber of the wall being verry hard our auger handles gave out and hindered us longer than we expected we applied to a friend and a verry slight uncautious act gave rise to some suspition and before we could fully succeed our plan was discovered and we had evry thing in readiness but the last stone and we could have made our escape in one minute and should have succeeded admirably had it not been for a little imprudance or over anxiety on the part of our friend. The sheriff and jailor did not blame us for our attempt it was a fine breach and cost the county a round sum but publick opinion says that we ought to have been permitted to have made our escape that then the disgrace would have been on us but now it must come on the state. that there cannot be any charge sustained against us and that the conduct of the mob, the murders committed at hawns mill,[7] and the exterminating order of the Governer, and the one sided rascally proceedings of the Legislature has damned the state of Missouri to all eternity I would just name also that Genl Atchison[8] has proved himself to be as contemtible as any of them we have tryed for a long time to get our lawyers to draw us some petitions to the supream Judges of this state. but they uterly refused we have examined the law and drawn the petitions ourselve and have obtained abundance of proof to counter act all the testimony that was against us, so that if the supream Judge deos not grant us our liberty he has got to act without cause contrary to honor evidence law or justice shearly to please the devil but we hope better things and trust that before many days God will so order our case that we shall be set at liberty and take up our habitation with the saints we received some letters last evening one from Emma one from Don C. Smith[9] and one from Bishop Partridge all breathing a kind and consoling spirit we were much gratified with there contence we had been a long time without information and when we read those letters they were to our souls ~~soles~~ as the gentle air, is refreshing but our joy was mingled with greaf because of the suffering of the poor and much injured saints and we need not say to you that the flood gates of our harts were hoisted and our eyes were a fountain of tears but those who have not been inclosed in the walls of a prison without cause or provication can have but little ideah how sweat [sweet] the voice of a friend is one token of friendship from any sorce whatever a wakens and calles into action evry simpathetick feeling it brings up in an instant evry thing that is pased it sesses [siezes] the presant with a vivasity of lightening it grasps after the future with the fearsness of a tiger it rhetrogrades from one thing to an other untill finally all enmity malice and hatred and past diferances misunderstandings and mismanagements be slain victoms at the feet of hope and when the hart is sufficiently contrite ~~and~~ then the voice of inspiration steals along and whispers my son peace be unto thy soal thine advirsity and thy afflictions shall be but a small moment and then if thou indure it well God shall exalt the[e] on high thou shalt tryumph over all thy foes thy friends do stand by the[e] and they shall hail the[e] again with warm harts and friendly hands thou art not yet as Job thy friends do not contend again[st] the[e] neither charge the[e] with transgretion as they did Job and they who do ~~the w~~ charge the[e] with transgretion there hope shall be blasted and there prospects shall melt away as the hory frost melteth before the burning rays of the rising sun and also that God hath set to his hand and seal to change the times and seasons and to blind their minds that they may not understand his marvilas workings that he may prove them also and take them in there own craftiness also because their harts are corrupt and the thing which they are willing to bring upon others and love to have others suffer may come upon themselves to the verry utmost that they may be disappointed also and their hopes may be cut off and not many years hence that they and their pasterity shall be swept from under heaven saith God that not one of them is left to stand by the wall cursed are all those that shall lift up the heal against mine anointed saith the Lord and cry they have sined when they have not sined before me saith the Lord but have done that which was meat in mine eyes and which I commanded them but those who cry transgresion do it becaus they are the servants of sin and are the children of disobediance themselvs and those who swear false against my servants that they might bring them unto bond-age and death. Wo unto them because they have offended my little ones they shall be severed from the ordinances of mine house their basket shall not be full their houses and their barnes shall famish and they themselvs shall be dispised by those that flattered them they shall not have the right to the priesthood nor their posterity after them from generation to generation it had been better for them that a millstone had been hanged about their necks and they drowned in the depth of the see[10] wo unto all those that discomfort my people and drive and murder and testify against them saith the Lord of host[s] a generation of viper[s] shall not escape the damnation of hell behold mine eye seeth and knoweth all their works and I have in reserve a swift judgement in the season thereoff for them all for there is a time appointed ~~for~~ to evry man according ~~their~~ as his work shall be and now beloved Brethren we say unto [you] that in asmuch as ~~good~~ God hath said that he would have a tried people that he would purge them as gold now we think that this time he has chosen his own crusible wherein we have been tryed and we think if we get through with any degree of safty and shall have kept the faith that it will be a sign to this generation alltogether sufficient to leave them without excuse and we think also that it will be a tryal of our faith equal to that of Abraham and that the ansionts [ancients] will not have were off [whereof] to bost over us in the day of judgment as being called to pass through heavier afflictions that we may hold an even waight in the balances with them but now after having suffered so grate a sacrifis and having pased through so grate a seane of sorrow we trust that a Ram may be caught in the thicket[11] speedily to releave the sons and daughters of Abraham from their ~~grate~~ great anxiety and to light up the lamp of salvation upon their countinances that they may hold up on now after having gone so far unto everlasting life. Now brethren conserning the places for the location of the saints we cannot counsyl you as we could if we were presant with you and as to the thi things that ware writen heartofore we did not concider them any thing verry binding therfore we now say once for all that we think it most proper that the general affairs of the church which are nessisary to be concidered while your humble servants remains in bondage s[h]ould be transacted by a general conferance of the most faithfull and the most respectible of the authorities of the church and a minute of those transactions may be kept and fo[r]warded from time to time to your humble servant and if there should be any corrections by the word ~~of the word of~~ the Lord they shall be f[r]eely transmitted and your humble servant will approve all ~~tha~~ things what soever is acceptable unto God if any thing should have been sejusted [suggested] by us or any names mentioned expt by commandment or thus saith the Lord we do not concider it binding. therefore our harts shall not be greaved if diferant arraingments should be entered into nevertheless we would sejest the propriety of being awar of an aspiring spirit which spirit has oftentimes urged men fo[r]wards to make foul speaches and influaance the church ~~and~~ to reject milder councils and has eventually been by the means of bringing much death and sorrow upon the church we would say be awar of pride also for well and truly hath the wise man s[a]id that pride goeth before distruction and a haughty spirit before a fall,[12] and Again outward appearance is not always a Criterean for us to Judge our fellow man but the lips betray the haughty and over baring imm[a]ginations of the heart, by his words by and his deeds let him be scaned flaterly [flattery] also is a deadly poison a frank an[d] open Rebuke provoketh a good man to Emulation and in the hour of trouble he will be your best friend, but on the other hand it will draw out all the corruption of a corrupt heart And lying and the poison of asps shall be under their tongues and they do cause the pure in heart to be cast in to prison because they want them out of thare way, A fanciful and flowely [flowery] and heated immagination be aware of be cause the things of God Are of deep import and time and expeariance and carful and pondurous and solom though[ts] can only find them out. thy mind O Man, if thou wilt lead a soul unto salvation must streach as high as the utmost Heavens, and sear[c]h in to and contemplate the ~~loest~~ lowest conside[r]ations of the darkest abyss, and Expand upon the broad considerations of Eternal Expance, he must commune with God. how much more dignifide and noble are the thoughts of God, than the vain immaginations of the human heart, none but fools, will triful, with the souls of men, how vane and trifling, have ben our spirits, our Conferencs our Coun[c]ils our ~~private~~ Meetings our pri[v]ate as well as public Conversations to low to mean to vulgar to condecending, for the dignifide Characters of the Cald and Chosen of God, according to the purposes of his ~~word~~ will from befo[re] the foundation of the world. to hold the keys of the mistress [mysteries] of those things that have ben kept hid from the foundation untill now, for of which som have tasted a little and which many of them are to be pored down from heaven upon the heads of babes, yea the weak obscure and dispizable ones of this earth. tharefore We beseath of you bretheren that you bear ~~bare~~ with those [w]ho do not feel themselves more worthey than yourselves, while we Exort one another, to a refermation, with on an[d] all. both old and young. teachers amd taugh[t] both high and low rich and poor bond and free Male and female. let honesty and sobriety, and cander and solemnity, and virtue, and pureness, and meekness, and simplisity, Crown our heads in every place, and in fine becum as little Children[13] without mallice guile or ~~high pockrichy~~ Hypokrisy: and now Brethren after your tribulations if you do these things, and exercise fervant prayer, and faith in the sight of God Always he shall give unto you knowledge by his holy spirit yea by the unspeakable gift of the holy-Ghost that has not been revealed since the world was untill now which our fathers have wated with anxious expectation to be revealed in the last times which their minds were pointed to by the Angels as held in reserve for the fullness of their glory a time to come in the which nothing shall be with held whither there be one god or many gods they shall be manifest all thrones and dominions principalities and powers shall be revealed and set forth upon all who have indured valiently for the gospel of Jesus Christ and also if there be bounds set to the heavens or to the seas or to the dry land or to the sun moon or starrs all the times of their revolutions all their appointed days month[s] and years and all the Days of their days, months and years, and all their glories laws and set times shall be reveald in the days of the dispensation of the fullness of times[14] according to that which was ordained in the midst of the councyl of the eternal God of all other Gods[15] before this world was that should be reserved unto the finishing and the end thereoff ~~when~~ when evry man shall enter into his eternal presants and into his immortal rest but I beg leave to say unto you Brethren that ignorance supe[r]stition and bigotry placing itself where it ought not is often times in the way of the prosperity of this church like the torant of rain from the mountains that floods the most pure and christle stream with mire and dirt and filthyness and obscures evry thing that was clear before and all hurls along in one general deluge but time tethers wethers tide and notwithstanding we are roled in for the time being by the mire of the flood the next surge peradventure as times roles on may bring us to the fountain as clear as cristal and as pure as snow while all the filthiness flood wood and rubbish is left and purged out by the way. How long can rowling watters remain impure what power shall stay the heavens as well might man streach forth his puny arm to stop the Missouri River in its dicread cours or to turne it up stream as to hinder the Almighty from pooring down knoledge from heaven upon the heads of the Latter day saints what is Boggs or his murderous party but wimbling willoes upon the shore to catch the flood wood as well might we argue that watter is not watter because ~~the~~ the mountain torants send down mire and riles the cristle stream altho afterwords renders it more pure than before or that fire is not fire because it is of a quenchable nature by pooring on the flood, as to say that our cause is down because runegadoes lyers preasts theavs and murderers who are all alike tenatious of their crafts and creeds have poord down from their spiritual wickedness in high places and from their strong holds of the divi[ne] a flud of dirt and mire and filthiness and vomit upon our heads no God forbid hell may poor forth its rage like the burning lavy of mount vesuvias or of Etna or of the most terible of the burning mountains and yet shall mormonism stand. watter, fire, truth, and god are all the same truth is [as] mormonism God is the author of it he is our shield it is by him we received our birth, it was by his voice that we were called to a dispensation of his gospel in the beginning of the fullness of times it was by him we received the book of mormon and it was by him that we remain unto this day and by him we shall remain if it shall be for our glory and in his almighty name we are determined to indure tribulation as good soldiers unto the end but brethren we shall continue to offer further reflections in our next epistle you will learn by the time you have read this and if you do not learn it you may learn it that walls and iron doors and sreaking hinges ~~is only calcu~~ and half scard to death Guards and jailors grining like some damned spirit lest an inocent man should make his escape to bring to light the damnible deeds of a murderous mob is cal[c]ulated in its verry nature to make the sole of an honest man feel stronger than the powers of hell. But we must bring our epistle to a close.

we send our respects to Fathers, Mothers, wives, and children, Brothers, and Sisters. we hold them in the most sacred remembrances ~~I send this epistle to Emma that she may have the first perusal of it~~ we feel to inquire after Elder Rigdon[16] if he has not forgotten us it has not been signified to us by his ~~pen~~ scrawl. Brother George W Robinson also and Elder Cahoon we remember him but would like to jog his memory a little on the fable of the [bear] and the two friends who mutually agreed to stand by each other and prehaps it would not be amis to mention Unkle John and various others, a word of consolation and a blessing would not come amiss from any body while we are being so closly whispered by the Bair but we feel to excuse evry body and evry thing. Yea the more readily when we contemplate that we are in the hands of a wors[e] than a Bair for the Bair would not pray upon a dead carcus. Our respects and love and fellowship to all the virtious saints we are your brethren and fellow sufferers and prisoners of Jesus Christ for the gospels sake and for the hope of glory which is in us. Amen.

Joseph Smith Jr
Hyrum Smith
Lyman Wight
Caleb Baldwin
Alexander McRae

Continued to the church of Latter-day-saints.

We continue to offer further reflections to Bishop Partridge and to the church of Jesus Christ of Latter-day-saints whom we love with ferveant love and do allways bear them in mind in all our prayers to the throne of God. It still seems to bear heavily in our minds that the church would do well to secure to themselves the contract of the Land which is proposed to them by Mr Isaac Galland.[17] and to cultivate the friendly feelings of that gentleman in as much as ~~he~~ he shall proove himself to be a man of honor and a friend to humanity. We really think that his letter breaths that kind of spirit if we can judge correctly. and Isaac Van Allen Esqr. the attorney General of Iowa Territory that peradventure such men may be wraught upon by the providence of God to do good unto his people. Governor Lucas[18] also. We sejust [suggest] the ideah of praying fervently for all men who manifest any degree of sympothy for the suffering children of God. We think that peradventure the United States survayer of the Iowa Territory may be one of grate benefeit to the church if it be the will of God to this end if ritiousness should be manifested as the girdle of our loins It seems to be deeply impressed upon our minds that the saints ought to lay hold of evry door that shall seem to be opened for ~~the saints~~ unto them to obtain foot ~~hol~~ hold on the Earth and be making all the preperations that is within the power of posibles for the terible storms that are now gethering in the heavens with darkness and gloominess and thick darkness as spoken of by the prophets who cannot be now of a long time lingering. For there seems to be a whispering that the angels of heaven who have been intrusted with the councils of these matters for the last days have taken council together and among the rest of the general affairs that have to be trasnsacted in their hono[r]able council they have taken cognisance of the testimony of those who were murdered at Hawns mills and also those who were martered ~~wi~~ with D. W. Patten. and else where and have passed some desisions peradventure in favor of the saints and those who were called to suffer without cause. These decisions will be made known in there time and they will ~~shall~~ take into concideration all those things that offend. We have a fervant desire that in your general conferances that evry thing should be discused with a grate deal of care and propriety lest you grieve the holy spirit which shall be poured out at all times upon your heads when you are exercised with those principals of ritiousness that are agreeable to the mind of God. and are properly affected one toward another and are carefull by all means to remember those who are in bondage and in heaviness and in deep aflection for your sakes and if there are any among you who aspire after their own aggrandisement and seek their own oppulance while their brethren are groning in poverty and are under sore trials and temptations they cannot be benefeited by the intersesions of the holy spirit which maketh intersesion for us day and knight with gronings which cannot be uttered.[19] We ought at all times to be verry carefull that such highmindedness never have place in our harts but condesend to men of low estate and with all long suffering bare the infirmities of the weak. Behold there are many called but few are chosen. And why are they not chosen? Because their hearts are set so much upon the things of this world and aspire to the honors of men that they do not learn this one lesson. that the rights of priesthood are inseperably connected with the powers of heaven and that the powers of heaven cannot be controled nor handled only upon the principals of rightiousness that they may be confered upon us it is tru[e] but when we undertake to cover our sins to or to gratify our pride or vaine ambition or to exercise controle or dominion or compulsion upon the souls of the children of men in any degree of unritiousness behold the heavens with draw themselves the spirit of the Lord is grieved and when it has withdrawn amen to the priesthood or the authroity of that man behold ere he is aware ~~he is aware~~ he is left unto himself to kick against the pricks[20] to persecute the saints and to fight against God. We have learned by sad experiance that it is the nature and disposition of almost all men as soon as they get a little authority as they suppose they will imediatly begin to exercise unritious dominion hence many are called, but few are chosen. No power or influance can or ought to be maintained by virtue of the priesthood, only by persuasion by long suffering, by gentleness and meakness and by love unfaigned, by kindness by pure knowledge which shall geratly enlarge the soul without highpocracy and without guile reproving ~~by~~ betimes with ~~shar~~ sharpness when moved upon by the holy ghost and then chowing forth afterwords an increas of love to ward him whom thou hast reproved lest he esteem the[e] to be his enemy that he may know that thy faithfulness is stronger than the cords of death thy bowells also being full of charity to ward all men and to the household of faith and virtue garnish thy thoughts unseasingly then shall thy confidence wax strong in the presants of God and the doctrines of the priesthood destell upon thy soul as the dews from heaven the Holy Ghost shall be thy constant companion and thy septer an unchanging septer of ritiousness and truth and thy dominion shall be an everlasting dominion and without compulsory means it shall flow unto thee for eve[r] and ever the ends of the Earth shall inquire after thy name and fools shall have thee in derision and hell shall rage against thee while the pure in heart and the wise and the noble and the virtuous shall seak council and authority and blesings constantly from under thy hand and thy people shall never be turned against thee by the testimony of traters and although their influance shall cast the[e] into trouble and into barrs and walls thou shalt be had in honor and but for a small moment and thy voice shall be more terrible in the midst of thine enemies than the fierce Lion because of thy ritiousness and thy God shall stand by the[e] for ever and ever. If thou art called to pass through tribulation if thou art in perel among false brethren if thou art in perel amongst robbers if thou art in peral by land or by sea if thou art accused with all maner of false accusations if thine enemies fall upon the[e] if they tear the[e] from the society of thy father and mother and brethren and sisters and if with a drawn sword thine enemies tear the[e] from the bosom of thy wife and of thine off springs and thine elder ~~one~~ son although but six years of age shall cling to thy garment and shall say my father O my father why cant you stay with us o my father what are the men agoing to do with you and if then he shall be thrust from the[e] by the sword and thou be draged to prison and thine enemies prowl around the[e] like wolves for the blood of the Lamb and if thou shouldest be cast into the pit and or into the hand of murdere[r]s and the sentance of death pased upon thee if thou be cast into the deep if the bilowing surge conspire against thee if the fearse winds become thine enemy if the heavens gether blackness and all the elements combine to hedge up thy way and above all if the verry jaws of hell shall gap open her mouth wide after thee know thou my son that all these things shall give thee experiance and shall be for thy good The son of man hath desended below them all art thou greater than he therefore hold on thy way and the priesthood shall remain with thee for their bounds are set they cannot pass thy days are known and thy years shall not be numbered less therefore fear not what man can do for God shall be with you for ever and ever now Brotheren I would sejest for the concideration of the conference of its being carefully and wisely understood by the council or conference that our brethren scattered abroad ~~that~~ who understand the spirit of the gethering that they fall into the places of refuge and safty that God shall open unto them betwean Kirtland and Far West Those from the East and from the West and from far countries let them fall in some where betwean those two bounderies in the most safe and quiet places they can find and let this be the presant understanding untill God shall open a more effectual door for us for

further conciderations. And again we further sejest for the concideration of the council that there be no organizations of large bodies upon
common ~~sto~~ stock princepals in property or of large companies of
firms ~~firm~~ untill the Lord shall signify it in a proper maner as it opens
such a dredfull field for the avericious and the indolent and corrupt
hearted to pray upon the inocent and virtious and honest we have
reason to believe that many things were introduced among the saints
before God had signified the times and not withstanding the principles and plans may have been good ~~innocent and virtitous~~ yet aspiring
men or in other words men who had not the substance of Godliness
among them perhaps undertook to handle edge tools children you
know are fond of tools while they are not yet able to use them. Time
and experiance however is the only safe remidy against such ~~people~~
evils there are many teachers but perhaps not many fathers there are
times coming when God will signify many things which are expedeant
for the well being of the saints but the times have not yet come but
will come as fast as there can be found place and reception for them
And again we would ~~sejest~~ sugjest for your concideration the propriety of all the saints gethering up a knoledge of all the facts and
sufferings and abuses put upon them by the people of this state and
also of all the property and amount of damages which they have
sustained both of character & personal injuries as well as real property and also the names of all persons that have had a hand in their
oppressions as far as they can get hold of them and find them out.
And perhaps a committe can be appointed to find out these things
and to take statements and affidafeits and also to gether up the
libilous publications that are a float and all that are in the magazines
and in the Insiclopedias and all the libillious histories that are published and that are writing and by whom and present the whole
concatination of diabolicalily rascality and nefarious and murderous
~~impositions that have been practised upon this people~~ that we may
not only publish to all the world but present them to the heads of the
government in all there dark and hellish hugh as the last effort which
is injoined on us by our heavenly father before we can fully and
completely claim that promise which ~~sha~~ shall call him forth from his
hiding place and also that the whole nation may be left without excuse
before he can ~~let fall that which the~~ send forth the power of his mighty
arme it is an imperios duty that we owe to God to angels with whom
we shall be braught to stand and also to ourselves to our wives and
our children who have been made to bow down with greaf sorrow and
care under the most damning hand of murder tyronny and appression

supported and urged on and upheld by the influance of that spirit which hath so strongly rivited the creeds of the fathers who have inherited lies upon ~~their~~ ·the harts of the children and filled the world with confusion and has been growing stronger and stronger and is now the verry main spring of all corruption ~~the corruption~~ in the world. and the whole Earth grones under the wait of its iniquity. It is an iron yok it is a strong band they are the verry hand cufs and chains and shackles and fetters of hell therefore it is an imperious duty that we owe not only to our own wives and children but to the widdow and fatherless whose husbands and fathers have been murdered under its iron hand which dark and blackning deeds are enough to make hell itself shudder and to stand aghas[t] and pail and the hands of the verry devile ~~palsy~~ tremble and palsy and also it is an imperious duty that we owe to all the rising generation and to all the pure in heart which there are many yet on the Earth among all sects parties and denominations who are blinded by the suttle craftiness of men where by they ly in wait to decieve[21] and only kept from the truth because they know not where to find it therefore that we should waist and ware out our lives in bringing to light all the hidden things of darkness where in we know them and they are truly manifest from heaven. These should then be attended to with greate earnestness Let no man count them as small things for there is much which lieth in futurity pertaining to the saints which depends upon these things you know brethren that a verry large ship is benefeited verry much by a verry small helm in the time of a storme by being kept work ways with the wind and the waves therefore dearly beloved brethren let us chearfully do all things that layeth in our power and then may we stand still with the utmost asurance to see the salvation of God and for his arm to be revealed. And again I would further sejest the impropriety of the organization of bands or companies by covenant or oaths by penalties or sercrecies but let the time past of our experiance and suferings by the wickedness of Doctor Avard[22] suffise and let our covenant be that of the everlasting covenant as is contained in the Holy writ. and the things that God hath revealed unto us. Pure friendship always becomes weakened the verry moment you undertake to make it stronger by penal oaths and secrecy. Your humble servant or servants intend from hence forth to disapprobate every thing that is not in accordance with the fullness of the gospel of Jesus Christ and is not of a bold and frank and an upright nature they will not hold their peace as in times past when they see iniquity begining to rear its head for fear of traitors or the concequinces that shall flow by reproving those who creap in unawairs that they may get something to destroy the flock we believe that the experience of the saints in times past has been sufficient that they will from henceforth be always ready to obey the truth without having mens persons in admiration because of advantage it is expediant that we should be awair of such things. and we ought always to be awair of those prejudices which sometimes so strongly presented themselves and are so congenial to human nature against our neighbors friends and bretheren of the world who choose to differ with us in opinion and in matters of faith. Our religeon is betwean us and our God their religeon is betwean them and their God there is a tie ~~which belongs~~ from God that should be excercised to wards those of our faith who walk uprightly which is peculiar to itself but it is without prejudice but gives scope to the mind which inables us to conduct ourselves with grater liberality to word all others that are not of our faith than what they exercise to wards one another these principal[s] approximate nearer to the mind of God because it is like God or God like There is a principal also which we are bound to be exercised with that is in common with all men such as governments and laws and regulations in the civil conserns of life this principal garentees to all parties sects and denominations and clases of religeon equal ~~and~~ coherant [and] indefeasible rights they are things that pertain to this life therefore all are alike interested they make our responcibilities ~~things~~ one toward another in matters of corruptable things while the former principals do not distroy the latter but bind us stronger and make our responcibilities not only one to another but unto God also hence we say that the constitution of the Unit[ed] States is a glorious standard it is founded [in] the wisdom of God it is a heavenly banner it is to all those who are privilaged with the sweats of its liberty like the cooling shades and refreshing waters of a greate rock in a thirsty and a weary land it is like a greate tree under whose branches men from evry clime can be shielded from the burning raies of a inclement sun. We bretheren are deprived of the protection of this glorious principal by the cruelty of the cruele by those who only look for the time being for pasterage like the beasts of the field only to fill themselves and forget that the mormons as well as the pr[e]sbitareans and those of evry other class and discription have equal rights to ~~pluck~~ partake of the fruit of the great tree of our national liberty but notwithstanding we see what we see and we feel what [we] feel and know what we know yet that fruit is no les presious and delisious to our taist we cannot be weaned from the milk nether can we be drawn from the breast neither will we deny our relegeon because of the hand of oppresion but we will hold on untill death we say that God is true that the book of [mor]m[on] is true that the book of covenants [is] that the constitution of the United States is [true] that the Bible is true tru[e] that Christ is true that the ministering [angels sen]t forth from God are true and [that we know] that we have an house not made [with hands] eternal in the heavens, whose [builder and m]aker is God[23] a consolation [which our opp]resers cannot feel when for[tune, or fate, sh]all lay its iron hand on them [as it has on us] now we ask what is man [remember breth]ren that time and chance hape[neth to all men] we shall continue our reflect[ions in our nex]t We subscribe ourselves your sin[cere friends and] bretherin in the bonds of the everlasting gospel prisoners of Jesus Christ for the sake of the gospel and the saints. we pronounce the blesing of heaven upon the heads of the saints who seek to serve God with an undevid[ed] heart in the name of Jesus Christ Amen.

Joseph Smith Jr,
Hyrum Smith
Lyman Wight
Caleb Balwin
Alexander McRae

Mrs. Emma Smith
Quincy

Notes

1. Edward Partridge (1793–1840) was the General Bishop of the Church. He had joined the Church in December, 1830, and was appointed to his assignment in February of 1831.
2. These four men were co-prisoners with Joseph.
3. Cf. 2 Peter 1:5–8.
4. Cf. Romans 8:38–39.
5. That is, Sheol, the Hebrew word for the world of the deserted. Hence, Joseph is using Sheol as a synonym for Hell.
6. Revelation 6:12.
7. A group of Latter-day Saint settlers in Haun's Mill, Missouri, (Caldwell County) were attacked on October 28, 1838, by a Missouri militia. Seventeen Mormons were killed.
8. David Atchison (1807–1886) was one of the men appointed as legal counsel for the Mormons in Liberty Jail.
9. Don Carlos Smith was the Prophet's younger brother.
10. Cf. Matthew 18:6.

11. Cf. Genesis 22:13.
12. Proverbs 16:18.
13. Matthew 18:3.
14. The Latter-day Saints believe this era to be the final gospel dispensation—the dispensation of the fulness of times. It is viewed as that final epoch when the Lord will "gather together in one all things in Christ, both which are in the heaven, and which are on earth; even in him." (Eph 1:10.)
15. This is one of the earliest references to a plurality of Gods in Joseph Smith's writings or sermons.
16. Sidney Rigdon was a counselor to Joseph Smith in the presidency of the Church.
17. Isaac Galland offered land to the Saints in Illinois.
18. Robert Lucas was the Govenor of Iowa Territory.
19. See Romans 8:26.
20. Cf. Acts 9:5.
21. Cf. Ephesians 4:14.
22. Samson Avard led a group of vigilante Mormons known as the "Danites."
23. Cf. Hebrews 11:10.

7. WELCOME TO A PRODIGAL (1840)

William Wine Phelps joined the Church in the early Kirtland period and was appointed as a printer for the Church. (See Doctrine and Covenants, *Section 55.) He was chosen to serve in the leadership of the Church in Missouri, but was chastened and excommunicated in March in 1838 for going contrary to counsel and also mixing ecclesiastical and personal finances. In bitterness he testified before legal bodies that Joseph Smith had advocated resistance to the laws of the land, which testimony contributed to the imprisonment of Mormon Church leaders. On June 29, 1840, as a broken and lonely man he wrote to Joseph Smith and begged for forgiveness and reinstatement in the Church. The Prophet's tender response is this letter dated June 22, 1840; it is found in* Personal Writings of Joseph Smith, *pp. 472–73.*

> *Nauvoo Hancock Co Ill.*
> *July 22nd 1840*

Dear Brother Phelps

I must say it is with no ordinary feelings I endeavour to write a few lines to you in answer to yours of the 29th Ultimo, at the same time I am rejoiced at the priveledge granted me. You may in some measure realise what my feelings, as well as Elder Rigdon's & Bro Hyrum's were when we read your letter, truly our hearts were melted into tenderness and compassion when we assertained your resolves &c

I can assure you I feel a disposition to act on your case in a manner that will meet the approbation of Jehovah (whose servant I am) and agreeably to the principles of truth and righteousness which have been revealed and inasmuch as long-suffering patience and mercy have ever characterized the dealings of our heavenly Father towards the humble and penitent, I feel disposed to copy the example and cherish the same principles, by so doing be a Savior of my fellow men

It is true, we have suffered much in consequence of your behavior—*the cup of gall already full enough* for mortals to drink, was indeed *filled to overflowing* when you turned against us: One with whom we had oft taken sweet council together, and enjoyed many refreshing seasons from the Lord "Had it been an enemy we could have borne it" In the day that thou stoodest on the other side, in the day when Strangers carried away captive his forces, and foreigners entered into his gates and cast lots upon Far West even thou wast as one of them. But thou shouldst not have ["]looked on the day of thy brother, in the day that he became a stranger neither shouldst thou have spoken proudly in the day of distress" However the Cup has been drunk, the will of our heavenly Father has been done, and we are yet alive for which we thank the Lord. And having been delivered from the hands of wicked men by the mercy of our God, we say it is your privilidge to be delivered from the power of the Adversary—be brought into the liberty of God's dear children, and again take your stand among the Saints of the Most High, and by diligence humility and love unfeigned, commend yourself to our God and your God and to the church of Jesus Christ.

Believing your confession to be real and your repentance genuine, I shall be happy once again to give you the right hand of fellowship, and rejoice over the returning prodigal.

Your letter was read to the Saints last Sunday and an expression of their feeling was taken, when it was unanimously resolved that W. W. Phelps should be received into fellowship.

"Come on dear Brother since the war is past,
For friends at first are friends again at last."

Yours as Ever,
Joseph Smith Jr

8. A LETTER TO JOHN WENTWORTH (1842)

John Wentworth, editor of the Chicago Democrat, *wrote to Joseph Smith on behalf of a friend (according to Joseph's account, a Mr. Barstow) who was preparing a history of New Hampshire and desired information concerning the rise and growth of Mormonism. The following is known as the "Wentworth Letter" and represents one of the excellent brief histories of the Church. It appeared in the* Times and Seasons, *the official Church newspaper in Nauvoo, Illinois, in the March 1, 1842, issue. Note that the end of the letter contains the thirteen statements of belief known as the "Articles of Faith." Records indicate that a history of New Hampshire did appear in 1842 written by a George Barstow, but the information contained in the Wentworth letter was nowhere to be found in that history. This text is from* Personal Writings of Joseph Smith, *pp. 213–20.*

I was born in the town of Sharon Windsor co., Vermont on the 23rd of December, A. D. 1805. When ten years old my parents removed to Palmyra New York, where we resided about four years, and from thence we removed to the town of Manchester.

My father was a farmer and taught me the art of husbandry. When about fourteen years of age I began to reflect upon the importance of being prepared for a future state, and upon enquiring the plan of salvation I found that there was a great clash in religious sentiment; if I went to one society they referred me to one plan, and another to another; each one pointing to his own particular creeds as the summon bonum of perfection: considering that all could not be right, and that God could not be the author of so much confusion I determined to investigate the subject more fully, believing that if God had a church it would not be split up into factions, and that if he taught one society to worship one way, and administer in one set of ordinances, he would not teach another principles which were diametrically opposed. Believing the word of God I had confidence in the declaration of James; "If any man lack wisdom let him ask of God who giveth to all men liberally and upbraideth not and it shall be given him," I retired to a secret place in a grove and began to call upon the Lord, while fervently engaged in supplication my mind was taken away from the objects with which I was surrounded, and I was enwrapped in a heavenly vision and saw two glorious personages who exactly resembled each other in features, and likeness, surrounded with a brilliant light which eclipsed the sun at noon-day. They told me that all religious denominations were believing in incorrect doctrines, and that none of them was acknowledged of God as his church and kingdom. And I was expressly commanded to "go not after them," at the same time receiving a promise that the fulness of the gospel should at some future time be made known unto me.

On the evening of the 21st of September, A. D. 1823, while I was praying unto God, and endeavoring to exercise faith in the precious promises of scripture on a sudden a light like that of day, only of a far purer and more glorious appearance, and brightness burst into the room, indeed the first sight was as though the house was filled with consuming fire; the appearance produced a shock that affected the whole body; in a moment a personage stood before me surrounded with a glory yet greater than that with which I was already surrounded. This messenger proclaimed himself to be an angel of God sent to bring the joyful tidings, that the covenant which God made with ancient Israel was at hand to be fulfilled, that the preparatory work for the second coming of the Messiah was speedily to commence; that the time was at hand for the gospel, in all its fulness to be preached in power, unto all nations that a people might be prepared for the millennial reign.

I was informed that I was chosen to be an instrument in the hands of God to bring about some of his purposes in this glorious dispensation.

I was also informed concerning the aboriginal inhabitants of this country, and shown who they were, and from whence they came; a brief sketch of their origin, progress, civilization, laws, governments, of their righteousness and iniquity, and the blessings of God being finally withdrawn from them as a people was made known unto me: I was also told where there was deposited some plates on which were engraven an abridgement of the records of the ancient prophets that had existed on this continent. The angel appeared to me three times the same night and unfolded the same things. After having received many visits from the angels of God unfolding the majesty, and glory of the events that should transpire in the last days, on the morning of the 22d of September A. D. 1827, the angel of the Lord delivered the records into my hands.

These records were engraven on plates which had the appearance of gold, each plate was six inches wide and eight inches long and not quite so thick as common tin. They were filled with engravings, in Egyptian characters and bound together in a volume, as the leaves of a book with three rings running through the whole. The volume was something near six inches in thickness, a part of which was sealed.

The characters on the unsealed part were small, and beautifully engraved. The whole book exhibited many marks of antiquity in its construction and much skill in the art of engraving. With the records was bound a curious instrument which the ancients called "Urim and Thummin," which consisted of two transparent stones set in the rim of a bow fastened to a breastplate.

Through the medium of the Urim and Thummin I translated the record by the gift, and power of God.

In this important and interesting book the history of ancient America is unfolded, from its first settlement by a colony that came from the tower of Babel, at the confusion of languages to the beginning of the fifth century of the Christian era. We are informed by these records that America in ancient times has been inhabited by two distinct races of people. The first were called Jaredites and came directly from the tower of Babel. The second race came directly from the city of Jerusalem, about six hundred years before Christ. They were principally Israelites, of the descendants of Joseph. The Jaredites were destroyed about the time that the Israelites came from Jerusalem, who succeeded them in the inheritance of the country. The principal nation of the second race fell in battle towards the close of the fourth century. The remnant are the Indians that now inhabit this country. This book also tells us that our Saviour made his appearance upon this continent after his resurrection, that he planted the gospel here in all its fulness, and richness, and power, and blessing; that they had apostles, prophets, pastors, teachers and evangelists; the same order, the same priesthood, the same ordinances, gifts, powers, and blessing, as was enjoyed on the eastern continent, that the people were cut off in consequence of their transgressions, that the last of their prophets who existed among them was commanded to write an abridgement of their prophesies, history &c., and to hide it up in the earth, and that it should come forth and be united with the bible for the accomplishment of the purposes of God in the last days For a more particular account I would refer to the Book of Mormon, which can be purchased at Nauvoo, or from any of our travelling elders.

As soon as the news of this discovery was made known, false reports, misrepresentation and slander flew as on wings of the wind in every direction, the house was frequently beset by mobs, and evil designing persons, several times I was shot at, and very narrowly escaped, and every device was made use of to get the plates away from me, but the power and blessing of God attended me, and several began to believe my testimony.

On the 6th of April, 1830, the "Church of Jesus Christ of Latter-day Saints," was first organized in the town of Manchester, Ontario co., state of New York. Some few were called and ordained by the spirit of revelation, and prophesy, and began to preach as the spirit gave them utterance, and though weak, yet were they strengthened by the power of God, and many were brought to repentance, were immersed in the water, and were filled with the Holy Ghost by the laying on of hands. They saw visions and prophesied, devils were cast out and the sick healed by the laying on of hands. From that time the work rolled forth with astonishing rapidity, and churches were soon formed in the states of New York, Pennsylvania, Ohio, Indiana, Illinois and Missouri; in the last named state a considerable settlement was formed in Jackson co.; numbers joined the church and we were increasing rapidly; we made large purchases of land, our farms teemed with plenty, and peace and happiness was enjoyed in our domestic circle and throughout our neighborhood; but as we could not associate with our neighbors who were many of them of the basest of men and had fled from the face of civilized society, to the frontier country to escape the hand of justice, in their midnight revels, their sabbath breaking, horse racing, and gambling, they commenced at first ridicule, then to persecute, and finally an organized mob assembled and burned our houses, tarred, and feathered, and whipped many of our brethren and finally drove them from their habitations; who houseless, and homeless, contrary to law, justice and humanity, had to wander on the bleak prairies till the children left the tracks of their blood on the prairie, this took place in the month of November, and they had no other covering but the canopy of heaven, in this inclement season of the year; this proceeding was winked at by the government and although we had warrantee deeds for our land, and had violated no law we could obtain no redress.

There were many sick, who were thus inhumanly driven from their houses, and had to endure all this abuse and to seek homes where they could be found. The result was, that a great many of them being deprived of the comforts of life, and the necessary attendances, died; many children were left orphans; wives, widows; and husbands widowers.—Our farms were taken possession of by the mob, many thousands of cattle, sheep, horses, and hogs, were taken and our household goods, store goods, and printing press, and type were broken, taken, or otherwise destroyed.

Many of our brethren removed to Clay[1] where they continued until 1836, three years; there was no violence offered but there were threatenings of violence. But in the summer of 1836, these threatenings began to assume a more serious form; from threats, public meetings were called, resolutions were passed, vengeance and destruction were threatened, and affairs again assumed a fearful attitude, Jackson county was a sufficient precedent, and as the authorities in that county did not interfere, they boasted that they would not in this, which on application to the authorities we found to be too true, and after much violence, privation and loss of property we were again driven from our homes.

We next settled in Caldwell, and Davies counties, where we made large and extensive settlements, thinking to free ourselves from the power of oppression, by settling in new counties, with very few inhabitants in them; but here we were not allowed to live in peace, but in 1838 we were again attacked by mobs an exterminating order was issued by Gov. Boggs, and under the sanction of law was organized banditti ranged through the country, robbed us of our cattle, sheep, horses, hogs &c., many of our people were murdered in cold blood, the chastity of our women was violated, and we were forced to sign away our property at the point of the sword, and after enduring every indignity that could be heaped upon us by an inhuman, ungodly band of marauders, from twelve to fifteen thousand souls men, women, and children were driven from their own fire sides, and from lands that they had warrantee deeds of, houseless, friendless, and homeless (in the depth of winter,) to wander as exiles on the earth or to seek an asylum in a more genial clime, and among a less barbarous people.

Many sickened and died, in consequence of the cold, and hardships they had to endure; many wives were left widows, and children orphans, and destitute. It would take more time than is allotted me here to describe the injustice, the wrongs, the murders, the bloodshed, the theft, misery and woe that has been caused by the barbarous, inhuman, and lawless, proceedings of the state of Missouri.

In the situation before alluded to we arrived in the state of Illinois in 1839, where we found a hospitable people and a friendly home; a people who were willing to be governed by the principles of law and humanity. We have commenced to build a city called "Nauvoo" in Hancock co., we number from six to eight thousand here besides vast numbers in the county around and in almost every county of the state. We have a city charter granted us and a charter for a legion the troops of which now number 1500. We have also a charter for a university, for an agricultural and manufacturing society, have our own laws and administrators, and possess all the privileges that other free and enlightened citizens enjoy.

Persecution has not stopped the progress of truth, but has only added fuel to the flame, it has spread with increasing rapidity, proud of the cause which they have espoused and conscious of their innocence and of the truth of their system amidst calumny and reproach have the elders of this church gone forth, and planted the gospel in almost every state in the Union; it has penetrated our cities, it has spread over our villages, and has caused thousands of our intelligent, noble, and patriotic citizens to obey its divine mandates, and be governed by its sacred truths. It has also spread into England, Ireland, Scotland and Wales: in the year of 1839 where a few of our missionaries were sent over five thousand joined the standard of truth, there are numbers now joining in every land.

Our missionaries are going forth to different nations, and in Germany, Palestine, New Holland, the East Indies, and other places, the standard of truth has been erected: no unhallowed hand can stop the work from progressing, persecutions may rage, mobs may combine, armies may assemble, calumny may defame, but the truth of God will go forth boldly, nobly, and independent till it has penetrated every continent, visited every clime, swept every country, and sounded in every ear, till the purposes of God shall be accomplished and the great Jehovah shall say the work is done.

We believe in God the Eternal Father, and in his son Jesus Christ, and in the Holy Ghost.

We believe that men will be punished for their own sins and not for Adam's transgression.

We believe that through the atonement of Christ all mankind may be saved by obedience to the laws and ordinances of the Gospel.

We believe that these ordinances are 1st, Faith in the Lord Jesus Christ; 2d, Repentance; 3d, Baptism by immersion for the remission of sins; 4th, Laying on of hands for the gift of the Holy Ghost.

We believe that a man must be called of God by "prophesy, and by laying on of hands" by those who are in authority to preach the gospel and administer in the ordinances thereof.

We believe in the same organization that existed in the primitive church, viz: apostles, prophets, pastors, teachers, evangelists &c.

We believe in the gift of tongues, prophesy, revelation, visions, healing, interpretation of tongues &c.

We believe the bible to be the word of God as far as it is translated correctly; we also believe the Book of Mormon to be the word of God.

We believe all that God has revealed, all that he does now reveal, and we believe that he will yet reveal many great and important things pertaining to the kingdom of God.

We believe in the literal gathering of Israel and in the restoration of the Ten Tribes. That Zion will be built upon this continent. That Christ will reign personally upon the earth, and that the earth will be renewed and receive its paradasaic glory.

We claim the privilege of worshipping Almighty God according to the dictates of our conscience, and allow all men the same privilege let them worship how, where, or what they may.

We believe in being subject to kings, presidents, rulers, and magistrates, in obeying, honoring and sustaining the law.

We believe in being honest, true, chaste, benevolent, virtuous, and in doing good to *all men;* indeed we may say that we follow the admonition of Paul "we believe all things we hope all things," we have endured many things and hope to be able to endure all things. If there is any thing virtuous, lovely, or of good report or praise worthy we seek after these things.[2] Respectfully &c.,

JOSEPH SMITH

Notes

1. Clay County in Missouri.
2. Cf. 1 Corinthians 13:7; Philippians 4:8.

9. HAPPINESS: THE OBJECT OF
OUR EXISTENCE (1842)

The Latter-day Saints believe that the principle of plural marriage had been revealed to Joseph Smith as early as 1831, but that the revelation commanding its practice had not been recorded until July 12, 1843. (See Doctrine and Covenants, *132.) The following appears to be a letter written to Nancy Rigdon, daughter of Sidney Rigdon, with regard to the spiritual rationale behind the practice of polygamy. This letter was first seen in the August 19, 1842, issue of the* Sangamo Journal, *contained in an attacking statement by John C. Bennett, former mayor of Nauvoo but finally disaffected member of the Church. It is now in* Personal Writings of Joseph Smith, *pp. 507–9.*

Happiness is the object and design of our existence, and will be the end thereof if we pursue the path that leads to it; and this path is virtue, uprightness, faithfulness, holiness, and keeping all the commandments of God. But we cannot keep all the commandments without first knowing them, and we cannot expect to know all, or more than we now know, unless we comply with or keep those we have already received. That which is wrong under one circumstance, may be and often is, right under another. God said thou shalt not kill,[1]—at another time he said thou shalt utterly destroy.[2] This is the principle on which the government of heaven is conducted—by revelation adapted to the circumstances in which the children of the kingdom are placed. Whatever God requires is right, no matter what it is, although we may not see the reason thereof till long after the events transpire. If we seek first the kingdom of God, all good things will be added.[3] So with Solomon—first he asked wisdom, and God gave it him, and with it every desire of his heart, even things which may be considered abominable to all who do not understand the order of heaven only in part, but which, in reality, were right, because God gave and sanctioned by special revelation.[4] A parent may whip a child, and justly too, because he stole an apple; whereas, if the child had asked for the apple, and the parent had given it, the child would have eaten it with a better appetite, there would have been no stripes—all the pleasures of the apple would have been received, all the misery of stealing lost. This principle will justly apply to all of God's dealings with his children. Every thing that God gives us is lawful and right, and 'tis proper that we should enjoy his gifts and blessings whenever and wherever he is disposed to bestow; but if we should seize upon these same blessings and enjoyments without the law, without revelation, without commandment, those blessings and enjoyments would prove cursings and vexations in the end, and we should have to go down in sorrow and wailings of everlasting regret. But in obedience there is joy and peace unspotted, unalloyed, and as God has designed our happiness, the happiness of all his creatures, he never has, he never will institute an ordinance, or give a commandment to his people that is not calculated in its nature to promote that happiness which he has designed, and which will not end in the greatest amount of good and glory to those who become the recipients of his laws and ordinances. Blessings offered, but rejected are no longer blessings, but become like the talent hid in the earth by the wicked and slothful servant—the proffered good returns of the giver, the blessing is bestowed on those who will receive, and occupy; for unto him that hath shall be given, and he shall have abundantly; but unto him that hath not, or will not receive, shall be taken away that which he hath, or might have had.

> "Be wise to-day, 'tis madness to defer.
> Next day the fatal precedent may plead;

Thus on till wisdom is pushed out of time," Into eternity. Our heavenly father is more liberal in his views, and boundless in his mercies and blessings, than we are ready to believe or receive, and at the same time is as terrible to the workers of iniquity, more awful in the executions of his punishments, and more ready to detect every false way than we are apt to suppose him to be. He will be enquired of by his children—he says ask and ye shall receive, seek and ye shall find; but if ye will take that which is not your own, or which I have not given you, you shall be rewarded according to your deeds, but no good thing will I withhold from them who walk uprightly before me, and do my will in all things, who will listen to my voice, and to the voice of my servant whom I have sent, for I delight in those who seek diligently to know my precepts, and abide by the laws of my kingdom, for all things shall be made known unto them in mine own due time, and in the end they shall have joy.

Notes

1. Exodus 20:13.
2. See, for example, Exodus 32:26–28; 1 Samuel 15:3.
3. Matthew 6:33.
4. Joseph seems to be making specific but veiled reference to Soloman's many wives.

10. AN EXPRESSION OF GRATITUDE (1842)

Willard Richards was an able and devoted personal secretary to Joseph Smith and later a competent compiler of the Prophet's history. Richards' faithfulness to his many assignments often kept him from contact with his family. The letter to Willard's wife is a token of appreciation from one who recognized the family's sacrifice and contribution to the ongoing kingdom. This letter is found is Personal Writings of Joseph Smith, *pp. 521–22.*

Nauvoo June 23rd 1842

Sister Jennetta Richards;

Agreabley to your request, in the midst of all the bustle, and buisness of the day, and the care of all the Churches boath at home and abroad, I now imbrace a moment to adress a few words to you thinking peradventure it may be a consolation to you to know that you too are remembered by me as well as all the saints. my hearts desire and prayr to God is all the day long for all the saints and in an especial and poticular manner for those whom he hath chosen and anointed to bear the heaviest burthens in the heat of the day among which number is your husband received a man in whom I have the most implicit confidence and trust you say I have got him so I have in the which I rejoice, for he has done me great good and taken a great burden off my shoulders since his arrival in Nauvoo never did I have greater intimacy with any man than with him may the blessings of Elijah[1] crown his head forever and ever. we are about to send him in a few days after his dear familyy he shall have our pray'rs fervently for his safe arrival to their imbraces and may God speed his Journey and return him quickly to our society, and I want you beloved Sister to be a Genral in this matter, in helping him along, which I know you will he will be able to teach you many things which you never have heard you may have implicit confidence in the same. I have heard much about you by the twelve[2] and in consequence of the great friendship that exists between your husband and me and the information they all have given me of your virtue and strong attachment to the truth of the work of God in the Last Days I have formed a very strong Brotherly friendship and attachment for you in the bonds of the Gosple, Although I never saw you I shall be exceedingly glad to see you face to face and be able to administer in the name of the Lord some of the words of Life to your consolation and I hope that you may be kept steadfast in the faith even unto the end, I want you should give my love and tender reguard to Br Richards familey and those who are friendly enough to me to enquire after me in that region of Country, not having but little time to apportion to anyone & having stolen this oppertunity I therefore subscribe myself in haste your most obedient Brother in the fulness of the Gosple

Joseph Smith

P.S. Bro Richards having been with me for a long time can give you any information which you need and will tell you all about me. I shall be very anxious for his return he is a grate prop to me in my Labours.

Mrs. Jenetta Richards
Richmond
Massachusetts

Notes

1. Joseph Smith seems to be making reference to the sealing powers restored by Elijah in the Kirtland Temple in 1836. The Prophet taught that the powers of Elijah were those necessary to assure salvation. (*History of the Church,* 6:252).
2. That is, from members of the Quorum of Twelve Apostles.

11. AN INVITATION TO RETURN
TO CHURCH ACTIVITY (1844)

The following brief letter is an invitation to a Mr. Abijah Tewksbury in Boston to return to the Church which he had once joined but since left. From Personal Writings of Joseph Smith, *pp. 580–81.* Nauvoo Ill. June 4, 1844.

Sir: We understand that you have been cut off from the church of Jesus Christ of Latter-Day Saints, and feeling an ardent desire for the salvation of the souls of men, we take pleasure in feeling after you: and therefore would in the sincerity of men of God advise you to be rebaptized by Elder Nickerson one of the servants of God that you may again receive the sweet influences of the holy Ghost, and enjoy the fellowship of the Saints the law of God requires it and you cannot be too good Patience is heavenly; obedience is noble: forgiveness is merciful; and exhaltation is Godly: and he that holds out faithful to the end shall in no wise lose his reward. A good man will endure all things to honor Christ, and dispose of the whole world and all in it to save his soul grace for grace is a heavenly decree, and union is power where wisdom guides

> Respectfully even
> Joseph Smith
> Hyrum Smith

12. LETTER TO EMMA:
HOURS BEFORE THE MARTYRDOM (1844)

In June of 1844 a dissident element in Nauvoo, Illinois, published an issue of a paper entitled the Nauvoo Expositer, *in which a number of damaging statements were made with regard to Joseph Smith and Mormonism. Joseph declared the paper "a public nuisance" and ordered the press destroyed. Thereafter the Prophet was arrested for riot associated with the suppression of freedom of the press. He was in prison in Carthage, Illinois, the county seat, when he wrote the following letter to his wife. The letter was begun on June 26 but finished the next morning, only a matter of hours before a mob of 150–200 men stormed the jail, and shot and killed Joseph and his brother Hyrum. The letter is in* Personal Writings of Joseph Smith, *pp. 611–12.*

> *Carthage Jail Jun. 27th 1844*
> *20. Past 8. A M.*

Dear Emma

The Gov continues his courtesies, and permits us to see our friends. We hear this morning that the Governor will not go down with his troops to day (to Nauvoo) as was anticipated last Evening but, if he does come down with his troops you will be protected, & I want to tell you to tell Bro Dunham[1] to instruct the people to stay at home and attend to their own business and let there be no groups or gathering together unless by permission of the Gov—they are called together to receive communications from the Gov—which would please our people, but let the Gov. direct. —Bro Dunham of course, will obey the orders of the Government officers, and render them the assistance they require. There is no danger of any "exterminating order" Should there be a mutiny among the troops, (which we do not anticipate, excitement is abating,) a part will remain loyal, and stand for the defence of the state & our rights; There is one principle which is Eternal, it is the duty of all men to protect their lives from every and the lives of their households whenever occasion necessity requires. and no power has a right to forbid id it. when w[. .]et should the last extreme arrive,—but *I anticipate no such extreme,* —but caution is the patent of safety.—

> Joseph Smith

PS Dear Emma,

I am very much resigned to my lot knowing I am Justified and have done the best that could be done give my love to the children and all my Friends Mr Brower[2] and all who in after inquire after me and as for treason I know that I have not commited any and they cannot prove one apearance of any thing of the kind So you need not have any fears that any harme can happen to us on that score may God bll bless you all Amen

Joseph Smith

Notes

1. Jonathan Dunham was acting major general of the Nauvoo Legion, a trained military force in the City of the Saints.
2. Perhaps a Colonel J. Brewer, a U.S. Army officer who visited Nauvoo a few days earlier.

IV.

SERMONS

In the winter of 1834–35, Joseph Smith organized a group of men into what came to be known as the "School of Prophets" or "School of the Elders." This project came as a result of a commandment to do so in revelations to the Prophet. (See Doctrine and Covenants 88:127, 136–41; 90:7.) Among the areas of study for this body (in addition to English grammar and Biblical Hebrew) was the principle of Faith. It appears that Joseph Smith and perhaps some of the leaders of the Church (e.g., Signey Rigdon, William W. Phelps) prepared seven theological lectures for presentation to the School of the Prophets, and this material came to be known as the "Lectures on Faith." In the words of Joseph Smith, these teachings were put forward to demonstrate what faith is, the objects on which it rests, and the fruits which flow from it. The lectures were included in the first edition (1835) of the Doctrine and Covenants, *and were a part of that book of LDS Scripture until 1921. The following four sermons are from the collection of* Lectures on Faith.

1. FAITH: A PRINCIPLE OF POWER (1834–35)

1. Faith being the first principle in revealed religion, and the foundation of all righteousness, necessarily claims the first place in a course of lectures which are designed to unfold to the understanding the doctrine of Jesus Christ.

2. In presenting the subject of faith, we shall observe the following order—

3. First, faith itself—what it is.

4. Secondly, the object on which it rests. And,

5. Thirdly, the effects which flow from it.

6. Agreeable to this order we have first to show what faith is.

7. The author of the epistle to the Hebrews, in the eleventh chapter of that epistle and first verse, gives the following definition of the word faith:

8. "Now faith is the substance [assurance] of things hoped for, the evidence of things not seen."

9. From this we learn that faith is the assurance which men have of the existence of things which they have not seen, and the principle of action in all intelligent beings.

10. If men were duly to consider themselves, and turn their thoughts and reflections to the operations of their own minds, they would readily discover that it is faith, and faith only, which is the moving cause of all action in them; that without it both mind and body would be in a state of inactivity, and all their exertions would cease, both physical and mental.

11. Were this class to go back and reflect upon the history of their lives, from the period of their first recollection, and ask themselves what principles excited them to action, or what gave them energy and activity in all their lawful avocations, callings, and pursuits, what would be the answer? Would it not be that it was the assurance which they had of the existence of things which they had not seen as yet? Was it not the hope which you had, in consequence of your belief in the existence of unseen things which stimulated you to action and exertion in order to obtain them? Are you not dependent on your faith, or belief, for the acquisition of all knowledge, wisdom, and intelligence? Would you exert yourselves to obtain wisdom and intelligence, unless you did believe that you could obtain them? Would you have ever sown, if you had not believed that you would reap? Would you have ever planted, if you had not believed that you would gather? Would you have ever asked, unless you had believed that you would have found? Or, would you have ever knocked, unless you had believed that it would have been opened unto you? In a word, is there anything that you would have done, either physical or mental, if you had not previously believed? Are not all your exertions of every kind, dependent on your faith? Or, may we not ask, what have you, or what do you possess, which you have not obtained by reason of your faith? Your food, your raiment, your lodgings, are they not all by reason of your faith? Reflect, and ask yourselves if these things are not so. Turn your thoughts on your own minds, and see if faith is not the moving cause of all action in yourselves; and if the moving cause in you, is it not in all other intelligent beings?

12. And as faith is the moving cause of all action in temporal concerns, so it is in spiritual; for the Saviour has said, and that truly, that "He that *believeth* and is baptized, shall be saved." Mark xvi.16.

13. And as we receive by faith all temporal blessings that we do receive, so we in like manner receive by faith all spiritual blessings that we do receive. But faith is not only the principle of action, but of power also, in all intelligent beings, whether in heaven or on earth. Thus says the author of the epistle to the Hebrews, xi. 3——

14. "Through faith we understand that the worlds were framed by the word of God; so that things which are seen were not made of things which do appear."

15. By this we understand that the principle of power which existed in the bosom of God, by which the worlds were framed, was faith: and that it is by reason of this principle of power existing in the Deity, that all created things exist; so that all things in heaven, on earth, or under the earth exist by reason of faith as it existed in HIM.

16. Had it not been for the principle of faith the worlds would never have been framed, neither would man have been formed of the dust. It is the principle by which Jehovah works, and through which he exercises power over all temporal as well as eternal things. Take this principle or attribute—for it is an attribute—from the Deity, and he would cease to exist.

17. Who cannot see, that if God framed the worlds by faith, that it is by faith that he exercises power over them, and that faith is the principle of power? And if the principle of power, it must be so in man as well as in the Deity? This is the testimony of all the sacred writers, and the lesson which they have been endeavouring to teach to man.

18. The Saviour says (Matthew xvii. 19, 20), in explaining the reason why the disciples could not cast out the devil, that it was because of their unbelief—"For verily I say unto you" (said he), "if ye have faith as a grain of mustard seed, ye shall say unto this mountain, Remove hence to yonder place, and it shall remove; and nothing shall be impossible unto you."

19. Moroni, while abridging and compiling the record of his fathers, has given us the following account of faith as the principle of power. He says, page 509, that it was the faith of Alma and Amulek which caused the walls of the prison to be rent, as recorded on the 246th page; it was the faith of Nephi and Lehi which caused a change to be wrought upon the hearts of the Lamanites, when they were immersed with the Holy Spirit and with fire, as seen on the 380th page; and that it was by faith the mountain Zerin was removed when

the brother of Jared spake in the name of the Lord. See also 511th page.

20. In addition to this we are told in Hebrews xi. 32, 33, 34, 35, that Gideon, Barak, Samson, Jephthah, David, Samuel, and the prophets, through faith subdued kingdoms, wrought righteousness, obtained promises, stopped the mouths of lions, quenched the violence of fire, escaped the edge of the sword; out of weakness were made strong, waxed valiant in fight, turned to flight the armies of the aliens, and that women received their dead raised to life again, &c., &c.

21. Also, Joshua, in the sight of all Israel, bade the sun and moon to stand still, and it was done. Joshua x: 12.

22. We here understand, that the sacred writers say that all these things were done by faith. It was by faith that the worlds were framed. God spake, chaos heard, and worlds came into order by reason of the faith there was in HIM. So with man also; he spake by faith in the name of God, and the sun stood still, the moon obeyed, mountains removed, prisons fell, lion's mouths were closed, the human heart lost its enmity, fire its violence, armies their power, the sword its terror, and death its dominion; and all this by reason of the faith which was in him.

23. Had it not been for the faith which was in men, they might have spoken to the sun, the moon, the mountains, prisons, the human heart, fire, armies, the sword, or to death in vain!

24. Faith, then, is the first great governing principle which has power, dominion, and authority over all things; by it they exist, by it they are upheld, by it they are changed, or by it they remain, agreeable to the will of God. Without it there is no power, and without power there could be no creation nor existence!

2. THE CHARACTER AND PERFECTIONS OF GOD:
LECTURES ON FAITH #4, 5 (1834–35)

1. . . . Correct ideas of the character of God are necessary in order to the exercise of faith in him unto life and salvation; and that without correct ideas of his character the minds of men could not have sufficient power with God to the exercise of faith necessary to the enjoyment of eternal life; and that correct ideas of his character lay a foundation, as far as his character is concerned, for the exercise of faith, so as to enjoy the fullness of the blessing of the gospel of

Jesus Christ, even that of eternal glory; we shall now proceed to show the connection there is between correct ideas of the attributes of God, and the exercise of faith in him unto eternal life.

2. Let us here observe, that the real design which the God of heaven had in view in making the human family acquainted with his attributes, was, that they, through the ideas of the existence of his attributes, might be enabled to exercise faith in him, and through the exercise of faith in him, might obtain eternal life; for without the idea of the existence of the attributes which belong to God, the minds of men could not have the power to exercise faith in him so as to lay hold upon eternal life. The God of heaven, understanding most perfectly the constitution of human nature, and the weakness of men, knew what was necessary to be revealed, and what ideas must be planted in their minds in order that they might be enabled to exercise faith in him unto eternal life.

3. Having said so much, we shall proceed to examine the attributes of God as set forth in his revelations to the human family, and to show how necessary correct ideas of his attributes are to enable men to exercise faith in him; for without these ideas being planted in the minds of men it would be out of the power of any person or persons to exercise faith in God so as to obtain eternal life. So that the divine communications made to men in the first instance were designed to establish in their minds the ideas necessary to enable them to exercise faith in God, and through this means to be partakers of his glory.

4. We have, in the revelations which he has given to the human family, the following account of his attributes:

5. First—Knowledge. Acts xv. 18: "Known unto God are all his works from the beginning of the world." Isaiah xlvi. 9, 10: "Remember the former things of old: for I am God, and there is none else; I am God, and there is none like me *declaring the end from the beginning,* and from ancient time the things that are not yet done, saying 'My counsel shall stand, and I will do all my pleasure.' "

6. Secondly—Faith or power. Hebrews xi. 3: "Through faith we understand that the worlds were framed by the word of God." Genesis i. 1: "In the beginning God created the heaven and the earth." Isaiah xiv. 24, 27: "The Lord of hosts hath sworn saying, "Surely as I have thought, so shall it come to pass: and as I have purposed so shall it stand. For the Lord of Hosts hath purposed, and who shall disannul it? and his hand is stretched out, and who shall turn it back?' "

7. Thirdly—Justice. Psalm lxxxix. 14: "Justice and judgment

are the habitation of thy throne." Isaiah xlv. 21: "Tell ye, and bring them near; yea, let them take counsel together: who hath declared this from the ancient time? have not I the Lord? and there is no God else beside me; a just God and a Saviour." Zephaniah iii. 5. "The just Lord is in the midst thereof." Zechariah ix. 9" "Rejoice greatly, O daughter of Zion; shout, O daughter of Jerusalem; behold thy King cometh unto thee: he is just and having salvation."

8. Fourthly—Judgment. Psalm lxxxix. 14: "Justice and judgment are the habitation of thy throne." Deuteronomy xxxii 4: "He is the Rock, his work is perfect; for all his ways are judgment: a God of truth and without iniquity, just and right is he." Psalm ix.7: "But the Lord shall endure for ever. He hath prepared his throne for judgment." Psalm ix. 16: "The Lord is known by the judgment which he executeth."

9. Fifthly—Mercy. Psalm lxxxix. 14: "Mercy and truth shall go before his face." Exodus xxxiv. 6: "And the Lord passed by before him, and proclaimed, 'The Lord, the Lord God, is merciful and gracious.' " Nehemiah ix. 17: "But thou art a God ready to pardon, gracious and merciful."

10. And sixthly—Truth. Psalm lxxxix. 14: "Mercy and truth shall go before thy face." Exodus xxxiv. 6: "Long suffering and abundant in goodness and truth." Deuteronomy xxxii. 4: "He is the Rock, his work is perfect; for all his ways are judgment: a God of truth and without iniquity, just and right is he." Psalm xxxi. 5: "Into Thine hand I commit my spirit: thou hast redeemed me, O Lord God of Truth."

11. By a little reflection it will be seen that the idea of the existence of these attributes in the Deity is necessary to enable any rational being to exercise faith in him; for without the idea of the existence of these attributes in the Deity men could not exercise faith in him for life and salvation; seeing that without the knowledge of all things, God would not be able to save any portion of his creatures; for it is by reason of the knowledge which he has of all things, from the beginning to the end, that enables him to give that understanding to his creatures by which they are made partakers of eternal life; and if it were not for the idea existing in the minds of men that God had all knowledge it would be impossible for them to exercise faith in him.

12. And it is not less necessary that men should have the idea of the existence of the attribute power in the Deity; for unless God had power over all things, and was able by his power to control all things, and thereby deliver his creatures who put their trust in him from the power of all beings that might seek their destruction, whether in heaven, on earth, or in hell, men could not be saved. But with the

idea of the existence of this attribute planted in the mind, men feel as though they had nothing to fear who put their trust in God, believing that he has power to save all who come to him to the very uttermost.

13. It is also necessary, in order to the exercise of faith in God unto life and salvation, that men should have the idea of the existence of the attribute justice in him; for without the idea of the existence of the attribute justice in the Deity, men could not have confidence sufficient to place themslves under his guidance and direction; for they would be filled with fear and doubt lest the judge of all the earth would not do right, and thus fear or doubt, existing in the mind, would preclude the possibility of the exercise of faith in him for life and salvation. But when the idea of the existence of the attribute justice in the Deity is fairly planted in the mind, it leaves no room for doubt to get into the heart, and the mind is enabled to cast itself upon the Almighty without fear and without doubt, and with the most unshaken confidence, believing that the Judge of all the earth will do right.

14. It is also of equal importance that men should have the idea of the existence of the attribute judgment in God, in order that they might exercise faith in him for life and salvation; for without the idea of the existence of this attribute in the Deity, it would be impossible for men to exercise faith in him for life and salvation, seeing that it is through the exercise of this attribute that the faithful in Christ Jesus are delivered out of the hands of those who seek their destruction; for if God were not to come out in swift judgment against the workers of iniquity and the powers of darkness, his saints could not be saved; for it is by judgment that the Lord delivers his saints out of the hands of all their enemies, and those who reject the gospel of our Lord Jesus Christ. But no sooner is the idea of the existence of this attribute planted in the minds of men, than it gives power to the mind for the exercise of faith and confidence in God, and they are enabled by faith to lay hold on the promises which are set before them, and wade through all the tribulations and afflictions to which they are subjected by reason of the persecution from those who know not God, and obey not the gospel of our Lord Jesus Christ, believing that in due time the Lord will come out in swift judgment against their enemies, and they shall be cut off from before him, and that in his own due time he will bear them off conquerors, and more than conquerors, in all things.

15. And again, it is equally important that men should have the idea of the existence of the attribute mercy in the Deity, in order to excrcise faith in him for life and salvation; for without the idea of the existence of this attribute in the Deity, the spirits of the saints would

faint in the midst of the tribulations, afflictions, and persecutions which they have to endure for righteousness' sake. But when the idea of the existence of this attribute is once established in the mind it gives life and energy to the spirits of the saints, believing that the mercy of God will be poured out upon them in the midst of their afflictions, and that he will compassionate them in their sufferings, and that the mercy of God will lay hold of them and secure them in the arms of his love, so that they will receive a full reward for all their sufferings.

16. And lastly, but not less important to the exercise of faith in God, is the idea of the existence of the attribute truth in him; for without the idea of the existence of this attribute the mind of man could have nothing upon which it could rest with certainty—all would be confusion and doubt. But with the idea of the existence of this attribute in the Deity in the mind, all the teachings, instructions, promises, and blessings, become realities, and the mind is enabled to lay hold of them with certainty and confidence, believing that these things, and all that the Lord has said, shall be fulfilled in their time; and that all the cursings, denunciations and judgments, pronounced upon the heads of the unrighteous, will also be executed in the due time of the Lord: and, by reason of the truth and veracity of him, the mind beholds its deliverance and salvation as being certain.

17. Let the mind once reflect sincerely and candidly upon the ideas of the existence of the before-mentioned attributes in the Deity, and it will be seen that, as far as his attributes are concerned, there is a sure foundation laid for the exercise of faith in him for life and salvation. For inasmuch as God possesses the attribute knowledge, he can make all things known to his saints necessary for their salvation; and as he possesses the attribute power, he is able thereby to deliver them from the power of all enemies; and seeing, also, that justice is an attribute of the Deity, he will deal with them upon the principles of righteousness and equity, and a just reward will be granted unto them for all their afflictions and sufferings for the truth's sake. And as judgment is an attribute of the Deity also, his saints can have the most unshaken confidence that they will, in due time, obtain a perfect deliverance out of the hands of their enemies, and a complete victory over all those who have sought their hurt and destruction. And as mercy is also an attribute of the Deity, his saints can have confidence that it will be exercised towards them, and through the exercise of that attribute towards them comfort and consolation will be administered unto them abundantly, amid all their afflictions and tribulations. And, lastly, realizing that truth is an attribute of the Deity, the

mind is led to rejoice amid all its trials and temptations, in hope of that glory which is to be brought at the revelation of Jesus Christ, and in view of that crown which is to be placed upon the heads of the saints in the day when the Lord shall distribute rewards unto them, and in prospect of that eternal weight of glory which the Lord has promised to bestow upon them, when he shall bring them in the midst of his throne to dwell in his presence eternally.

18. In view, then, of the existence of these attributes, the faith of the saints can become exceedingly strong, abounding in righteousness unto the praise and glory of God, and can exert its mighty influence in searching after wisdom and understanding until it has obtained a knowledge of all things that pertain to life and salvation.

19. Such, then, is the foundation which is laid, through the revelation of the attributes of God, for the exercise of faith in him for life and salvation; and seeing that these are attributes of the Deity, they are unchangeable—being the same yesterday, to-day, and for ever—which gives to the minds of the Latter-day Saints the same power and authority to exercise faith in God which the Former-day Saints had; so that all the saints, in this respect, have been, are, and will be, alike until the end of time; for God never changes, therefore his attributes and character remain forever the same. And as it is through the revelation of these that a foundation is laid for the exercise of faith in God unto life and salvation, the foundation, thereof, for the exercise of faith was, is, and ever will be, the same; so that all men have had, and will have, an equal privilege.

1. In our former lectures we treated of the being, character, perfections, and attributes of God. What we mean by perfections is, the perfections which belong to all the attributes of his nature. We shall, in this lecture, speak of the Godhead—we mean the Father, Son, and Holy Spirit.

2. There are two personages who constitute the great, matchless, governing, and supreme power over all things, by whom all things were created and made, that are created and made, whether visible or invisible, whether in heaven, on earth, or in the earth, under the earth, or throughout the immensity of space. They are the Father and the Son—the Father being a personage of spirit,[1] glory, and power, possessing all perfection and fullness, the Son, who was in the bosom of the Father, a personage of tabernacle, made or fashioned like unto man, or being in the form and likeness of man, or rather man was formed after his likeness and in his image; he is also the express image and likeness of the personage of the Father, possess-

ing all the fullness of the Father, or the same fullness with the Father; being begotten of him, and ordained from before the foundation of the world to be a propitiation for the sins of all those who should believe on his name,[2] and is called the Son because of the flesh, and descended in suffering below that which man can suffer; or, in other words, suffered greater sufferings, and was exposed to more powerful contradictions than any man can be.[3] But, notwithstanding all this, he kept the law of God, and remained without sin,[4] showing thereby that it is in the power of man to keep the law and remain also without sin; and also, that by him a righteous judgment might come upon all flesh, and that all who walk not in the law of God may justly be condemned by the law, and have no excuse for their sins. And he being the Only Begotten of the Father, full of grace and truth, and having overcome, received a fullness of the glory of the Father, possessing the same mind with the Father, which mind is the Holy Spirit, that bears record of the Father and the Son, and these three are one; or, in other words, these three constitute the great, matchless, governing and supreme power over all things; by whom all things were created and made that were created and made, and these three constitute the Godhead, and are one;[5] the Father and the Son possessing the same mind, the same wisdom, glory, power, and fullness—filling all in all; the Son being filled with the fullness of the mind, glory, and power; or, in other words, the spirit, glory, and power, of the Father, possessing all knowledge and glory, and the same kingdom, sitting at the right hand in power, in the express image and likeness of the Father, mediator for man, being filled with the fullness of the mind of the Father; or, in other words, the Spirit of the Father, which Spirit is shed forth upon all who believe on his name and keep his commandments; and all those who keep his commandments shall grow up from grace to grace, and become heirs of the heavenly kingdom, and joint heirs with Jesus Christ;[6] possessing the same mind, being transformed into the same image or likeness, even the express image of him who fills all in all; being filled with the fullness of his glory, and become one in him, even as the Father, Son and Holy Spirit are one.

3. From the foregoing account of the Godhead, which is given in his revelations, the saints have a sure foundation laid for the exercise of faith unto life and salvation, through the atonement and mediation of Jesus Christ; by whose blood they have a forgiveness of sins, and also a sure reward laid up for them in heaven, even that of partaking of the fullness of the Father and the Son through the Spirit. As the Son partakes of the fullness of the Father through the Spirit, so the saints are, by the same Spirit, to be partakers of the same

fullness, to enjoy the same glory; for as the Father and the Son are one, so, in like manner, the saints are to be one in them. Through the love of the Father, the mediation of Jesus Christ, and the gift of the Holy Spirit, they are to be heirs of God, and joint heirs with Jesus Christ.

Notes

1. See Introduction, note 35.
2. Romans 3:25; 1 John 2:2; 4:10.
3. Hebrews 12:3.
4. 2 Corinthians 5:21; Hebrews 4:15; 1 Peter 2:22.
5. Joseph Smith taught the oneness of the members of the Godhead in regard to mind, purpose, and glory, but maintained from the beginning of his ministry a belief that they were separate and distinct persons. "I have always declared God to be a distinct personage, Jesus Christ a separate and distinct personage from God the Father, and that the Holy Ghost was a distinct personage and a Spirit: and these three constitute three distinct personages and three Gods." (*History of the Church,* 6:474.)
6. Romans 8:17.

3. SACRIFICE AND THE BLESSINGS OF HEAVEN: LECTURE ON FAITH #6 (1834–35)

1. Having treated in the preceding lectures of the ideas, of the character, perfections, and attributes of God, we next proceed to treat of the knowledge which persons must have, that the course of life which they pursue is according to the will of God, in order that they may be enabled to exercise faith in him unto life and salvation.[1]

2. This knowledge supplies an important place in revealed religion; for it was by reason of it that the ancients were enabled to endure as seeing him who is invisible. An actual knowledge to any person, that the course of life which he pursues is according to the will of God, is essentially necessary to enable him to have that confidence in God without which no person can obtain eternal life. It was this that enabled the ancient saints to endure all their afflictions and persecutions, and to take joyfully the spoiling of their goods, knowing (not believing merely) that they had a more enduring substance. Hebrews x. 34.

3. Having the assurance that they were pursuing a course which

was agreeable to the will of God, they were enabled to take not only the spoiling of their goods, and the wasting of their substance, joyfully, but also to suffer death in its most horrid forms; knowing (not merely believing) that when this earthly house of their tabernacle was dissolved, they had a building of God, a house not made with hands, eternal in the heavens. 2 Corinthians v. 1.

4. Such was, and always will be, the situation of the saints of God, that unless they have an actual knowledge that the course they are pursuing is according to the will of God they will grow weary in their minds, and faint; for such has been, and always will be, the opposition in the hearts of unbelievers and those that know not God against the pure and unadulterated religion of heaven (the only thing which insures eternal life), that they will persecute to the uttermost all that worship God according to his revelations, receive the truth in the love of it, and submit themselves to be guided and directed by his will; and drive them to such extremities that nothing short of an actual knowledge of their being the favorites of heaven, and of their having embraced the order of things which God has established for the redemption of man, will enable them to exercise that confidence in him, necessary for them to overcome the world, and obtain that crown of glory which is laid up for them that fear God.

5. For a man to lay down his all, his character and reputation, his honor, and applause, his good name among men, his houses, his lands, his brothers and sisters, his wife and children, and even his own life also—counting all things but filth and dross for the excellency of the knowledge of Jesus Christ—requires more than mere belief or supposition that he is doing the will of God; but actual knowledge, realizing that, when these sufferings are ended, he will enter into eternal rest, and be a partaker of the glory of God.

6. For unless a person does know that he is walking according to the will of God, it would be offering an insult to the dignity of the Creator were he to say that he would be a partaker of his glory when he should be done with the things of this life. But when he has this knowledge, and most assuredly knows that he is doing the will of God, his confidence can be equally strong that he will be a partaker of the glory of God.

7. Let us here observe, that a religion that does not require the sacrifice of all things never has power sufficient to produce the faith necessary unto life and salvation; for, from the first existence of man, the faith necessary unto the enjoyment of life and salvation never could be obtained without the sacrifice of all earthly things. It was through this sacrifice, and this only, that God has ordained that men

should enjoy eternal life; and it is through the medium of the sacrifice of all earthly things that men do actually know that they are doing the things that are well pleasing in the sight of God. When a man has offered in sacrifice all that he has for the truth's sake, not even withholding his life, and believing before God that he has been called to make this sacrifice because he seeks to do his will, he does know, most assuredly, that God does and will accept his sacrifice and offering, and that he has not, nor will not seek his face in vain. Under these circumstances, then, he can obtain the faith necessary for him to lay hold on eternal life.

8. It is in vain for persons to fancy themselves that they are heirs with those, or can be heirs with them, who have offered their all in sacrifice, and by this means obtain faith in God and favor with him so as to obtain eternal life, unless they, in like manner, offer unto him the same sacrifice, and through that offering obtain the knowledge that they are accepted of him.

9. It was in offering sacrifices that Abel, the first martyr, obtained knowledge that he was accepted of God. And from the days of righteous Abel to the present time, the knowledge that men have that they are accepted in the sight of God is obtained by offering sacrifice. And in the last days, before the Lord comes, he is to gather together his saints who made a covenant with him by sacrifice. Psalm 1: 3, 4, 5: "Our God shall come, and shall not keep silence: a fire shall devour before him, and it shall be very tempestuous round about him. He shall call to the heavens from above, and to the earth, that he may judge his people. Gather my saints together unto me; those that have made a covenant with me by sacrifice."

10. Those, then, who make the sacrifice, will have the testimony that their course is pleasing in the sight of God; and those who have this testimony will have faith to lay hold on eternal life, and will be enabled, through faith, to endure unto the end, and receive the crown that is laid for them that love the appearing of our Lord Jesus Christ. But those who do not make the sacrifice cannot enjoy this faith, because men are dependent upon this sacrifice in order to obtain this faith: therefore, they cannot lay hold upon eternal life, because the revelations of God do not guarantee unto them the authority so to do, and without this guarantee faith could not exist.

11. All the saints of whom we have account, in all the revelations of God which are extant, obtained the knowledge which they had of their acceptance in his sight through the sacrifice which they offered unto him; and through the knowledge thus obtained their faith became sufficiently strong to lay hold upon the promise of eter-

nal life, and to endure as seeing him who is invisible; and were enabled, through faith, to combat the powers of darkness, contend against the wiles of the adversary, overcome the world, and obtain the end of their faith, even the salvation of their souls.

12. But those who have not made this sacrifice to God do not know the course which they pursue is well pleasing in his sight; for whatever may be their belief or their opinion, it is a matter of doubt and uncertainty in their mind; and where doubt and uncertainty are there faith is not, nor can it be. For doubt and faith do not exist in the same person at the same time; so that persons whose minds are under doubts and fears cannot have unshaken confidence; and where unshaken confidence is not there faith is weak; and where faith is weak the persons will not be able to contend against all the opposition, tribulations, and afflictions which they have to encounter in order to be heirs of God, and joint heirs with Christ Jesus; and they will grow weary in their minds, and the adversary will have power over them and destroy them.

Note

1. In the third lecture, Joseph explained that three things are necessary in order for any person to generate saving faith: (a) the idea that God actually exists; (b) a correct idea of his character, perfections, and attributes; and (c) an actual knowledge that the course in life one is pursuing is according to the will of God. That is, the first two prerequisites for faith are associated with his knowledge of and confidence in God; the third is related to his confidence in himself.

4. HOW GOD CAME TO BE GOD (1844)

On March 9, 1844, a man named King Follett was killed in Nauvoo in an accident involving the construction of a well. He was a well-known and beloved member of the Church, and so Joseph Smith utilized the April, 1844, conference of the Church to eulogize Follett. In so doing, the Prophet delivered one of his most profound and searching sermons, a statement which, in fact, is also one of the most controversial of all of Joseph Smith's teachings. As early as 1832 Joseph had learned in a revelation (Doctrine and Covenants 76) that man has the capacity to become as God is. In the Lectures on Faith (Lecture #5, 1834–35), he taught a similar message—that man has the power through the Atonement, of becoming joint heirs with Christ to all that the Father has. It was in the King Follett Sermon, delivered on April 7, 1844, that the Mormon Leader not only reaffirmed that man may become as God, but also taught the singularly Mormon doctrine that God is an exalted man, and that he once lived a mortal life like our own. Sources indicate that the sermon was recorded in some detail by Willard Richards, William Clayton, and Thomas Bullock—all scribes or secretaries to Joseph Smith—and by Wilford Woodruff, a member of the Quorum of the Twelve Apostles and a superb note taker/journal keeper. The text which follows is an amalgamation of the sermon from the notes of all four of the above-mentioned scribes, as contained in The Prophet Joseph Smith's King Follett Discourse: A Six-Column Comparison of Original Notes and Amalgamation, Introduction and Commentary by Donald Q. Cannon and Larry E. Dahl (Provo, Utah: Brigham Young University Printing Services, 1983).

Beloved Saints, I will call the attention of this congregation while I address you on the subject of the dead. The decease of our beloved brother Elder King Follett, who was crushed in a well by the falling of a tub of rock, has more immediately led to that subject. I have been requested to speak by his friends and relatives, but inasmuch as there are a great many in this congregation who live in this city as well as elsewhere, who have lost friends, I feel disposed to speak on the subject in general, and offer you my ideas, so far as I have ability, and so far as I shall be inspired by the Holy Spirit to dwell on this subject.

I want your prayers and faith that I may have the instruction of Almighty God and the gift of the Holy Ghost, so that I may set forth things that are true and which can be easily comprehended by you and that the testimony may carry conviction to your hearts and minds of the truth of what I shall say. Pray that the Lord may strengthen my lungs, stay the winds, and let the prayers of the Saints to heaven appear, that they may enter into the ears of the Lord of Sabaoth, for the effectual prayers of the righteous avail much. There is strength here, and I verily believe that your prayers will be heard. Before I enter fully into the investigation of the subject which is lying before me, I wish to pave the way and bring up the subject from the beginning, that you may understand it. I will make a few preliminaries, in order that you may understand the subject when I come to it. I do not intend to please your ears with superfluity of words or oratory or with much learning;[1] but I intend to edify you with the simple truths from heaven.

In the first place, I wish to go back to the beginning—to the morn of creation. There is the starting point for us to look to, in order to understand and be fully acquainted with the mind, purposes and decrees of the Great Elohim, who sits in yonder heavens as he did at the creation of this world. It is necessary for us to have an understanding of God himself in the beginning. If we start right it is easy to go right all the time; but if we start wrong, we may go wrong, and it be a hard matter to get right.

There are but a very few beings in the world who understand rightly the character of God. The great majority of mankind do not comprehend anything, either that which is past, or that which is to come, as it respects their relationship to God. They do not know, neither do they understand the nature of that relationship; and consequently they know but little above the brute beast, or more than to eat, drink and sleep. This is all man knows about God or his existence, unless it is given by the inspiration of the Almighty.

If a man learns nothing more than to eat, drink and sleep, and does not comprehend any of the designs of God, the beast comprehends the same things. It eats, drinks, sleeps, and knows nothing more about God; yet it knows as much as we, unless we are able to comprehend by the inspiration of Almighty God. If men do not comprehend the character of God, they do not comprehend themselves. I want to go back to the beginning, and so lift your minds into a more lofty sphere and a more exalted understanding than what the human mind generally aspires to.

I want to ask this congregation, every man, woman and child, to answer the question in their own heart, what kind of a being God is? Ask yourselves; turn your thoughts into your hearts, and say if any of you have seen, heard, or communed with him. This is a question that may occupy your attention for a long time. I again repeat the question—What kind of a being is God? Does any man or woman know? Have any of you seen him, heard him, or communed with him? Here is the question that will, peradventure, from this time henceforth occupy your attention. The scriptures inform us that "This is life eternal that they may know thee, the only true God, and Jesus Christ whom thou hast sent."[2]

If any man does not know God, and inquires what kind of a being he is—if he will search diligently his own heart—if the declaration of Jesus and the apostles be true, he will realize that he has not eternal life; for there can be eternal life on no other principle.

My first object is to find out the character of the only wise and true God, and what kind of a being he is; and if I am so fortunate as to be the man to comprehend God, and explain or convey the principles to your hearts, so that the Spirit seals them upon you, then let every man and woman henceforth sit in silence, put their hands on their mouths, and never lift their hands or voices, or say anything against the man of God or the servants of God again. But if I fail to do it, it becomes my duty to renounce all further pretensions to revelations and inspirations, or to be a prophet; and I should be like the rest of the world—a false teacher, be hailed as a friend, and no man would seek my life. But if all religious teachers were honest enough to renounce their pretensions to godliness when their ignorance of the knowledge of God is made manifest, they will all be as badly off as I am, at any rate; and you might as well take the lives of other false teachers as that of mine, if I am false.[3] If any man is authorized to take away my life because he thinks and says I am a false teacher, then, upon the same principle, we should be justified in taking away the life of every false teacher, and where would be the end of blood? And who would not be the sufferer?

But meddle not with any man for his religion: and all governments ought to permit every man to enjoy his religion unmolested. No man is authorized to take away life in consequence of difference of religion, which all laws and governments ought to tolerate and protect, right or wrong. Every man has a natural, and, in our country, a constitutional right to be a false prophet, as well as a true prophet. If I show, verily, that I have the truth of God, and show that ninety-nine out of every hundred professing religious ministers are false teachers, having no authority, while they pretend to hold the keys of God's kingdom on earth, and was to kill them because they are false teachers it would deluge the whole world with blood.

I will prove that the world is wrong, by showing what God is. I am going to enquire after God; for I want you all to know him, and to be familiar with him; and if I am bringing you to a knowledge of him, all persecutions against me ought to cease. You will then know that I am his servant; for I speak as one having authority.

I will go back to the beginning before the world was, to show what kind of being God is. What sort of a being was God in the beginning? Open your ears and hear all ye ends of the earth for I am going to prove it to you by the Bible, and to tell you the designs of God in relation to the human race, and why He interferes with the affairs of man.

God himself was once as we are now, and is an exalted man, and sits enthroned in yonder heavens! That is the great secret. If the veil were rent today, and the great God who holds this world its in orbit, and who upholds all worlds and all things by his power, was to make himself visible—I say, if you were to see him today you would see him like a man in form—like yourselves in all the person, image, and very form as a man; for Adam was created in the very fashion, image and likeness of God, and received instruction from, and walked, talked and conversed with him, as one man talks and communes with another.

In order to understand the subject of the dead, for consolation of those who mourn for the loss of their friends, it is necessary we should understand the character and being of God and how he came to be so; for I am going to tell you how God came to be God. We have imagined and supposed that God was God from all eternity. I will refute that idea, and take away the veil, so that you may see.

These are incomprehensible ideas to some, but they are simple. It is the first principle of the Gospel to know for a certainty the Character of God, and to know that we may converse with him as one man converses with another, and that he was once a man like us; yea, that God himself, the Father of us all, dwelt on an earth, the same as Jesus Christ himself did; and I will show it from the Bible.

I wish I was in a suitable place to tell it, and that I had the trump of an archangel, so that I could tell the story in such a manner that persecution would cease for ever. What did Jesus say? (Mark it, Elder Rigdon!) The Scriptures inform us that Jesus said, As the Father hath power in Himself, even so hath the Son power[4]—to do what? Why, what the Father did. The answer is obvious—in a manner to lay down His body and take it up again. Jesus, what are you going to do? To lay down my life as my Father did, and take it up again. Do we believe it? If you do not believe it, you do not believe the Bible. The Scriptures say it, and I defy all the learning and wisdom and all the combined powers of earth and hell together to refute it.

Here, then, is eternal life—to know the only wise and true God;[5] and you have got to learn how to be Gods yourselves, and to be kings and priests to God, the same as all Gods have done before you, namely, by going from one small degree to another, and from a small capacity to a great one; from grace to grace, from exaltation to exaltation, until you attain to the resurrection of the dead, and are able to dwell in everlasting burnings, and to sit in glory, as do those who sit enthroned in everlasting power. And I want you to know that God, in the last days, while certain individuals are proclaiming his name, is not trifling with you or me.

These are the first principles of consolation. How consoling to the mourners when they are called to part with a husband, wife, father, mother, child, or dear relative, to know that, although the earthly tabernacle is laid down and dissolved, they shall rise again to dwell in everlasting burnings[6] in immortal glory, not to sorrow, suffer, or die any more; but they shall be heirs of God and joint heirs with Jesus Christ.[7] What is it? To inherit the same power, the same glory and the same exaltation until you arrive at the station of a God, and ascend the throne of eternal power, the same as those who have gone before. What did Jesus do? Why; I do the things I saw my Father do[8] when worlds came rolling into existence. My Father worked out his kingdom with fear and trembling, and I must do the same; and when I get my kingdom, I shall present it to my Father, so that he may obtain kingdom upon kingdom, and it will exalt him in glory. He will then take a higher exaltation, and I will take his place, and thereby become exalted myself. So that Jesus treads in the tracks of his Father, and inherits what God did before; and God is thus glorified and exalted in the salvation and exaltation of all his children. It is plain beyond disputation, and you thus learn some of the first principles of the Gospel, about which so much hath been said.

When you climb up a ladder, you must begin at the bottom, and ascend step by step, until you arrive at the top; and so it is with the principles of the Gospel—you must begin with the first, and go on until you learn all the principles of exaltation. But it will be a great while after you have passed through the veil before you will have learned them. It is not all to be comprehended in this world; it will be a great work to learn our salvation and exaltation even beyond the grave. I suppose I am not allowed to go into an investigation of anything that is not contained in the Bible. If I do, I think there are so many over-wise men here, that they would cry "treason" and put me to death. So I will go to the old Bible and turn commentator today.

I shall comment on the very first Hebrew word in the Bible; I will make a comment on the very first sentence of the history of creation in the Bible—Berosheit. I want to analyze the word. Baith—in, by, through, and everything else. Rosh—the head. Sheit—grammatical termination. When the inspired man wrote it, he did not put the baith there. An old Jew without any authority added the word; he thought it too bad to begin to talk about the head! It read first, "The head one of the Gods brought forth the Gods." That is the true meaning of the words. Baurau signifies to bring forth. If you do not believe it, you do not believe the learned man of God. Learned men can teach you no more than what I have told you. Thus the head God brought forth the Gods in the grand council.

I will transpose and simplify it in the English language. Oh, ye lawyers, ye doctors, and ye priests, who have persecuted me, I want to let you know that the Holy Ghost knows something as well as you do. The head God called together the Gods and sat in grand council to bring forth the world. The grand councilors sat at the head in yonder heavens and contemplated the creation of the worlds which were created at the time. When I say doctors and lawyers, I mean the doctors and lawyers of the Scriptures. I have done so hitherto without explanation, to let the lawyers flutter and everybody laugh at them. Some learned doctors might take a notion to say the Scriptures say thus and so; and we might believe the Scriptures; they are not to be altered. But I am going to show you an error in them.

I have an old edition of the New Testament in the Latin, Hebrew, German and Greek languages. I have been reading the German, and find it to be the most [nearly] correct translation, and to correspond nearest to the revelations which God has given to me for the last fourteen years. It tells about Jacobus, the son of Zebedee. It means Jacob. In the English New Testament it is translated James. Now, if Jacob had the keys, you might talk about James through all eternity and never get the keys. In the 21st of the fourth chapter of Matthew, my old German edition gives the word Jacob instead of James.

The doctors (I mean doctors of law, not physic) say, "If you preach anything not according to the Bible, we will cry treason." How can we escape the damnation of hell, except God be with us and reveal to us? Men bind us with chains. The Latin says Jacobus, which means Jacob; the Hebrew says Jacob, the Greek says Jacob and the German says Jacob; here we have the testimony of four against one. I thank God that I have got this old book but I thank him more for the gift of the Holy Ghost. I have got the oldest book in the world; but I [also] have the oldest book in my heart, even the gift of the Holy Ghost. I have all the four Testaments. Come here, ye learned men, and read, if you can. I should not have introduced this testimony, were it not to back up the word rosh—the head, the Father of the Gods. I should not have brought it up, only to show that I am right.

In the beginning, the head of the Gods called a council of the Gods; and they came together and concocted a plan to create the world and people it. When we begin to learn this way, we begin to learn the only true God, and what kind of a being we have got to worship. Having a knowledge of God, we begin to know how to approach him, and how to ask so as to receive an answer. When we understand the character of God, and know how to come to him, he begins to unfold the heavens to us, and to tell us all about it. When we are ready to come to him, he is ready to come to us.

Now, I ask all who hear me, why the learned men who are preaching salvation, say that God created the heavens, and the earth out of nothing?[9] The reason is, that they are unlearned in the things of God, and have not the gift of the Holy Ghost; they account it blasphemy in any one to contradict their idea. If you tell them that God made the world out of something, they will call you a fool. But I am learned, and know more than all the world put together. The Holy Ghost does, anyhow, and He is within me, and comprehends more than all the world; and I will associate myself with Him.

You ask the learned doctors why they say the world was made out of nothing; and they will answer, "Doesn't the Bible say He created the world?" And they infer, from the word create, that it must have been made out of nothing. Now, the word create came from the word baurau, which does not mean to create out of nothing; it means to organize; the same as a man would organize materials and build a ship. Hence, we infer that God had materials to organize the world out of chaos—chaotic matter, which is element, and in which dwells all the glory. Element had an existence from the time he had. The pure principles of element are principles which can never be destroyed; they may be organized and re-organized, but not destroyed. They had no beginning, and can have no end.[10]

I have another subject to dwell upon, which is calculated to exalt man; but it is impossible for me to say much on this subject. I shall therefore just touch upon it, for time will not permit me to say all. It is associated with the subject of the resurrection of the dead—namely, the soul—the mind of man—the immortal spirit. Where did it come from? All learned men and doctors of divinity say that God created it in the beginning; but it is not so; the very idea lessens man in my estimation. I do not believe the doctrine; I know better. Hear it, all ye ends of the world; for God has told me so; and if you don't believe me, it will not make the truth without effect. I will make a man appear a fool before I get through if he does not belive it. I am going to tell of things more noble.

We say that God himself is a self-existent being. Who told you so? It is correct enough; but how did it get into your heads? Who told you that man did not exist in like manner upon the same principles? Man does exist upon the same principles. God made a tabernacle and put a spirit into it, and it became a living soul. (Refers to the old Bible.) How does it read in the Hebrew? It does not say in the

Hebrew that God created the spirit of man. It says "God made man out of the earth and put into him Adam's spirit, and so became a living body."

The mind or the intelligence which man possesses is co-equal with God himself.[11] I know that my testimony is true; hence, when I talk to these mourners, what have they lost? Their relatives and friends are only separated from their bodies for a short season: their spirits which existed with God have left the tabernacle of clay only for a little moment, as it were; and they now exist in a place where they converse together the same as we do on earth.

I am dwelling on the immortality of the spirit of man. Is it logical to say that the intelligence of spirits is immortal, and yet that it had a beginning? The intelligence of spirits had no beginning, neither will it have an end. That is good logic. That which has a beginning may have an end. There never was a time when there were not spirits; for they are co-equal [co-eternal] with our Father in heaven.

I want to reason more on the spirit of man; for I am dwelling on the body and spirit of man—on the subject of the dead. I take my ring from my finger and liken it unto the mind of man—the immortal part, because it has no beginning. Suppose you cut it in two; then it has a beginning and an end; but join it again, and it continues one eternal round. So with the spirit of man. As the Lord liveth, if it has a beginning, it will have an end. All the fools and learned wise men from the beginning of creation, who say that the spirit of man had a beginning, prove that it must have an end; and if that doctrine is true, then the doctrine of annihilation would be true. But if I am right, I might with boldness proclaim from the house-tops that God never had the power to create the spirit of man at all. God himself could not create himself.

Intelligence is eternal and exists upon a self-existent principle. It is a spirit from age to age, and there is no creation about it. All the minds and spirits that God ever sent into the world are susceptible of enlargement.

The first principles of man are self-existent with God. God himself, finding he was in the midst of spirits and glory, because he was more intelligent, saw proper to institute laws whereby the rest could have a privilege to advance like himself. The relationship we have with God places us in a situation to advance in knowledge. He has power to institute laws to instruct the weaker intelligences, that they may be exalted with himself, so that they might have one glory upon another, and all that knowledge, power, glory, and intelligence, which is requisite in order to save them in the world of spirits.

This is good doctrine. It tastes good. I can taste the principles of eternal life, and so can you. They are given to me by the revelations of Jesus Christ; and I know that when I tell you these words of eternal life as they are given to me, you taste them, and I know that you believe them. You say honey is sweet, and so do I. I can also taste the spirit of eternal life. I know it is good; and when I tell you of these things which were given me by inspiration of the Holy Spirit, you are bound to receive them as sweet, and rejoice more and more.

I want to talk more of the relation of man to God. I will open your eyes in relation to your dead. All things whatsoever God in his infinite wisdom has seen fit and proper to reveal to us, while we are dwelling in mortality, in regard to our mortal bodies, are revealed to us in the abstract, and independent of affinity of this mortal tabernacle, but we are revealed to our spirits precisely as though we had no bodies at all; and those revelations which will save our spirits will save our bodies. God reveals them to us in view of no eternal dissolution of the body, or tabernacle. Hence the responsibility, the awful responsibility, that rests upon us in relation to our dead; for all the spirits who have not obeyed the Gospel in the flesh must either obey it in the spirit or be damned.[12] Solemn thought!—dreadful thought! Is there nothing to be done?—no preparation—no salvation for our fathers and friends who have died without having had the opportunity to obey the decrees of the Son of Man?[13]

Would to God that I had forty days and nights in which to tell you all! I would let you know that I am not a "fallen prophet."

What promises are made in relation to the subject of the salvation of the dead? and what kind of characters are those who can be saved, although their bodies are mouldering and decaying in the grave? When his commandments teach us, it is in view of eternity; for we are looked upon by God as though we were in eternity. God dwells in eternity, and does not view things as we do.

The greatest responsibility in this world that God has laid upon us is to seek after our dead. The Apostle says, "They without us cannot be made perfect;" (Hebrews 11:40) for it is necessary that the sealing power should be in our hands to seal our children and our dead for the fulness of the dispensation of times—a dispensation to meet the promises made by Jesus Christ before the foundation of the world for the salvation of man.

Now I will speak of them. I will meet Paul half way. I say to you, Paul, you cannot be perfect without us. It is necessary that those who are going before and those who come after us should have salvation in common with us; and thus hath God made it obligatory upon man.

Hence, God said, "I will send you Elijah the prophet before the coming of the great and dreadful day of the Lord: and he shall turn the heart of the fathers to the children, and the heart of the children to their fathers, lest I come and smite the earth with a curse." (Malachi 4:5.)[14]

I have a declaration to make as to the provisions which God hath made to suit the conditions of man—made from before the foundation of the world. What has Jesus said? All sin, and all blasphemies, and every transgression, except one, that man can be guilty of, may be forgiven;[15] and there is a salvation for all men, either in this world or the world to come, who have not committed the unpardonable sin, there being a provision either in this world or the world of spirits. Hence God hath made a provision that every spirit in the eternal world can be ferreted out and saved unless he has committed that unpardonable sin which cannot be remitted to him either in this world or the world of spirits. God has wrought out a salvation for all men, unless they have committed a certain sin; and every man who has a friend in the eternal world can save him, unless he has committed the unpardonable sin. And so you can see how far you can be a savior.

A man cannot commit the unpardonable sin after the dissolution of the body,[16] and there is a way possible for escape. Knowledge saves a man; and in the world of spirits[17] no man can be exalted but by knowledge. So long as a man will not give heed to the commandments, he must abide without salvation. If a man has knowledge, he can be saved; although, if he has been guilty of great sins, he will be punished for them. But when he consents to obey the Gospel, whether here or in the world of spirits, he is saved.

A man is his own tormentor and his own condemner. Hence the saying, They shall go into the lake that burns with fire and brimstone. The torment of disappointment in the mind of man is as exquisite as a lake burning with fire and brimstone. I say, so is the torment of man.

I know the Scriptures and understand them. I said, no man can commit the unpardonable sin after the dissolution of the body, nor in this life, until he receives the Holy Ghost; but they must do it in this world. Hence the salvation of Jesus Christ was wrought out for all men, in order to triumph over the devil; for if it did not catch him in one place, it would in another; for he stood up as a Savior. All will suffer until they obey Christ himself.

The contention in heaven[18] was—Jesus said there would be certain souls that would not be saved; and the devil said he could save them all, and laid his plans before the grand council, who gave their vote in favor of Jesus Christ. So the devil rose up in rebellion against

God, and was cast down, with all who put up their heads for him. (Book of Moses—Pearl of Great Price, Chap. 4:1–4; Book of Abraham, Chap. 3:23–28.)

All sins shall be forgiven, except the sin against the Holy Ghost; for Jesus will save all except the sons of perdition. What must a man do to commit the unpardonable sin? He must receive the Holy Ghost, have the heavens opened unto him, and know God, and then sin against Him. After a man has sinned against the Holy Ghost, there is no repentance for him. He has got to say that the sun does not shine while he sees it; he has got to deny Jesus Christ when the heavens have been opened unto him, and to deny the plan of salvation with his eyes open to the truth of it; and from that time he begins to be an enemy. This is the case with many apostates of the Church of Jesus Christ of Latter-day Saints.

Whan a man begins to be an enemy to this work, he hunts me, he seeks to kill me, and never ceases to thirst for my blood. He gets the spirit of the devil—the same spirit that they had who crucified the Lord of Life—the same spirit that sins against the Holy Ghost. You cannot save such persons; you cannot bring them to repentance; they make open war, like the devil, and awful is the consequence.

I advise all of you to be careful what you do, or you may by-and-by find out that you have been deceived. Stay yourselves; do not give way; don't make any hasty moves, you may be saved. If a spirit of bitterness is in you, don't be in haste. You may say, that man is a sinner. Well, if he repents, he shall be forgiven. Be cautious: await. When you find a spirit that wants bloodshed—murder, the same is not of God, but is of the devil. Out of the abundance of the heart of man the mouth speaketh.

The best men bring forth the best works. The man who tells you words of life is the man who can save you. I warn you against all evil characters who sin against the Holy Ghost; for there is no redemption for them in this world nor in the world to come.

I could go back and trace every subject of interest concerning the relationship of man to God, if I had the time. I can enter into the mysteries; I can enter largely into the eternal worlds; for Jesus said, "In my Father's house are many mansions; if it were not so, I would have told you. I go to prepare a place for you" (John 14:2). Paul says, "There is one glory of the sun, and another glory of the moon, and another glory of the stars; for one star differeth from another star in glory. So also is the resurrection of the dead" (I Cor. 15:41). What have we to console us in relation to the dead? We have reason to have the greatest hope and consolations for our dead of any people on the earth; for we have seen them walk worthily in our midst, and seen them sink asleep in the arms of Jesus; and those who have died in the faith are now in the celestial kingdom of God. And hence is the glory of the sun.[19]

You mourners have occasion to rejoice, speaking of the death of Elder King Follet; for your husband and father is gone to wait until the resurrection of the dead—until the perfection of the remainder; for at the resurrection your friend will rise in perfect felicity and go to celestial glory, while many must wait myriads of years before they can receive the like blessings;[20] and your expectations and hopes are far above what man can conceive; for why has God revealed it to us?

I am authorized to say, by the authority of the Holy Ghost, that you have no occasion to fear; for he is gone to the home of the just. Don't mourn, don't weep. I know it by the testimony of the Holy Ghost that is within me; and you may wait for your friends to come forth to meet you in the morn of the celestial world.

Rejoice, O Israel! Your friends who have been murdered for the truth's sake in the persecutions shall triumph gloriously in the celestial world, while their murderers shall welter for ages in torment, even until they shall have paid the uttermost farthing.[21] I say this for the benefit of strangers.

I have a father, brother, children and friends who have gone to a world of spirits. They are only absent for a moment. They are in the spirit, and we shall soon meet again. The time will soon arrive when the trumpet shall sound. When we depart, we shall hail our mothers, fathers, friends, and all whom we love, who have fallen asleep in Jesus. There will be no fear of mobs, persecutions, or malicious lawsuits and arrests; but it will be an eternity of felicity.

A question may be asked—"Will mothers have their children in eternity?" Yes! Yes! Mothers, you shall have your children; for they shall have eternal life, for their debt is paid. There is not damnation awaiting them[22] for they are in the spirit. But as the child dies, so shall it rise from the dead, and be for ever living in the learning of God. It will never grow [in the grave]; it will still be the child, in the same precise form [when it rises] as it appeared before it died out of its mother's arms, but possessing all the intelligence of a God. Children dwell in the mansions of glory and exercise power, but appear in the same form as when on earth. Eternity is full of thrones, upon which dwell thousands of children, reigning on thrones of glory, with not one cubit added to their stature.[23]

I will leave this subject here, and make a few remarks on the subject of baptism. The baptism of water, without the baptism of fire and the Holy Ghost attending it, is of no use; they are necessarily and inseparably connected. An individual must be born of water and the Spirit in order to get into the kingdom of God.[24] In the German, the text bears me out the same as the revelations which I have given and taught for the last fourteen years on that subject. I have the testimony to put in their teeth. My testimony has been true all the time. You will find it in the declaration of John the Baptist. (Reads from the German.) John says, "I baptize you with water, but when Jesus comes, who has the power (or keys), he shall administer the baptism of fire and the Holy Ghost."[25] Where is now all the sectarian world? And if this testimony is true, they are all damned as clearly as anathema can do it. I know the text is true. I call upon all you Germans who know that it is true to say, Aye. (Loud shouts of "Aye.")

Alexander Campbell, how are you going to save people with water alone?[26] For John said his baptism was good for nothing without the baptism of Jesus Christ. "Therefore, not leaving the principles of the doctrine of Christ, let us go on unto perfection; not laying again the foundation of repentance from dead works, and of faith toward God, of the doctrine of baptisms, and of laying on of hands, and of resurrection of the dead, and of eternal judgment. And this will we do, if God permit." (Heb. 6:1–3).

There is one God, one Father, one Jesus, one hope of our calling, one baptism. All these three baptisms only made one. Many talk of baptism not being essential to salvation; but this kind of teaching would lay the foundation of their damnation. I have the truth, and am at the defiance of the world to contradict me, if they can.

I have now preached a little Latin, a little Hebrew, Greek, and German; and I have fulfilled all. I am not so big a fool as many have taken me to be. The Germans know that I read the German correctly.

Hear it, all ye ends of the earth—all ye priests, all ye sinners, and all men. Repent! repent! Obey the Gospel. Turn to God; for your religion won't save you, and you will be damned. I do not say how long. There have been remarks made concerning all men being redeemed from hell; but I say that those who sin against the Holy Ghost cannot be forgiven in this world or in the world to come; they shall die the second death. Those who commit the unpardonable sin are doomed to Gnolom—to dwell in hell, worlds without end. As they concoct scenes of bloodshed in this world, so they shall rise to that resurrection which is as the lake of fire and brimstone. Some shall rise to the everlasting burnings of God; for God dwells in everlasting burnings, and some shall rise to the damnation of their own filthiness, which is as exquisite a torment as the lake of fire and brimstone.

I have intended my remarks for all, both rich and poor, bond and free, great and small. I have no enmity against any man. I love you all; but I hate some of your deeds. I am your best friend, and if persons miss their mark it is their own fault. If I reprove a man, and he hates me, he is a fool; for I love all men, especially these my brethren and sisters.

I rejoice in hearing the testimony of my aged friends. You don't know me; you never knew my heart. No man knows my history, I cannot tell it: I shall never undertake it. I don't blame any one for not believing my history. If I had not experienced what I have, I could not have believed it myself. I never did harm any man since I was born in the world. My voice is always for peace.

I cannot lie down until all my work is finished. I never think any evil, nor do anything to the harm of my fellow-man. When I am called by the trump of the archangel and weighed in the balance, you will all know me then. I add no more, God bless you all. Amen.

Notes

1. Joseph is probably making a reference to a talk given by Sidney Rigdon the day before, April 6. Rigdon was an accomplished orator.
2. John 17:3.
3. Groups of individuals in Nauvoo, Illinois, had taken issue with Smith on doctrinal matters, and particularly over the practice of plural marriage. Many called him a "fallen prophet."
4. John 5:26.
5. See again, John 17:3.
6. Cf. Isaiah 33:14.
7. Romans 8:17.
8. Cf. John 5:19.
9. That is, creation *ex nihilo*.
10. A revelation received in May of 1833 stated that "the elements are eternal." (*Doctrine and Covenants,* 93:33.)
11. "Man was also in the beginning with God. Intelligence, or the light of truth, was not created or made, neither indeed can be." (*Doctrine and Covenants* 93:29.)
12. This is a reference to the Latter-day Saint belief in "baptism for the dead," the idea that persons here on earth may be baptized on behalf of dead friends or relatives—this that all might have the opportunity to know the truth (being taught the gospel in the world of spirits after death) and receive the saving sacraments or

ordinances (performed by proxy). Joseph's first public discourse on this subject was in August of 1840.

13. The command to be baptized. See John 3:1–5.

14. Joseph Smith taught that Elijah restored the power to seal families together for eternity.

15. Matthew 12:31–32.

16. That is, one cannot go downhill spiritually after he has passed the tests of this life. He cannot deny the faith hereafter after having been loyal to the faith here.

17. The Latter-day Saints believe that the world of the spirits is the world beyond death but before the resurrection. See Robert L. Millet and Joseph Fielding McConkie, *The Life Beyond* (Salt Lake City: Bookcraft, 1986).

18. This refers to the premortal world.

19. See I Corinthians 15:40–42. The Celestial Kingdom is the highest heaven.

20. Latter-day Saint scriptures teach that the first resurrection or "resurrection of the just"—begun at the time of Jesus Christ's resurrection—will resume at the time of the Second Coming. After the 1,000 year period of the Millennium the "last resurrection" or "resurrection of the unjust" will take place.

21. Cf. Matthew 5:26.

22. The Book of Mormon, the *Doctrine and Covenants,* and the "Pearl of Great Price" all teach of the innocence of children, all deny the notion of an "original sin," and stress that one of the unconditional benefits of the atonement of Christ is the saved status of children who die before the time of accountability. (See Book of Mormon, Mosiah 3:16; 15:25; Moroni 8; *Doctrine and Covenants* 29:46–47; 137:10; "Pearl of Great Price," Moses 6:53–55.)

23. These statements by Joseph Smith led to subsequent misunderstanding over the years. Some members asserted that Joseph had taught that resurrected children will *never* grow, but will retain their child status forever. Joseph F. Smith, sixth president of the Church and nephew of the founding prophet, collected affidavits and testimonies from others who remembered Joseph's sermon. They claimed that what the Prophet has said (and intended) was that children who died before the age of accountability will be resurrected as children, and will not grow in death. See Joseph F. Smith, *Gospel Doctrine* (Salt Lake City: Deseret Book Co., 1971), pp. 452–54; also *Messages of the First Presidency,* 5:91–98.

24. John 3:3–5.
25. Mark 1:8.
26. One of the reasons for a break between Sidney Rigdon and Alexander Campbell in 1830 was the issue of authority necessary to lay on hands for the gift of the Holy Ghost, as well as the need for subsequent "gifts of the Spirit." (See F. Mark McKiernan, *The Voice of One Crying in the Wilderness: Sidney Rigdon, Religious Reformer, 1793–1876* [Lawrence, Kansas: Coronado Press, 1971], p. 27.)

V.

REVELATIONS

1. "THE VOICE OF THE LORD . . . UNTO ALL MEN": A PREFACE (1831)

At a conference of the Church held in November of 1831 it was decided to compile and publish the revelations received by Joseph Smith to date. On November 1, Joseph dictated a revelation which was designated as the "Preface to the Book of Commandments," the Book of Commandments being the name of the initial collection of revelations which was published in 1833. This revelation is now known as Section One of the Doctrine and Covenants, *and elucidates the Lord's description of things in the world—many people caught up in a form of idolatry—as well as his prescription for redemption—the call of a modern prophet and the initiation of a new gospel dispensation.*

1. Hearken, O ye people of my church, saith the voice of him who dwells on high, and whose eyes are upon all men; yea, verily I say: Hearken ye people from afar; and ye that are upon the islands of the sea, listen together.

2. For verily the voice of the Lord is unto all men, and there is none to escape; and there is no eye that shall not see, neither ear that shall not hear, neither heart that shall not be penetrated.

3. And the rebellious shall be pierced with much sorrow; for their iniquities shall be spoken upon the housetops, and their secret acts shall be revealed.

4. And the voice of warning shall be unto all people, by the mouths of my disciples, whom I have chosen in these last days.

5. And they shall go forth and none shall stay them, for I the Lord have commanded them.

6. Behold, this is mine authority, and the authority of my servants, and my preface unto the book of my commandments, which I have given them to publish unto you, O inhabitants of the earth.

7. Wherefore, fear and tremble, O ye people, for what I the Lord have decreed in them shall be fulfilled.

8. And verily I say unto you, that they who go forth, bearing these tidings unto the inhabitants of the earth, to them is power given to seal both on earth and in heaven, the unbelieving and rebellious;

9. Yea, verily, to seal them up unto the day when the wrath of God shall be poured out upon the wicked without measure—

10. Unto the day when the Lord shall come to recompense unto every man according to his work, and measure to every man according to the measure which he has measured to his fellow man.

11. Wherefore the voice of the Lord is unto the ends of the earth, that all that will hear may hear:

12. Prepare ye, prepare ye for that which is to come, for the Lord is nigh;

13. And the anger of the Lord is kindled, and his sword is bathed in heaven, and it shall fall upon the inhabitants of the earth.

14. And the arm of the Lord shall be revealed; and the day cometh that they who will not hear the voice of the Lord, neither the voice of his servants, neither give heed to the words of the prophets and apostles, shall be cut off from among the people;[1]

15. For they have strayed from mine ordinances, and have broken mine everlasting covenant;[2]

16. They seek not the Lord to establish his righteousness, but every man walketh in his own way, and after the image of his own god, whose image is in the likeness of the world, and whose substance is that of an idol, which waxeth old and shall perish in Babylon, even Babylon the great which shall fall.

17. Wherefore, I the Lord knowing the calamity which should come upon the inhabitants of the earth, called upon my servant Joseph Smith, Jun., and spake unto him from heaven, and gave him commandments;

18. And also gave commandments to others, that they should proclaim these things unto the world; and all this that it might be fulfilled, which was written by the prophets—

19. The weak things of the world shall come forth and break down the mighty and strong ones,[3] that man should not counsel his fellow man, neither trust in the arm of flesh—

20. But that every man might speak in the name of God the Lord, even the Savior of the world;

21. That faith also might increase in the earth;

22. That mine everlasting covenant might be established;

23. That the fulness of my gospel might be proclaimed by the weak and the simple unto the ends of the world, and before kings and rulers.

24. Behold, I am God and have spoken it; these commandments are of me, and were given unto my servants in their weakness, after the manner of their language, that they might come to understanding.[4]

25. And inasmuch as they erred it might be made known;

26. And inasmuch as they sought wisdom they might be instructed;

27. And inasmuch as they sinned they might be chastened, that they might repent;

28. And inasmuch as they were humble they might be made strong, and blessed from on high, and receive knowledge from time to time.

29. And after having received the record of the Nephites, yea, even my servant Joseph Smith, Jun., might have power to translate through the mercy of God, by the power of God, the Book of Mormon.

30. And also those to whom these commandments were given, might have power to lay the foundations of this church, and to bring it forth out of obscurity and out of darkness, the only true and living church upon the face of the whole earth, with which I, the Lord, am well pleased, speaking unto the church collectively and not individually—

31. For I the Lord cannot look upon sin with the least degree of allowance;

32. Nevertheless, he that repents and does the commandments of the Lord shall be forgiven;

33. And he that repents not, from him shall be taken even the light which he has received; for my Spirit shall not always strive with man, saith the Lord of Hosts.

34. And again, verily I say unto you, O inhabitants of the earth: I the Lord am willing to make these things known unto all flesh;

35. For I am no respecter of persons, and will that all men shall know that the day speedily cometh; the hour is not yet, but is nigh at hand, when peace shall be taken from the earth, and the devil shall have power over his own dominion.

36. And also the Lord shall have power over his saints, and shall reign in their midst, and shall come down in judgment upon Idumea, or the world.

37. Search these commandments, for they are true and faithful, and the prophecies and promises which are in them shall all be fulfilled.

38. What I the Lord have spoken, I have spoken, and I excuse not myself; and though the heavens and the earth pass away, my word shall not pass away, but shall all be fulfilled, whether by mine own voice of by the voice of my servants, it is the same.[5]

39. For behold, and lo, the Lord is God, and the Spirit beareth record, and the record is true, and the truth abidith forever and ever. Amen.

Notes

1. It is worth noting the similarity of language between this verse and the Deuteronomy passage regarding a special prophet to be raised up (Deut 18:15, 18–19; Acts 3:22).
2. Cf. Isaiah 24:5–6.
3. See 1 Corinthians 1:27.
4. George A. Smith, an early Mormon apostle said: "When the Lord reveals anything to men, He reveals it in language that accords with their own. If any of you were to converse with an angel, and you used strictly grammatical language he would do the same. But if you used two negatives in a sentence the heavenly messenger would use language to correspond with your understanding." (*Journal of Discourses*, 12:335.)
5. In speaking of the elders of the Church, a revelation received at about this same time period (November, 1831) explained: "And whatsoever they shall speak when moved upon by the Holy Ghost shall be scripture, shall be the will of the Lord, shall be the mind of the Lord, shall be the word of the Lord, shall be the voice of the Lord, and the power of God unto salvation." (*Doctrine and Covenants*, 68:4.)

2. JESUS CHRIST AND THE COMMAND TO REPENT (1830)

The following is a revelation given through Joseph Smith to Martin Harris, one of the earliest converts to Mormonism. Harris was one of the three men who attested by signature and written testimony as to the genuineness of the Book of Mormon plates. The attestations of the "Three Witnesses" have been located in the prefatory material of the Book of Mormon since the initial printings in 1830. Harris was a prominent and prosperous farmer in Palmyra, New York, who offered to mortgage a portion of his property to finance the first printing of the Book of Mormon. The revelation is a major doctrinal statement which also contains specific instructions to Harris. It is now Section 19 of the Doctrine and Covenants.

I am Alpha and Omega, Christ the Lord; yea, even I am he, the beginning and the end, the Redeemer of the world.

2. I, having accomplished and finished the will of him whose I am, even the Father, concerning me—having done this that I might subdue all things unto myself—

3. Retaining all power, even to the destroying of Satan and his works at the end of the world, and the last great day of judgment, which I shall pass upon the inhabitants thereof, judging every man according to his works and the deeds which he hath done.

4. And surely every man must repent or suffer, for I, God, am endless.

5. Wherefore, I revoke not the judgments which I shall pass, but woes shall go forth, weeping, wailing and gnashing of teeth, yea, to those who are found on my left hand.

6. Nevertheless, it is not written that there shall be no end to this torment, but it is written endless torment.

7. Again, it is written eternal damnation; wherefore it is more express than other scriptures, that it might work upon the hearts of the children of men, altogether for my name's glory.

8. Wherefore, I will explain unto you this mystery, for it is meet unto you to know even as mine apostles.

9. I speak unto you that are chosen in this thing, even as one, that you may enter into my rest.

10. For, behold, the mystery of godliness, how great is it! For, behold, I am endless, and the punishment which is given from my hand is endless punishment, for Endless is my name. Wherefore—

11. Eternal punishment is God's punishment.

12. Endless punishment is God's punishment.[1]

13. Wherefore, I command you to repent, and keep the commandments which you have received by the hand of my servant Joseph Smith, Jun., in my name;

14. And it is by my almighty power that you have received them;

15. Therefore I command you[2] to repent—repent, lest I smite

you by the rod of my mouth, and by my wrath, and by my anger, and your sufferings be sore—how sore you know not, how exquisite you know not, yea, how hard to bear you know not.

16. For behold, I, God, have suffered these things for all, that they might not suffer if they would repent;

17. But if they would not repent they must suffer even as I;

18. Which suffering caused myself, even God, the greatest of all, to tremble because of pain, and to bleed at every pore, and to suffer both body and spirit—and would that I might not drink the bitter cup, and shrink—[3]

19. Nevertheless, glory be to the Father, and I partook and finished my preparations unto the children of men.

20. Wherefore, I command you again to repent, lest I humble you with my almighty power; and that you confess your sins, lest you suffer these punishments of which I have spoken, of which in the smallest, yea, even in the least degree you have tasted at the time I withdrew my Spirit.[4]

21. And I command you that you preach naught but repentance, and show not these things[5] unto the world until it is wisdom in me.

22. For they cannot bear meat now, but milk they must receive; wherefore, they must not know these things, lest they perish.

23. Learn of me, and listen to my words; walk in the meekness of my Spirit, and you shall have peace in me.

24. I am Jesus Christ; I came by the will of the Father, and I do his will.

25. And again, I command thee that thou shalt not covet thy neighbor's wife; nor seek thy neighbor's life.

26. And again, I command thee that thou shalt not covet thine own property, but impart it freely to the printing of the Book of Mormon, which contains the truth and the word of God—

27. Which is my word to the Gentile, that soon it may go to the Jew, of whom the Lamanites are a remnant,[6] that they may believe the gospel, and look not for a Messiah to come who has already come.

28. And again, I command thee that thou shalt pray vocally as well as in thy heart; yea, before the world as well as in secret, in public as well as in private.

29. And thou shalt declare glad tidings, yea publish it upon the mountains, and upon every high place, and among every people that thou shalt be permitted to see.

30. And thou shalt do it with all humility, trusting in me, reviling not against revilers.

31. And of tenets thou shalt not talk, but thou shalt declare repentance and faith on the Savior, and remission of sins by baptism and by fire, yea, even the Holy Ghost.

32. Behold, this is a great and the last commandment which I shall give unto you concerning this matter; for this shall suffice for thy daily walk, even unto the end of thy life.

33. And misery thou shalt receive if thou wilt slight these counsels, yea, even the destruction of thyself and property.

34. Impart a portion of thy property, yea, even part of thy lands, and all save the support of thy family.

35. Pay the debt thou hast contracted with the printer. Release thyself from bondage.

36. Leave thy house and home, except when thou shalt desire to see thy family;

37. And speak freely to all; yea, preach, exhort, declare the truth, even with a loud voice, with a sound of rejoicing, crying—Hosanna, hosanna, blessed by the name of the Lord God!

38. Pray always, and I will pour out my Spirit upon you, and great shall be your blessing—yea, even more than if you should obtain treasures of earth and corruptibleness to the extent thereof.

39. Behold, canst thou read this without rejoicing and lifting up thy heart for gladness?

40. Or canst thou run about longer as a blind guide?

41. Or canst thou be humble and meek, and conduct thyself wisely before me? Yea, come unto me thy Savior. Amen.

Notes

1. In Joseph Smith's translation of Genesis, we see the words 'endless' and 'eternal' used as names of God, and thus come to appreciate the Latter-day Saint concept of "endless" punishment and "eternal damnation" (as used in this section of the *Doctrine and Covenants*) as qualitative descriptions of God's retribution for sin. (See Moses 1:3; 7:35.)
2. In the 1833 Book of Commandments we read: "Therefore I command you *by my name, and by my Almighty power,* that you repent—repent, lest I smite you by the rod of my mouth—"
3. This verse is a part of the scriptural basis for the Latter-day Saint belief that Christ's suffering in the Garden of Gethsemane (Mt 26:36–36; Mk 14:32–42; Lk 22:39–46) was an integral part of the act of atonement. His bleeding at every pore (cf. Lk 22:44; Book of Mormon, Mosiah 3:7) was an evidence of his suffering the

effects of the world's sins. Thus, Joseph Smith taught that what began in Gethsemane was consummated on the cross of Calvary. Brigham Young spoke the following regarding why Christ sweat blood: "The Father withdrew his spirit from His Son, at the time he was to be crucified. . . . At the very moment, at the hour when the crisis came for him to offer up his life, the Father withdrew His Spirit, and cast a vail over him. That is what made him sweat blood." (*Journal of Discourses,* 3:206.)

4. Martin Harris served for a time as a scribe to Joseph Smith in the translation of the Book of Mormon. After the twosome had completed 116 manuscript pages, Harris requested permission to take the translation and show it to his wife and selected family members. Joseph Smith inquired of God and the request was denied. Harris persisted on two subsequent occasions, until permission was finally granted; he was required to enter into a covenant to display the manuscript pages to designated individuals only. Martin Harris's zeal and desire for acceptance exceeded his wisdom, and the pages were lost. God's judgment was felt by Harris and the Smith family. Lucy Mack Smith, mother of Joseph, described the occasion as follows: "It seemed as though Martin Harris, for his transgression, suffered temporally as well as spiritually. . . . I will remember that day of darkness, both within and without. To us, at least, the heavens seemed clothed with blackness and the earth shrouded with gloom. I have often said within myself, that if a continual punishment, as severe as that which we experienced on that occasion, were to be inflicted upon the most wicked characters who ever stood upon the footstool of the Almighty—if even their punishment were no greater than that, I should feel to pity their condition." (*History of Joseph Smith by His Mother,* ed. Preston Nibley [Salt Lake City: Bookcraft, 1958], pp. 131–32.)

5. From the Book of Commandments: "And I command you that you preach naught but repentance, and show not these things *neither speak these things* unto the world until it is wisdom in me."

6. The Lamanites in the Book of Mormon, though of the tribe of Joseph (Alma 10:3), are known as "Jews" inasmuch as they "came out from Jerusalem." (2 Nephi 30:4; 33:8.)

3. A REVELATION TO EMMA SMITH,
WIFE OF THE PROPHET (1830)

Emma Hale and Joseph Smith were married in January of 1827. The couple were the parents of eleven children, five of whom lived to maturity. She was baptized just two months after the formal organization of the Church. She was the first president of the Church's organization for women, the "Relief Society," which position she was called to assume in Nauvoo, Illinois in March of 1842. Following the death of Joseph, Emma became disaffected from the Church and had at best a strained relationship with Brigham Young, her husband's successor. In 1860 Joseph and Emma's son, Joseph III (born November 6 1832) was appointed president of a group of members who proposed succession in the Church presidency according to lineal descent. Emma thereafter affiliated with the Reorganized Church of Jesus Christ of Latter-day Saints. The following revelation, received in July 1830, is now Section 25 of the Doctrine and Covenants.

Hearken unto the voice of the Lord your God, while I speak unto you, Emma Smith, my daughter; for verily I say unto you, all those who receive my gospel are sons and daughters in my kingdom.

2. A revelation I give unto you concerning my will; and if thou art faithful and walk in the paths of virtue before me, I will preserve thy life, and thou shalt receive an inheritance in Zion.

3. Behold, thy sins are forgiven thee, and thou art an elect lady,[1] whom I have called.

4. Murmur not because of the things which thou has not seen,[2] for they are withheld from thee and from the world, which is wisdom in me in a time to come.

5. And the office of thy calling shall be for a comfort unto my servant, Joseph Smith, Jun., thy husband, in his afflictions with consoling words, in the spirit of meekness.

6. And thou shalt go with him at the time of his going, and be unto him for a scribe,[3] while there is no one to be a scribe for him, that I may send my servant, Oliver Cowdery, whithersoever I will.

7. And thou shalt be ordained under his hand to expound scriptures, and to exhort the church, according as it shall be given thee by my Spirit.

8. For he shall lay his hands upon thee, and thou shalt receive the Holy Ghost,[4] and thy time shall be given to writing, and to learning much.

9. And thou needest not fear, for thy husband shall support thee in the church; for unto them is his calling, that all things might be revealed unto them, whatsoever I will, according to their faith.

10. And verily I say unto thee that thou shalt lay aside the things of this world, and seek for the things of a better.

11. And it shall be given thee, also, to make a selection of sacred hymns,[5] as it shall be given thee, which is pleasing unto me, to be had in my church.

12. For my soul delighteth in the song of the heart; yea, the song of the righteous is a prayer unto me, and it shall be answered with a blessing upon their heads.

13. Wherefore, lift up thy heart and rejoice, and cleave unto the covenants which thou has made.

14. Continue in the spirit of meekness, and beware of pride. Let thy soul delight in thy husband, and the glory which shall come upon him.

15. Keep my commandments continually, and a crown of righteousness thou shalt receive. And except thou do this, where I am you cannot come.

16. And verily, verily, I say unto you, that this is my voice unto all. Amen.

Notes

1. Cf. 2 John 1:1.
2. The reference here seems to be to the golden plates from which the Book of Mormon was translated.
3. Emma Smith probably served for a time as a scribe to her husband in his translation of the King James Bible. (See Matthews, "A Plainer Translation," pp. 27, 95.) This verse cannot have reference to the translation of the Book of Mormon, since the first edition of the Book of Mormon had been released in March of 1830.
4. Though Emma had been baptized in June, she was not confirmed (did not receive the gift of the Holy Ghost by the laying on of hands) until August. (*History of the Church,* 1:88, 108.)
5. Emma's selection of hymns was first published in 1835.

4. THE PLACE OF SPIRITUAL GIFTS IN THE CHURCH (1831)

One of the constant pleadings of Book of Mormon prophets is that the people of God never "deny the revelations and gifts of God." One of the Articles of Faith of the LDS church is stated thus: "We believe in the gift of tongues, prophecy, revelation, visions, healing, interpretation of tongues, and so forth." (Article of Faith #7) The following text, now Section 46 of the Doctrine and Covenants, *is a revelation given to the Church on March 8, 1831, and specifies the types of gifts and powers which ought to be evident in the Latter-day Church of Christ.*

Hearken, O ye people of my church; for verily I say unto you that these things were spoken unto you for your profit and learning.

2. But notwithstanding those things which are written, it always has been given to the elders of my church from the beginning, and ever shall be, to conduct all meetings as they are directed and guided by the Holy Spirit.

3. Nevertheless ye are commanded never to cast any one out from your public meetings which are held before the world.

4. Ye are also commanded not to cast any one who belongeth to the church out of your sacrament meetings; nevertheless, if any have trespassed, let him not partake until he makes reconciliation.[1]

5. And again I say unto you, ye shall not cast any out of your sacrament meetings who are earnestly seeking the kingdom—I speak this concerning those who are not of the church.

6. And again I say unto you, concerning your confirmation meetings, that if there be any that are not of the church, that are earnestly seeking after the kingdom, ye shall not cast them out.

7. But ye are commanded in all things to ask of God, who giveth liberally; and that which the Spirit testifies unto you even so I would that ye should do in all holiness of heart, walking uprightly before me, considering the end of your salvation, doing all things with prayer and thanksgiving, that ye may not be seduced by evil spirits, or doctrines of devils, or the commandments of men; for some are of men, and others of devils.

8. Wherefore, beware lest ye are deceived; and that ye may not be deceived seek ye earnestly the best gifts, always remembering for what they are given;

9. For verily I say unto you, they are given for the benefit of those who love me and keep all my commandments, and him that

seeketh so to do; that all may be benefited that seek or that ask of me, that ask and not for a sign that they may consume it upon their lusts.

10. And again, verily I say unto you, I would that ye should always remember, and always retain in your minds what those gifts are, that are given unto the church.

11. For all have not every gift given unto them; for there are many gifts, and to every man is given a gift by the Spirit of God.[2]

12. To some is given one, and to some is given another, that all may be profited thereby.

13. To some it is given by the Holy Ghost to know that Jesus Christ is the Son of God, and that he was crucified for the sins of the world.

14. To others it is given to believe on their words, that they also might have eternal life if they continue faithful.

15. And again, to some it is given by the Holy Ghost to know the differences of administration, as it will be pleasing unto the same Lord, according as the Lord will, suiting his mercies according to the conditions of the children of men.

16. And again, it is given by the Holy Ghost to some to know the diversities of operations, whether they be of God, that the manifestations of the Spirit may be given to every man to profit withal.

17. And again, verily I say unto you, to some is given, by the Spirit of God, the word of wisdom.

18. To another is given the word of knowledge, that all may be taught to be wise and to have knowledge.

19. And again, to some it is given to have faith to be healed;

20. And to others it is given to have faith to heal.

21. And again, to some is given the working of miracles;

22. And to others it is given to prophesy;

23. And to others the discerning of spirits.

24. And again, it is given to some to speak with tongues;

25. And to another is given the interpretation of tongues;

26. And all these gifts come from God, for the benefit of the children of God.

27. And unto the bishop of the church, and unto such as God shall appoint and ordain to watch over the church and to be elders unto the church, are to have it given unto them to discern all those gifts lest there shall be any among you professing and yet be not of God.

28. And it shall come to pass that he that asketh in Spirit shall receive in Spirit;

29. That unto some it may be given to have all those gifts, that there may be a head, in order that every member may be profited thereby.[3]

30. He that asketh in the Spirit asketh according to the will of God; wherefore it is done even as he asketh.

31. And again, I say unto you, all things must be done in the name of Christ, whatsoever you do in the Spirit;

32. And ye must give thanks unto God in the Spirit for whatsoever blessings ye are blessed with.

33. And ye must practice virtue and holiness before me continually. Even so. Amen.

Notes

1. Cf. 1 Corinthians 11:26–30.
2. In regard to the following, cf. 1 Corinthians 12.
3. A later revelation speaks of the President of the Church as "a seer, a revelator, a translator, and a prophet, having all the gifts of God which he bestows upon the head of the church." (*Doctrine and Covenants,* 107:92.)

5. A REVELATION TO THE SHAKERS (1831)

In May of 1831 a new convert to the faith, Leman Copley, came to Joseph Smith and requested that missionaries be sent to his former religious associates, the "United Society of Believers in Christ's Second Appearing," known simply as "the Shakers." The Shakers resided in a communal group in North Union, Ohio, fifteen miles from Kirtland. The following revelation, given through Joseph Smith to Copley, Sidney Rigdon, and Parley P. Pratt, specifies numerous doctrinal errors that the Mormon missionaries were to bring to the attention of the Shakers. Quoting from the Preface to Section 49 of the Doctrine and Covenants *(1981 edition), "Some of the beliefs of the Shakers were that Christ's Second Coming had already occurred and he had appeared in the form of a woman, Ann Lee; baptism by water was not considered essential; the eating of pork was specifically forbidden, and many did not eat any meat; and a celibate life was considered higher than marriage." This revelation was taken to the Shaker community and read to the assembled congregation, but was completely rejected.*

Hearken unto my word, my servants Sidney, and Parley, and Leman; for behold, verily I say unto you, that I give unto you a commandment that you shall go and preach my gospel which ye have received, even as ye have received it, unto the Shakers.

2. Behold, I say unto you, that they desire to know the truth in part, but not all, for they are not right before me and must needs repent.

3. Wherefore, I send you, my servants Sidney and Parley, to preach the gospel unto them.

4. And my servant Leman shall be ordained unto this work, that he may reason with them, not according to that which he has received of them, but according to that which shall be taught him by you my servants; and by so doing I will bless him, otherwise he shall not prosper.

5. Thus saith the Lord; for I am God, and have sent mine Only Begotten Son into the world for the redemption of the world, and have decreed that he that receiveth him shall be saved, and he that receiveth him not shall be damned—

6. And they have done unto the Son of Man even as they listed; and he has taken his power on the right hand of his glory, and now reigneth in the heavens, and will reign till he descends on the earth to put all enemies under his feet, which time is nigh at hand—

7. I, the Lord God, have spoken it; but the hour and the day no man knoweth, neither the angels in heaven, nor shall they know until he comes.[1]

8. Wherefore, I will that all men shall repent, for all are under sin, except those which I have reserved unto myself, holy men that ye know not of.

9. Wherefore, I say unto you that I have sent unto you mine everlasting covenant, even that which was from the beginning.

10. And that which I have promised I have so fulfilled, and the nations of the earth shall bow to it; and, if not of themselves, they shall come down for that which is now exalted of itself shall be laid low of power.

11. Wherefore, I give unto you a commandment that ye go among this people, and say unto them, like unto mine apostle of old, whose name was Peter;[2]

12. Believe on the name of the Lord Jesus, who was on the earth, and is to come, the beginning and the end;

13. Repent and be baptized in the name of Jesus Christ, according to the holy commandment, for the remission of sins;

14. And whoso doeth this shall receive the gift of the Holy Ghost, by the laying on of the hands of the elders of the church.

15. And again, verily I say unto you, that whoso forbiddeth to marry is not ordained of God, for marriage is ordained of God unto man.

16. Wherefore, it is lawful that he should have one wife, and they twain shall be one flesh, and all this that the earth might answer the end of its creation;

17. And that it might be filled with the measure of man, according to his creation before the world was made.

18. And whoso forbiddeth to abstain from meats, that man should not eat the same, is not ordained of God;

19. For, behold, the beasts of the field and the fowls of the air, and that which cometh of the earth, is ordained for the use of man for food and for raiment, and that he might have in abundance.

20. But it is not given that one man should possess that which is above another, wherefore the world lieth in sin.

21. And wo be unto man that sheddeth blood or that wasteth flesh and hath no need.

22. And again, verily I say unto you, that the Son of Man cometh not in the form of a woman, neither of a man traveling on the earth.

23. Wherefore, be not deceived, but continue in steadfastness, looking forth for the heavens to be shaken, and the earth to tremble and to reel to and fro as a drunken man, and for the valleys to be exalted, and for the mountains to be made low, and for the rough places to become smooth—and all this when the angel shall sound his trumpet.[3]

24. But before the great day of the Lord shall come, Jacob shall flourish in the wilderness, and the Lamanites shall blossom as the rose.

25. Zion shall flourish upon the hills and rejoice upon the mountains, and shall be assembled together unto the place which I have appointed,

26. Behold, I say unto you, go forth as I have commanded you; repent of all your sins; ask and ye shall receive; knock and it shall be opened unto you.

27. Behold, I will go before you and be your rearward; and I will be in your midst, and you shall not be confounded.

28. Behold, I am Jesus Christ and I come quickly. Even so. Amen.

Notes

1. Cf. Mark 13:32.
2. Acts 2:37–39.
3. That is to say, the Second Coming will be cataclysmic in scope—will be known to all.

6. THREE DEGREES OF GLORY:
MANY MANSIONS OF THE FATHER (1832)

Joseph Smith and his scribes worked fairly consistently on the Bible translation of the Old Testament from June of 1830 until March 7, 1831, at which time they were instructed to begin work on the New Testament. By February of 1832 they had progressed in the work to the Gospel of John. On February 16, Joseph and his scribe, Sidney Rigdon, working in the home of John Johnson in Hiram, Ohio, translated the fifth chapter of John and made changes in verse 29 which deals with "they that have done good, unto the resurrection of life; and they that have done evil, unto the resurrection of damnation." Joseph altered the text to read the "resurrection of the just" and the "resurrection of the unjust." While pondering upon the importance of their alteration to the King James text, the following vision was received. Joseph Smith later wrote of this occasion: "From sundry revelations which had been received, it was apparent that many important points touching the salvation of man had been taken from the Bible, or lost before it was compiled. It appeared self-evident from what truths were left, that if God rewarded every one according to the deeds done in the body, the term 'Heaven,' as intended for the Saints' eternal home, must include more kingdoms than one. Accordingly, while translating St. John's Gospel, myself and Elder Rigdon saw the following vision." (History of the Church, 1:245.) The following is Section 76 of the Doctrine and Covenants, and is the basis for the Latter-day Saint belief in three major kingdoms of glory in the hereafter.

Hear, O ye heavens, and give ear, O earth,[1] and rejoice ye inhabitants thereof, for the Lord is God, and beside him there is no Savior.

2. Great is his wisdom, marvelous are his ways, and the extent of his doings none can find out.

3. His purposes fail not, neither are there any who can stay his hand.

4. From eternity to eternity he is the same, and his years never fail.

5. For thus saith the Lord—I, the Lord, am merciful and gracious unto those who fear me, and delight to honor those who serve me in righteousness and in truth unto the end.

6. Great shall be their reward and eternal shall be their glory.

7. And to them will I reveal all mysteries, yea, all the hidden mysteries of my kingdom from days of old, and for ages to come, will I make known unto them the good pleasure of my will concerning all things pertaining to my kingdom.

8. Yea, even the wonders of eternity shall they know, and things to come will I show them, even the things of many generations.

9. And their wisdom shall be great, and their understanding reach to heaven; and before them the wisdom of the wise shall perish, and the understanding of the prudent shall come to naught.[2]

10. For by my Spirit will I enlighten them, and by my power will I make known unto them the secrets of my will—yea, even those things which eye has not seen, nor ear heard, nor yet entered into the heart of man.

11. We, Joseph Smith, Jun., and Sidney Rigdon, being in the Spirit on the sixteenth day of February, in the year of our Lord one thousand eight hundred and thirty-two—

12. By the power of the Spirit our eyes were opened and our understandings were enlightened, so as to see and understand the things of God—

13. Even those things which were from the beginning before the world was, which were ordained of the Father, through his Only Begotten Son, who was in the bosom of the Father, even from the beginning;

14. Of whom we bear record; and the record which we bear is the fulness of the gospel of Jesus Christ, who is the Son, whom we saw and with whom we conversed in the heavenly vision.

15. For while we were doing the work of translation, which the Lord had appointed unto us, we came to the twenty-ninth verse of the fifth chapter of John, which was given unto us as follows—

16. Speaking of the resurrection of the dead, concerning those who shall hear the voice of the Son of Man:

17. And shall come forth; they who have done good, in the resurrection of the just; and they who have done evil, in the resurrection of the unjust.

18. Now this caused us to marvel, for it was given unto us of the Spirit.

19. And while we meditated upon these things, the Lord touched the eyes of our understandings and they were opened, and the glory of the Lord shone round about.

20. And we beheld the glory of the Son, on the right hand of the Father, and received of his fulness;

21. And saw the holy angels, and them who are sanctified before his throne, worshiping God, and the Lamb, who worship him forever and ever.

22. And now, after the many testimonies which have been given of him, this is the testimony, last of all, which we give of him: That he lives!

23. For we saw him, even on the right hand of God; and we heard the voice bearing record that he is the Only Begotten of the Father—

24. That by him, and through him, and of him, the worlds are and were created, and the inhabitants thereof are begotten sons and daughters unto God.

25. And this we saw also, and bear record, that an angel of God who was in authority in the presence of God, who rebelled against the Only Begotten Son whom the Father loved and who was in the bosom of the Father, was thrust down from the presence of God and the Son,

26. And was called Perdition, for the heavens wept over him—he was Lucifer, a son of the morning.

27. And we beheld, and lo, he is fallen! is fallen, even a son of the morning![3]

28. And while we were yet in the Spirit, the Lord commanded us that we should write the vision; for we beheld Satan, that old serpent, even the devil, who rebelled against God, and sought to take the kingdom of our God and his Christ—

29. Wherefore, he maketh war with the saints of God, and encompasseth them round about.

30. And we saw a vision of the sufferings of those with whom he made war and overcame, for thus came the voice of the Lord unto us;

31. Thus saith the Lord concerning all those who know my power, and have been made partakers thereof, and suffered themselves through the power of the devil to be overcome, and to deny the truth and defy my power—

32. They are they who are the sons of perdition,[4] of whom I say that it had been better for them never to have been born;

33. For they are vessels of wrath, doomed to suffer the wrath of God, with the devil and his angels in eternity;

34. Concerning him I have said there is no forgiveness in this world nor in the world to come—[5]

35. Having denied the Holy Spirit after having received it, and having denied the Only Begotten Son of the Father, having crucified him unto themselves and put him to an open shame.

36. These are they who shall go away into the lake of fire and brimstone, with the devil and his angels—

37. And the only ones on whom the second death shall have any power;

38. Yea, verily, the only ones who shall not be redeemed in the due time of the Lord, after the sufferings of his wrath.

39. For all the rest[6] shall be brought forth by the resurrection of the dead, through the triumph and the glory of the Lamb, who was slain, who was in the bosom of the Father before the worlds were made.

40. And this is the gospel, the glad tidings, which the voice out of the heavens bore record unto us—

41. That he came into the world, even Jesus, to be crucified for the world, and to bear the sins of the world, and to sanctify the world, and to cleanse it from all unrighteousness;

42. That through him all might be saved whom the Father had put into his power and made by him;

43. Who glorifies the Father, and saves all the works of his hands, except those sons of perdition who deny the Son after the Father has revealed him.

44. Wherefore, he saves all except them—they shall go away into everlasting punishment, which is endless punishment, which is eternal punishment, to reign with the devil and his angels in eternity, where their worm dieth not, and the fire is not quenched, which is their torment—[7]

45. And the end thereof, neither the place thereof, nor their torment, no man knows;

46. Neither was it revealed, neither is, neither will be revealed unto man, except to them who are made partakers thereof;

47. Nevertheless, I, the Lord, show it by vision unto many, but straightway shut it up again;

48. Wherefore, the end, the width, the height, the depth, and the misery thereof, they understand not, neither any man except those who are ordained unto this condemnation.

49. And we heard the voice, saying: Write the vision, for lo, this is the end of the vision of the sufferings of the ungodly.

50. And again we bear record—for we saw and heard, and this is the testimony of the gospel of Christ concerning them who shall come forth in the resurrection of the just—

51. They are they who received the testimony of Jesus, and believed on his name and were baptized after the manner of his burial, being buried in the water in his name, and this according to the commandment which he has given—

52. That by keeping the commandments they might be washed and cleansed from all their sins, and receive the Holy Spirit by the laying on of the hands of him who is ordained and sealed unto the power;

53. And who overcome by faith, and are sealed by the Holy Spirit of promise, which the Father sheds forth upon all those who are just and true.

54. They are they who are the church of the Firstborn.[8]

55. They are they into whose hands the Father has given all things—

56. They are they who are priests and kings, who have received of his fulness, and of his glory;

57. And are priests of the Most High, after the order of Melchizedek, which was after the order of Enoch, which was after the order of the Only Begotten Son.[9]

58. Wherefore, as it is written, they are gods,[10] even the sons of God—

59. Wherefore, all things are theirs, whether life or death, or things present, or things to come, all are theirs and they are Christ's, and Christ is God's.

60. And they shall overcome all things.

61. Wherefore, let no man glory in man, but rather let him glory in God, who shall subdue all enemies under his feet,[11]

62. These shall dwell in the presence of God and his Christ forever and ever.

63. These are they whom he shall bring with him, when he shall come in the clouds of heaven to reign on the earth over his people.

64. These are they who shall have part in the first resurrection.

65. These are they who shall come forth in the resurrection of the just.

66. These are they who are come unto Mount Zion, and unto the city of the living God, the heavenly place, the holiest of all.

67. These are they who have come to an innumerable company of angels, to the general assembly and church of Enoch, and of the Firstborn.[12]

68. These are they whose names are written in heaven, where God and Christ are the judge of all.

69. These are they who are just men made perfect through Jesus the mediator of the new covenant, who wrought out this perfect atonement through the shedding of his own blood.

70. These are they whose bodies are celestial, whose glory is that of the sun, even the glory of God, the highest of all, whose glory the sun of the firmament is written of us being typical.

71. And again, we saw the terrestrial world, and behold and lo, these are they who are of the terrestrial, whose glory differs from that of the church of the Firstborn who have received the fulness of the Father, even as that of the moon differs from the sun in the firmament.

72. Behold, these are they who died without law;[13]

73. And also they who are the spirits of men kept in prison, whom the Son visited, and preached the gospel unto them, that they might be judged according to men in the flesh;

74. Who received not the testimony of Jesus in the flesh, but afterwards received it.[14]

75. These are they who are honorable men of the earth, who were blinded by the craftiness of men.

76. These are they who receive of his glory, but not of his fulness.

77. These are they who receive of the presence of the Son, but not of the fulness of the Father.

78. Wherefore, they are bodies terrestrial, and not bodies celestial, and differ in glory as the moon differs from the sun.

79. These are they who are not valiant in the testimony of Jesus; wherefore, they obtain not the crown over the kingdom of our God.

80. And now this is the end of the vision which we saw of the terrestrial, that the Lord commanded us to write while we were yet in the Spirit.

81. And again, we saw the glory of the telestial, which glory is that of the lesser, even as the glory of the stars differs from that of the glory of the moon in the firmament.

82. These are they who received not the gospel of Christ, neither the testimony of Jesus.

83. These are they who deny not the Holy Spirit.[15]

84. These are they who are thrust down to hell.

85. These are they who shall not be redeemed from the devil until the last resurrection, until the Lord, even Christ the Lamb, shall have finished his work.

86. These are they who receive not of his fulness in the eternal world, but of the Holy Spirit through the ministration of the terrestrial;

87. And the terrestrial through the ministration of the celestial.

88. And also the telestial receive it of the administering of angels who are appointed to minister for them, or who are appointed to be ministering spirits for them; for they shall be heirs of salvation.

89. And thus we saw, in the heavenly vision, the glory of the telestial, which surpasses all understanding;

90. And no man knows it except him to whom God has revealed it.

91. And thus we saw the glory of the terrestrial which excels in all things the glory of the telestial, even in glory, and in power, and in might, and in dominion.

92. And thus we saw the glory of the celestial, which excels in all things—where God, even the Father, reigns upon his throne forever and ever;

93. Before whose throne all things bow in humble reverence and give him glory forever and ever.

94. They who dwell in his presence are the church of the First-born; and they see as they are seen, and know as they are known, having received of his fullness and of his grace;

95. And he makes them equal in power, and in might, and in dominion.

96. And the glory of the celestial is one, even as the glory of the sun is one.

97. And the glory of the terrestrial is one, even as the glory of the moon is one.

98. And the glory of the telestial is one, even as the glory of the stars is one; for as one star differs from another star in glory, even so differs one from another in glory in the telestial world;[16]

99. For these are they who are of Paul, and of Apollos, and of Cephas.

100. These are they who say they are some of one and some of another—some of Christ and some of John, and some of Moses, and some of Elias, and some of Esaias, and some of Isaiah, and some of Enoch;[17]

101. But received not the gospel, neither the testimony of Jesus, neither the prophets, neither the everlasing covenant.

102. Last of all, these all are they who will not be gathered with the saints, to be caught up unto the church of the Firstborn, and received into the cloud.

103. These are they who are liars, and sorcerers, and adulterers, and whoremongers, and whosoever loves and makes a lie.[18]

104. These are they who suffer the wrath of God on earth.

105. These are they who suffer the vengeance of eternal fire.

106. These are they who are cast down to hell and suffer the wrath of Almighty God, until the fulness of times, when Christ shall have subdued all enemies under his feet, and shall have perfected his work;[19]

107. When he shall deliver up the kingdom, and present it unto the Father, spotless, saying: I have overcome and have trodden the wine-press alone, even the wine-press of the fierceness of the wrath of Almighty God.

108. Then shall he be crowned with the crown of his glory, to sit on the throne of his power to reign forever and ever.

109. But behold, and lo, we saw the glory and the inhabitants of the telestial world, that they were as innumerable as the stars in the firmament of heaven, or as the sand upon the seashore;

110. And heard the voice of the Lord saying: These all shall bow the knee, and every tongue shall confess to him who sits upon the throne forever and ever;

111. For they shall be judged according to their works, and every man shall receive according to his own works, his own dominion, in the mansions which are prepared;

112. And they shall be servants of the Most High; but where God and Christ dwell they cannot come, worlds without end.

113. This is the end of the vision which we saw, which we were commanded to write while we were yet in the Spirit.

114. But great and marvelous are the works of the Lord, and the mysteries of his kingdom which he showed unto us, which surpass all understanding in glory, and in might, and in dominion;

115. Which he commanded us we should not write while we were yet in the Spirit, and are not lawful for man to utter;

116. Neither is man capable to make them known, for they are only to be seen and understood by the power of the Holy Spirit, which God bestows on those who love him, and purify themselves before him;

117. To whom he grants this privilege of seeing and knowing for themselves;

118. That through the power and manifestation of the Spirit, while in the flesh, they may be able to hear his presence in the world of glory.

119. And to God and the Lamb be glory, and honor, and dominion forever and ever. Amen.

Notes

1. Cf. Isaiah 1:2.
2. Cf. Isaiah 29:14.
3. These verses describe what the Latter-day Saints call the "war in heaven" (Rev 12), a pre-mortal dispute between the forces of God and those of Lucifer, the one who became Satan or the Devil when cast to the earth. (See also Moses 4:1–4; Abraham 3:22–28.)
4. Joseph Smith taught in 1844: "What must a man do to commit the unpardonable sin? He must receive the Holy Ghost, have the heavens opened unto him, and know God, and then sin against Him. After a man has sinned against the Holy Ghost, there is no repentance for him. He has got to say that the sun does not shine while he sees it; he has got to deny Jesus Christ when the heavens have been opened unto him; and to deny the plan of salvation with his eyes open to the truth of it; and from that time he begins to be an enemy." (*History of the Church,* 6:314.)
5. Matthew 12:31–32.
6. The earliest known account of this revelation is the "Kirtland Revelation Book." From this record, the verses under consideration are as follows: "Yea, verily, the only ones who shall not be redeemed in the due time of the Lord, after the sufferings of his wrath. *Who* shall be brought forth by the resurrection of the dead. . . ." The earlier account (from Kirtland Revelation Book) is more in harmony with the Latter-day Saint belief that all persons who come into mortality—sons of perdition included—will eventually be resurrected.
7. Isaiah 66:24.
8. Hebrews 12:23. In Latter-day Saint thought, the "Church of the Firstborn" is the church of the exalted, the church composed of those who have the assurance of salvation. It is made up of those who, through faithfulness, have become co-inheritors or "joint heirs with Christ" (Rom 8:17), and are thus entitled to the blessings of the Firstborn.

9. The priesthood is "the power and authority of God, delegated to man on earth, to act in all things for the salvation of men." (Bruce R. McConkie, *Let Every Man Learn His Duty* [Salt Lake City: Deseret Book Co., 1976], p. 22.) A later revelation explained: "There are, in the Church, two priesthoods, namely the Melchizedek and Aaronic, including the Levitical Priesthood. Why the first is called the Melchizedek is because Melchizedek was such a great high priest. Before his day it was called the Holy Priesthood, after the Order of the Son of God. But out of respect or reverence to the name of the Supreme Being, to avoid the too frequent repetition of his name, they, the Church, in ancient days, called that priesthood after Melchizedek, or the Melchizedek Priesthood." (*Doctrine and Covenants*, 107: 1–4.)

10. This seems to be the first reference to the doctrine (later proclaimed in a public sermon) that man may become as God. It is doubtful whether the majority of the Saints grasped the implications of this verse as early as 1832.

11. 1 Corinthians 15:26.

12. Hebrews 12:22–24.

13. Joseph Smith taught that the "heathen nations" were those who died without law, those who therefore *as a nation* will never desire or qualify for the glories of the highest heaven.

14. These lines have reference to the Mormon belief concerning Christ's post-mortal ministry to the "world of spirits." See *Doctrine and Covenants*, 138; Robert L. Millet and Joseph Fielding McConkie, *The Life Beyond* (Salt Lake City: Bookcraft, 1986).

15. That is, they are wicked but not so corrupt as to become sons of perdition.

16. Cf. 1 Corinthians 15:40–42.

17. Cf. 1 Corinthians 1:12–13.

18. The list provided in the Apocalypse adds murderers (see Rev 21:8; 22:15).

19. That is to say, these are the ones who will be destroyed at the time of Christ's coming in glory. Their spirits pass quickly into that portion of the spirit world known as "hell" or "outer darkness." Here they will repent and suffer for the duration of the thousand year period known as the Millennium, the era when Christ will reign personally on the earth. At the end of the millennial era, those in hell will be resurrected in the "last" or second resurrection, the "resurrection of the unjust."

7. ON THE DUTY OF BISHOPS TO CARE FOR THE POOR (1832)

The following revelation specifies the role of bishops in the Church in seeing to the needs of the poor and implementing the Law of Consecration and Stewardship. It is from "Newel K. Whitney Papers," Harold B. Lee Library, Brigham Young University, Provo, Utah.

Verily thus saith the Lord unto you my servant Sidney[1] and Joseph:

2. I reveal unto you for your own profit and instruction concerning the Bishops of my church.

3. What is their duty in the church?

4. Behold, it is their duty to stand in the office of their Bishopric, and to fill the judgment seat, which I have appointed unto them, to administer the benefits of the church, or the overplusses[2] of all who are in their stewardships: according to the commandments as they are severally appointed.

5. And the property, or that which they receive of the church is not their own, but belongeth to the church.

6. Wherefore, it is the property of the Lord, and it is for the poor of the church, to be administered according to the law.

7. For it is the will of the Lord that the Church should be made equal in all things.

8. Wherefore the bishops are accountable before the Lord for their stewardships to administer of their stewardship in the which they are appointed by commandment jointly with you my servants unto the Lord, as well as you my servants or the rest of the church that the benefits of all may be dedicated unto the Lord that the Lord's storehouse may be filled always, that ye may all grow in temporal, as well as spiritual things.

9. And now verily I say unto you the bishops must needs be separated unto their bishopric and judgment seats from [the] care of business.

10. But not from claim, neither from counsel.

11. Wherefore I have given unto you commandment that you should be joined together by covenant and bond.

12. Wherefore see that ye do even as I have commanded.

13. And unto the office of the presidency of the high priesthood[3] I have given authority to preside with assistance of his councilors over all concerns of the church.

14. Wherefore stand ye fast, claim your Priesthood in authority, yet in meekness.

15. And I am able to make you abound, and be fruitful, and you shall never fall.

16. For unto you I have given the keys of the kingdom,[4] and if you transgress not they shall never be taken from you.

17. Wherefore feed my sheep. Even so, Amen.

Notes

1. Sidney Rigdon.
2. That is, the surplus.
3. The First Presidency: The President or Prophet, assisted by his two counselors.
4. "Keys" of the priesthood are understood to be the right of presidency, the directing powers.

8. THE CARE OF THE NEEDY (1832)

As indicated briefly in the Introduction, Joseph Smith's vision of spirituality comprehended the concept of a society of the pure in heart, a community wherein there was "no poor among them." The principles of the Law of Consecration and Stewardship were given to eliminate class distinctions and eradicate inequality. The following revelation (Section 83 of the Doctrine and Covenants), *received April 30, 1832, indicates those who had claim upon the "Storehouse," that is, those who were entitled to assistance from the Church through the established system.*

Verily, thus saith the Lord, in addition to the laws of the church concerning women and children, those who belong to the church, who have lost their husbands or fathers:

2. Women have claim on their husbands for their maintenance, until their husbands are taken;[1] and if they are not found transgressors they shall have fellowship in the church.

3. And if they are not faithful they shall not have fellowship in the church; yet they may remain upon their inheritances according to the laws of the land.

4. All children have claim upon their parents for their maintenance until they are of age.

5. And after that, they have claim upon the church, or in other words upon the Lord's storehouse, if their parents have not wherewith to give them inheritances.

6. And the storehouse shall be kept by the consecrations of the church; and widows and orphans shall be provided for, as also the poor. Amen.

Notes

1. An earlier revelation had explained: "Every man who is obliged to provide for his own family, let him provide, and he shall in nowise lose his crown; and let him labor in the church." (*Doctrine and Covenants,* 75:28.)

9. A PROPHECY ON WAR (1832)

The text of the prophecy below (Section 87 of the Doctrine and Covenants) *deals with the coming of the Civil War in particular, and with future wars in general. The context for this oracle is given in the following statement from Joseph Smith on December 25, 1832, the day on which this revelation was dictated: "Appearances of troubles among the nations became more visible this season than they had previously been since the Church began her journey out of the wilderness. The ravages of the cholera were frightful in almost all of the large cities on the globe. The plague broke out in India, while the United States, amid all her pomp and greatness, was threatened with immediate dissolution. The people of South Carolina, in convention assembled (in November), passed ordinances, declaring their state a free and independent nation; and appointed Thursday, the 31st day of January, 1833, as a day of humiliation and prayer, to implore Almighty God to vouchsafe His blessings, and restore liberty and happiness within their borders. President [Andrew] Jackson issued his proclamation against this rebellion, called out a force sufficient to quell it, and implored the blessings of God to assist the nation to extricate itself from the horrors of the approaching and solemn crisis." (History of the Church, 1:301.)*

Verily, thus saith the Lord concerning the wars that will shortly come to pass, beginning at the rebellion of South Carolina, which will eventually terminate in the death and misery of many souls;

2. And the time will come that war will be poured out upon all nations, beginning at this place.[1]

3. For behold, the Southern States shall be divided against the Northern States, and the South States will call on other nations, even the nation of Great Britain, as it is called, and they shall also call upon other nations, in order to defend themselves against other nations; and then war shall be poured out upon all nations.

4. And it shall come to pass, after many days, slaves shall rise up against their masters, who shall be marshaled and disciplined for war.

5. And it shall come to pass also that the remnants who are left of the land will marshal themselves, and shall become exceedingly angry, and shall vex the Gentiles with a sore vexation.

6. And thus, with the sword and by bloodshed the inhabitants of the earth shall mourn; and with famine, and plague, and earthquake, and the thunder of heaven, and the fierce and vivid lightning also, shall the inhabitants of the earth be made to feel the wrath, and indignation and chastening hand of an Almighty God, until the consumption decreed hath made a full end of all nations;

7. That the cry of the saints, and of the blood of the saints, shall cease to come up into the ears of the Lord of Sabaoth, from the earth, to be avenged of their enemies.

8. Wherefore, stand ye in holy places, and be not moved, until the day of the Lord come; for behold, it cometh quickly, saith the Lord. Amen.

Notes

1. Joseph Smith explained in April of 1834: "I prophesy, in the name of the Lord God, that the commencement of the difficulties which will cause much bloodshed previous to the coming of the Son of Man will be in South Carolina. It may probably arise through the slave question. This a voice declared to me, while I was praying earnestly on the subject, December 25th, 1832." (*Doctrine and Covenants,* 130: 12–13.)

10. THE WORD OF WISDOM:
A HEALTH CODE REVEALED (1833)

The background for this revelation is provided by Brigham Young as follows: "I think I am as well acquainted with the circum-

stances which led to the giving of the Word of Wisdom as any man in the Church, although I was not present at the time to witness them. The first school of the prophets was held in a small room situated over the Prophet Joseph's kitchen, in a house which belonged to Bishop [Newel K.] Whitney, and which was attached to his store, which store might be about fifteen feet square. In the rear of this building was a kitchen, probably ten by fourteen feet, containing rooms and pantries. Over this kitchen was situated the room in which the Prophet received revelations and in which he instructed his brethren. The brethren came to that place for hundreds of miles to attend school in a little room probably no larger than eleven by fourteen. When they assembled together in this room after breakfast, the first [thing] they did was to light their pipes, and, while smoking, talk about the great things of the kingdom, and spit all over the room, and as soon as the pipe was out of their mouths a large chew of tobacco would then be taken. Often when the Prophet entered the room to give the school instructions he would find himself in a cloud of tobacco smoke. This, and the complaints of his wife at having to clean so filthy a floor, made the Prophet think upon the matter, and he inquired of the Lord relating to the conduct of the Elders in using tobacco, and the revelation known as the Word of Wisdom was the result of his inquiry." (Journal of Discourses, *12:158.) The revelation, recorded on 27 February 1833, is now Section 89 of the* Doctrine and Covenants.

A Word of Wisdom, for the benefit of the council of high priests, assembled in Kirtland, and the church, and also the saints in Zion—

2. To be sent greeting; not by commandment or constraint, but by revelation and the word of wisdom, showing forth the order and will of God in the temporal salvation of all saints in the last days—

3. Given for a principle with promise, adapted to the capacity of the weak and the weakest of all saints, who are or can be called saints.[1]

4. Behold, verily, thus saith the Lord unto you: In consequence of evils and designs which do and will exist in the hearts of conspiring men in the last days, I have warned you, and forewarn you, by giving unto you this word of wisdom by revelation—

5. That inasmuch as any man drinketh wine or strong drink among you, behold it is not good, neither meet in the sight of your Father, only in assembling yourselves together to offer up your sacraments before him.

6. And, behold, this should be wine, yea, pure wine of the grape of the vine, or your own make.

7. And, again, strong drinks are not for the belly, but for the washing of your bodies.

8. And again, tobacco is not for the body, neither for the belly, and is not good for man, but is an herb for bruises and all sick cattle, to be used with judgment and skill.

9. And again, hot drinks are not for the body or belly.

10. And again, verily I say unto you, all wholesome herbs God hath ordained for the constitution, nature, and use of man—

11. Every herb in the season thereof, and every fruit in the season thereof; all these to be used with prudence and thanksgiving.

12. Yea, flesh also of beasts and of the fowls of the air, I, the Lord, have ordained for the use of man with thanksgiving; nevertheless they are to be used sparingly;

13. And it is pleasing unto me that they should not be used, only in times of winter, or of cold, or famine.

14. All grain is ordained for the use of man and of beasts, to be the staff of life, not only for man but for the beasts of the field, and the fowls of heaven, and all wild animals that run or creep on the earth;

15. And these hath God made for the use of man only in times of famine and excess of hunger.

16. All grain is good for the food of man; as also the fruit of the vine; that which yieldeth fruit, whether in the ground or above the ground—

17. Nevertheless, wheat for man, and corn for the ox, and oats for the horse, and rye for the fowls and for swine, and for all beasts of the field, and barley for all useful animals, and for mild drinks, as also other grain.

18. And all saints who remember to keep and do these sayings, walking in obedience to the commandments, shall receive health in their navel and marrow to their bones;

19. And shall find wisdom and great treasures of knowledge, even hidden treasures;

20. And shall run and not be weary, and shall walk and not faint.[2]

21. And I, the Lord, give unto them a promise, that the destroying angel shall pass by them, as the children of Israel, and not slay them. Amen.

Notes

1. Originally the first three verses were a part of the introduction to the revelation prepared by Joseph Smith. The Word of Wisdom was declared to be a commandment in 1908 by Joseph F. Smith, sixth President of the Church (Conference Report, October, 1908), and particularly since the 1930's has served as a major indication of Mormon orthodoxy. (See Paul H. Peterson, "An Historical Analysis of the Word of Wisdom," Unpublished Master's Thesis, Brigham Young University, 1972.)
2. Isaiah 40:31.

11. INSTRUCTIONS CONCERNING THE APOCRYPHA (1833)

On October 8, 1829, Joseph Smith and Oliver Cowdery purchased a large pulpit-style edition of the King James Bible from E.B. Grandin in Palmyra, New York, for $3.75. This was the Bible which was used in the work of "inspired translation." This Bible was printed in 1828 by the H. and E. Phinney Company at Cooperstown, New York, and contained the Old and New Testaments, with the Old Testament Apocrypha in the middle of the Bible (separating the testaments). In the midst of the translation, the Prophet Joseph came to the Apocrypha—this set of noncanonical works whose authenticity and authorship had been questioned by most of the Judaeo-Christian world for centuries—and wondered what he should do with regard to this section of his Bible. The following, received on March 9, 1833, and known as Section 91 of the Doctrine and Covenants, *is the answer to Joseph's query.*

Verily, thus saith the Lord unto you concerning the Apocrypha—There are many things contained therein that are true, and it is mostly translated correctly;

2. There are many things contained therein that are not true, which are interpolations by the hands of men.

3. Verily, I say unto you, that it is not needful that the Apocrypha should be translated.

4. Therefore, whoso readeth it, let him understand, for the Spirit manifesteth truth;

5. And whoso is enlightened by the Spirit shall obtain benefit therefrom;

6. And whoso receiveth not by the Spirit, cannot be benefited. Therefore it is not needful that it should be translated. Amen.

12. LIGHT AND TRUTH FORSAKE THE EVIL ONE (1833)

The following revelation, recorded in May of 1833, is perhaps one of the deepest and most doctrinally significant of Joseph's oracles. It deals with such matters as Christ's gradual progression to Godhood, the nature of pure worship, the pre-mortal existence of man, and the glory of God as intelligence. It also contains a vivid chastisement of the First Presidency of the Church for specific omissions and misdeeds. The following is Section 93 of the Doctrine and Covenants.

Verily, thus saith the Lord: It shall come to pass that every soul who forsaketh his sins and cometh unto me, and calleth on my name, and obeyeth my voice, and keepeth my commandments, shall see my face and know that I am; [1]

2. And that I am the true light that lighteth every man that cometh into the world;

3. And that I am in the Father, and the Father in me, and the Father and I are one—[1]

4. The Father because he gave me of his fulness, and the Son because I was in the world and made flesh my tabernacle, and dwelt among the sons of men.

5. I was in the world and received of my Father, and the works of him were plainly manifest.[2]

6. And John saw and bore record of the fulness of my glory, and the fulness of my glory, and the fulness of John's record is hereafter to be revealed.

7. And he bore record, saying: I saw his glory, that he was in the beginning, before the world was;

8. Therefore, in the beginning the Word was, for he was the Word, even the messenger of salvation—

9. The light and the Redeemer of the world; the Spirit of truth, who came into the world, because the world was made by him, and in him was the life of men and the light of men.

10. The worlds were made by him; men were made by him; all things were made by him, and through him, and of him.[3]

11. And I, John, bear record that I beheld his glory, as the glory

of the Only Begotten of the Father, full of grace and truth, even the Spirit of truth, which came and dwelt in the flesh, and dwelt among us.

12. And I, John, saw that he received not of the fulness at the first, but received grace for grace;[4]

13. And he received not of the fulness at first, but continued from grace to grace, until he received a fulness;

14. And thus he was called the Son of God, because he received not of the fulness at the first.

15. And I, John, bear record, and lo, the heavens were opened and the Holy Ghost descended upon him in the form of a dove, and sat upon him, and there came a voice out of heaven saying: This is my beloved Son.[5]

16. And I, John bear record that he received a fulness of the glory of the Father;

17. And he received all power, both in heaven and on earth, and the glory of the Father was with him, for he dwelt in him.

18. And it shall come to pass, that if you are faithful you shall receive the fulness of the record of John.

19. I give unto you these sayings that you may understand and know how to worship, and know what you worship,[6] that you may come unto the Father in my name, and in due time receive of his fulness.

20. For if you keep my commandments you shall receive of his fulness, and be glorified in me as I am in the Father; therefore, I say unto you, you shall receive grace for grace.

21. And now, verily I say unto you, I was in the beginning with the Father, and am the Firstborn;

22. And all those who are begotten through me are partakers of the glory of the same, and are the church of the Firstborn.

23. Ye were also in the beginning with the Father; that which is Spirit, even the Spirit of truth;[7]

24. And truth is knowledge of things as they are, and as they were, and as they are to come;

25. And whatsoever is more or less than this is the spirit of that wicked one who was a liar from the beginning.

26. The Spirit of truth is of God. I am the Spirit of truth, and John bore record of me, saying: He received a fulness of truth, yea, even of all truth;

27. And no man receiveth a fulness unless he keepeth his commandments.

28. He that keepeth his commandments receiveth truth and light, until he is glorified in truth and knoweth all things.

29. Man was also in the beginning with God. Intelligence, or the light of truth, was not created or made, neither indeed can be.

30. All truth is independent in that sphere in which God has placed it, to act for itself, as all intelligence also; otherwise there is no existence.

31. Behold, here is the agency of man, and here is the condemnation of man; because that which was from the beginning is plainly manifest unto them, and they receive not the light.

32. And every man whose spirit receiveth not the light is under condemnation.

33. For man is spirit. The elements are eternal, and spirit and element, inseparably connected, receive a fulness of joy;

34. And when separated, man cannot receive a fulness of joy.[8]

35. The elements are the tabernacle of God; yea, man is the tabernacle of God, even temples; and whatsoever temple is defiled, God shall destroy that temple.[9]

36. The glory of God is intelligence, or, in other words, light and truth.

37. Light and truth forsake that evil one.

38. Every spirit of man was innocent in the beginning; and God having redeemed man from the fall, men became again, in their infant state, innocent before God.[10]

39. And that wicked one cometh and taketh away light and truth through disobedience, from the children of men, and because of the tradition of their fathers.

40. But I have commanded you to bring up your children in light and truth.

41. But verily I say unto you, my servant Frederick G. Williams, you have continued under this condemnation;

42. You have not taught your children light and truth, according to the commandments; and that wicked one hath power, as yet, over you, and this is the cause of your affliction.

43. And now a commandment I give unto you—if you will be delivered you shall set in order your own house, for there are many things that are not right in your house.

44. Verily, I say unto my servant Sidney Rigdon, that in some things he hath not kept the commandments concerning his children; therefore, first set in order thy house.

45. Verily, I say unto my servant Joseph Smith, Jun., or in other

words, I will call you friends, for you are my friends, and ye shall have an inheritance with me—

46. I called you servants for the world's sake, and ye are their servants for my sake—

47. And now, verily I say unto Joseph Smith, Jun.—You have not kept the commandments, and must needs stand rebuked before the Lord;

48. Your family must needs repent and forsake some things, and give more earnest heed unto your sayings, or be removed out of their place.

49. What I say unto one I say unto all; pray always lest that wicked one have power in you, and remove you out of your place.

50. My servant Newel K. Whitney also, a bishop of my church, hath need to be chastened, and set in order his family, and see that they are more diligent and concerned at home, and pray always, or they shall be removed out of their place.

51. Now, I say unto you, my friends, let my servant Sidney Rigdon go on his journey, and make haste, and also proclaim the acceptable year of the Lord, and the gospel of salvation, as I shall give him utterance; and by your prayer of faith with one consent I will uphold him.

52. And let my servants Joseph Smith, Jun., and Frederick G. Williams make haste also, and it shall be given them even according to the prayer of faith; and inasmuch as you keep my sayings you shall not be confounded in this world, nor in the world to come.

53. And, verily I say unto you, that it is my will that you should hasten to translate my scriptures[11] and to obtain a knowledge of history, and of countries, and of kingdoms, of laws of God and man, and all this for the salvation of Zion. Amen.

Notes

1. Cf. John 10:30.
2. John 5:36; 10:25; 14:10.
3. John 1:1–4.
4. Cf. John 1:16.
5. John 1:32; Matthew 3:16–17.
6. This is one of the few places in Latter-day Saint scripture wherein "worship" is defined. According to the above pattern, worship consists in the imitation of Christ.

7. This is a reference to man's pre-mortal existence. See also verse 29.
8. Joseph Smith taught that total fulfillment or a fulness of joy may be had only in the resurrection, in a day when spirit and element (physical body) are inseparably connected.
9. 1 Corinthians 3:16–17; 6:19–20.
10. One of the doctrines taught again and again in the Book of Mormon is the "timeless" nature of Christ's atonement, the idea that the "Lamb slain from the foundation of the world" (Rev 13:8) offered himself as a ransom for men from the beginning to the end of time. (See Book of Mormon, Jarom 1:11; Mosiah 3:13; 16:6; Alma 24:13; 39:17–19.)
11. This has reference to Joseph's Bible translation which was interrupted regularly by the pressures of administering a growing church.

13. A VISION OF THE CELESTIAL OR HIGHEST HEAVEN (1836)

During the weeks prior to the dedication of the Kirtland, Ohio, Temple, the leaders of the Church had begun holding meetings in the uncompleted structure. In a series of meetings held on January 21, 1836, Joseph Smith, his counselors in the First Presidency, and Church leaders from Ohio and Missouri had participated in solemn ceremonies. While receiving a special blessing at the hands of the other leaders, the Prophet explained that he was caught away into a vision, the account of which is given below. The report of this experience, now designated as Section 137 of the Doctrine and Covenants, *was not added to the Mormon canon of scripture until 1976.*

The heavens were opened upon us, and I beheld the celestial kingdom of God, and the glory thereof, whether in the body or out I cannot tell.

2. I saw the transcendent beauty of the gate through which the heirs of that kingdom will enter, which was like unto circling flames of fire;

3. Also the blazing throne of God, whereon was seated the Father and the Son.

4. I saw the beautiful streets of that kingdom, which had the appearance of being paved with gold.[1]

5. I saw Father Adam and Abraham; and my father and my mother;[2] my brother Alvin, that has long since slept;[3]

6. And marveled how it was that he had obtained an inheritance in that kingdom, seeing that he had departed this life before the Lord had set his hand to gather Israel the second time, and had not been baptized for the remission of sins.

7. Thus came the voice of the Lord unto me, saying: All who have died without a knowledge of this gospel, who would have received it if they had been permitted to tarry, shall be heirs of the celestial kingdom of God;

8. Also all that shall die henceforth without a knowledge of it, who would have received it with all their hearts, shall be heirs of that kingdom;[4]

9. For I, the Lord, will judge all men according to their works, according to the desire of their hearts.

10. And I also beheld that all children who die before they arrive at the years of accountability[5] are saved in the celestial kingdom of heaven.[6]

Notes

1. Cf. John's vision in Revelation 21:10–27.
2. This vision was a glimpse into the future. Joseph Smith, Sr. was in the same room with his son at the time of the vision. He would live another four years. Lucy Mack Smith, the Prophet's mother, would live until 1855.
3. Alvin Smith, the oldest of the Smith children, was born in February of 1798 in Tunbridge, Vermont. He died suddenly in November of 1823, seven years before the Church was formally organized.
4. This revelation opened the door doctrinally to the idea that persons could receive the highest heaven hereafter while they had not received the fulness of the gospel here. Joseph Smith delivered his first public discourse on "Baptism for the Dead" on August 15, 1840 in Nauvoo, Illinois, and explained that persons here on earth could be baptized on behalf of their friends or loved ones who had not had opportunity for such ordinances (sacraments) while they were alive. Smith taught that this doctrine was of ancient origin, and pointed to the words of Paul in the New Testament: "Else what shall they do which are baptized

for the dead, if the dead rise not at all? Why are they then baptized for the dead?" (1 Cor 15:29.)

5. Joseph Smith taught that the child who reached the age of eight years had reached the "age of accountability." (See *Doctrine and Covenants,* 68: 25–28; JST, Genesis 17:11.)

6. This was an affirmation of the same doctrine taught in the Book of Mormon. (See Mosiah 3:16–18; 15:25; Moroni 8.)

14. ANGELS RETURN IN THE KIRTLAND TEMPLE (1836)

In 1833 the Mormons began the construction of a temple in Kirtland, Ohio. As the first-century Christians had been told that they would be "endued with power from on high" (Lk 24:49), so this Latter-day Saint Christian group anticipated a pentecostal era after the temple had been erected. The dedicatory services began on Sunday, March 27, 1836. During the week the people reported many unusual spiritual happenings—tongues, prophecy, visions, revelations, and appearances of angels. One week later, on April 3, Joseph Smith prefaced the visionary experience described below (now section 110 in the Doctrine and Covenants) *as follows: "In the afternoon, I assisted the other Presidents in distributing the Lord's Supper to the Church, receiving it from the Twelve, whose privilege it was to officiate at the sacred desk this day. After having performed this service to my brethren, I. . . bowed myself, with Oliver Cowdery, in solemn and silent prayer. After rising from prayer, the following vision was opened to both of us."* (History of the Church, *2:435–36.)*

The veil was taken from our minds, and the eyes of our understanding were opened.

2. We saw the Lord standing upon the breastwork of the pulpit, before us; and under his feet was a paved work of pure gold, in color like amber.

3. His eyes were as a flame of fire; the hair of his head was white like the pure snow; his countenance shone above the brightness of the sun and his voice was as the sound of the rushing of great waters, even the voice of Jehovah, saying:[1]

4. I am the first and the last; I am he who liveth, I am he who was slain, I am your advocate with the Father.[2]

5. Behold, your sins are forgiven you; you are clean before me; therefore, lift up your heads and rejoice.

6. Let the hearts of your brethren rejoice, and let the hearts of

all my people rejoice, who have, with their might, built this house to my name.

7. For behold, I have accepted this house, and my name shall be here; and I will manifest myself to my people in mercy in this house.

8. Yea, I will appear unto my servants, and speak unto them with mine own voice, if my people will keep my commandments, and do not pollute this holy house.

9. Yea the hearts of thousands and tens of thousands shall greatly rejoice in consequence of the blessings which shall be poured out, and the endowment[3] with which my servants have been endowed in this house.

10. And the fame of this house shall spread to foreign lands; and this is the beginning of the blessings which shall be poured out upon the heads of my people. Even so. Amen.

11. After this vision closed, the heavens were again opened unto us; and Moses appeared before us, and committed unto us the keys[4] of the gathering of Israel from the four parts of the earth, and the leading of the ten tribes from the land of the north.[5]

12. After this, Elias appeared, and committed the dispensation of the gospel of Abraham, saying that in us and our seed all generations after us should be blessed.[6]

13. After this vision had closed, another great and glorious vision burst upon us; for Elijah the prophet, who was taken to heaven without tasting death, stood before us, and said:

14. Behold, the time has fully come, which was spoken of by the mouth of Malachi—testifying that he [Elijah] should be sent, before the great and dreadful day of the Lord come—

15. To turn the hearts of the fathers to the children, and the hearts of the children to the fathers, lest the whole earth be smitten with a curse—[7]

16. Therefore, the keys of this dispensation are committed into your hands; and by this ye may know that the great and dreadful day of the Lord is near, even at the doors.[8]

Notes

1. Cf. Exodus 24:9–10; Revelation 1:14–15.
2. The modern Church accepts Jehovah as the pre-mortal name of Jesus Christ. See also Isaiah 44:6; 48:12; Revelation 1:17.
3. That "endowment" was believed to be twofold: (a) an outpouring of the Holy Spirit, an era of modern pentecost; and (b) certain

sacraments or ordinances—ritual performances—intended to cleanse and purify those who received them.

4. "Keys" are directing powers, the right of presidency.

5. The work of "gathering" is associated with proselyting and missionary work. A revelation dictated in September of 1830 stated: "And ye are called to bring to pass the gathering of mine elect; for mine elect hear my voice and harden not their hearts." (*Doctrine and Covenants*, 29:7.)

6. The specific identity of this person (Elias) is unknown. His keys opened the door for Joseph Smith to become a "modern Abraham." A later revelation to Joseph Smith declared: "And as I said unto Abraham concerning the kindreds of the earth, even so I say unto my servant Joseph: In thee and in thy seed shall the kindred of the earth be blessed." (*Doctrine and Covenants*, 124:58; cf. 132:30–32.) Mormons believe that through the ordinance of eternal marriage (performed only in temples), all persons may come to receive the blessings of Abraham, Isaac, and Jacob. (See Bruce R. McConkie, "The Promises Made to the Fathers," in *Studies in Scripture, Vol. 3: Genesis to 2 Samuel,* ed. Kent P. Jackson and Robert L. Millet [Sandy, Utah: Randall Book Co., 1985], pp. 47–62.)

7. Latter-day Saints believe Elijah restored the power to seal families together forever.

8. Of this visionary experience, Jan Shipps has written: "This transfiguration experience tied Mormonism to the Old Testament traditions and Hebraic scriptures as much as the transfiguration on the high mountain described in Matthew 17 tied Christianity to the traditions of the Old Testament. Whether or not this experience was mediated through the New Testament, it pointed to the flourishing afterward of the conception of Mormonism as the restoration of Israel that would become the ruling conception of Mormon restorationism in the years to come." (*Mormonism: The Story of a New Religious Tradition,* p. 82.)

15. A REVELATION ON ETERNAL AND PLURAL MARRIAGE (1843)

While historical sources indicate that Joseph Smith came to know of the principles of eternal and plural marriage as early as 1831—while he was engaged in the work of translation of the Old Testament—yet the full application and historical context of that which follows reflect its 1843 recording. The Mormon Leader shared many of the details of the revelation with intimate associates, particularly when he felt one could be trusted to value and preserve what he considered to be a sacred matter. A number of the leaders of the Church were instructed concerning the eternal marriage covenant, when that marriage was performed by one holding "sealing powers" of the Priesthood. In addition, between 1831 and 1843 certain persons were told of the doctrine of plurality of wives, and it was explained that eventually many would be called upon to comply with the will of the Lord in this regard. As one might expect, this doctrine was not easily received, even by those who were otherwise counted as faithful and loyal to Joseph. In spite of the fact that Smith taught that the idea had come from God as a part of the latter-day move to "restore all things," it proved to be one of the greatest trials and dividers of the Latter-day Saints in the entire history of the Church. One of those for whom the principle was particularly difficult was Emma Smith, wife of the Prophet. It appears, therefore, that one of the major reasons for the formal recording of the revelation in 1843 was to assist Emma to recognize the divine source of this practice. The following entry from the diary of William Clayton, secretary to Joseph, for July 12, 1843, is noteworthy: "This A.M. I wrote a Revelation consisting of 10 pages on the order of the priesthood, showing the designs in Moses, Abraham, David and Solomon having many wives & concubines & c. After it was wrote Prests. Joseph & Hyrum presented it and read it to E[mma]. who said she did not believe a word of it and appeared very rebellious." (Cited in Cook, Revelations of the Prophet Joseph Smith, *p. 294.) The revelation is now Section 132 of the* Doctrine and Covenants. *The following is an excerpt.*

Verily, thus saith the Lord unto you my servant Joseph, that inasmuch as you have inquired of my hand to know and understand wherein I, the Lord, justified my servants Abraham, Isaac, and Jacob, as also Moses, David and Solomon, my servants, as touching the principle and doctrine of their having many wives and concubines—

2. Behold, and lo, I am the Lord thy God, and will answer thee as touching this matter.

3. Therefore, prepare thy heart to receive and obey the instructions which I am about to give unto you; for all those who have this law revealed unto them must obey the same.

4. For behold, I reveal unto you a new and an everlasting covenant;[1] and if ye abide not that covenant, then are ye damned; for no one can reject this covenant and be permitted to enter into my glory.

5. For all who will have a blessing at my hands shall abide the

law which was appointed for that blessing, and the conditions thereof, as were instituted from before the foundation of the world.

6. And as pertaining to the new and everlasting covenant, it was instituted for the fulness of my glory; and he that receiveth a fulness thereof must and shall abide the law, or he shall be damned, saith the Lord God.

7. And verily I say unto you, that the conditions of this law are these: All covenants, contracts, bonds, obligations, oaths, vows, performances, connections, associations, or expectations, that are not made and entered into and sealed by the Holy Spirit of promise,[2] of him who is anointed, both as well for time and for all eternity, and that too most holy, by revelation and commandment through the medium of mine anointed, whom I have appointed on the earth to hold this power (and I have appointed unto my servant Joseph to hold this power in the last days, and there is never but one on the earth at a time on whom this power and the keys of this priesthood are conferred), are of no efficacy, virtue, or force in and after the resurrection from the dead; for all contracts that are not made unto this end have an end when men are dead.

8. Behold, mine house is a house of order, saith the Lord God, and not a house of confusion.

9. Will I accept of an offering, saith the Lord, that is not made in my name?

10. Or will I receive at your hands that which I have not appointed?

11. And will I appoint unto you, saith the Lord, except it be by law, even as I and my Father ordained unto you, before the world was?

12. I am the Lord thy God; and I give unto you this commandment—that no man shall come unto the Father but by me[3] or by my word, which is my law, saith the Lord.

13. And everything that is in the world, whether it be ordained of men, by thrones, or principalities, or powers, or things of name, whatsoever they may be, that are not by me or by my word, saith the Lord, shall be thrown down, and shall not remain after men are dead, neither in nor after the resurrection, saith the Lord your God.

14. For whatsoever things remain are by me; and whatsoever things are not by me shall be shaken and destroyed.

15. Therefore, if a man marry him a wife in the world, and he marry her not by me nor by my word, and he covenant with her so long as he is in the world and she with him, their covenant and marriage are not of force when they are dead, and when they are out

of the world; therefore, they are not bound by any law when they are out of the world.

16. Therefore, when they are out of the world they neither marry nor are given in marriage; but are appointed angels in heaven,[4] which angels are ministering servants, to minister for those who are worthy of a far more, and an exceeding, and an eternal weight of glory.

17. For these angels did not abide my law; therefore, they cannot be enlarged, but remain separately and singly, without exaltation, in their saved condition, to all eternity; and from henceforth are not gods, but are angels of God forever and ever.[5]

18. And again, verily I say unto you, if a man marry a wife, and make a covenant with her for time and for all eternity, if that covenant is not by me or by my word, which is my law, and is not sealed by the Holy Spirit of promise, through him whom I have anointed and appointed unto this power, then it is not valid neither of force when they are out of the world, because they are not joined by me, saith the Lord, neither by my word; when they are out of the world it cannot be received there, because the angels and the gods are appointed there, by whom they cannot pass; they cannot, therefore, inherit my glory; for my house is a house of order, saith the Lord God.

19. And again, verily I say unto you, if a man marry a wife by my word, which is my law, and by the new and everlasting covenant, and it is sealed unto them by the Holy Spirit of promise, by him who is anointed, unto whom I have appointed this power and the keys of this priesthood; and it shall be said unto them—Ye shall come forth in the first resurrection; and if it be after the first resurrection, in the next resurrection; and shall inherit thrones, kingdoms, principalities, and powers, dominions, all heights and depths—then shall it be written in the Lamb's Book of Life, that he shall commit no murder whereby to shed innocent blood, and if ye abide in my covenant, and commit no murder whereby to shed innocent blood, it shall be done unto them in all things whatsoever my servant hath put upon them, in time, and through all eternity; and shall be of full force when they are out of the world; and they shall pass by the angels, and the gods, which are set there, to their exaltation and glory in all things, as hath been sealed upon their heads, which glory shall be a fulness and a continuation of the seeds forever and ever.

20. Then shall they be gods, because they have no end; therefore shall they be from everlasting to everlasting, because they continue; then shall they be above all, because all things are subject unto

them. Then shall they be gods, because they have all power, and the angels are subject unto them.[6]

21. Verily, verily, I say unto you, except ye abide my law ye cannot attain to this glory.

22. For strait is the gate, and narrow the way[7] that leadeth unto the exaltation and continuation of the lives, and few there be that find it, because ye receive me not in the world neither do ye know me.

23. But if ye receive me in the world, then shall ye know me, and shall receive your exaltation; that where I am ye shall be also.

24. This is eternal lives—to know the only wise and true God, and Jesus Christ, whom he hath sent.[8] I am he. Receive ye, therefore, my law.

25. Broad is the gate, and wide the way that leadeth to the deaths;[9] and many there are that go in thereat, because they receive me not, neither do they abide in my law.

26. Verily, verily, I say unto you, if a man marry a wife according to my word, and they are sealed by the Holy Spirit of promise, according to mine appointment, and he or she shall commit any sin or transgression of the new and everlasting covenant whatever, and all manner of blasphemies, and if they commit no murder wherein they shed innocent blood, yet they shall come forth in the first resurrection, and enter into their exaltation; but they shall be destroyed in the flesh, and shall be delivered unto the buffetings of Satan unto the day of redemption, saith the Lord God.[10]

27. The blasphemy against the Holy Ghost, which shall not be forgiven in the world nor out of the world, is in that ye commit murder wherein ye shed innocent blood, and assent unto my death, after ye have received my new and everlasting covenant, saith the Lord God; and he that abideth not this law can in nowise enter into my glory, but shall be damned, saith the Lord.

28. I am the Lord thy God, and will give unto thee the law of my Holy Priesthood, as was ordained by me and my Father before the world was.

29. Abraham received all things, whatsoever he received, by revelation and commandment, by my word, saith the Lord, and hath entered into his exaltation and sitteth upon his throne.

30. Abraham received promises concerning his seed, and of the fruit of his loins—from whose loins ye are, namely, my servant Joseph—which were to continue so long as they were in the world; and as touching Abraham and his seed, out of the world they should continue; both in the world and out of the world should they continue

as innumerable as the stars; or, if you were to count the sand upon the seashore ye could not number them.[11]

31. This promise is yours also, because ye are of Abraham, and the promise was made unto Abraham; and by this law is the continuation of the works of my Father, wherein he glorifieth himself.

32. Go ye, therefore, and do the works of Abraham; enter ye into my law and ye shall be saved.[12]

33. But if ye enter not into my law ye cannot receive the promise of my Father, which he made unto Abraham.

34. God commanded Abraham, and Sarah gave Hagar to Abraham to wife.[13] And why did she do it? Because this was the law; and from Hagar sprang many people. This, therefore, was fulfilling, among other things, the promises.

35. Was Abraham, therefore, under condemnation? Verily I say unto you, Nay; for I, the Lord, commanded it.

36. Abraham was commanded to offer his son Isaac; nevertheless, it was written: Thou shalt not kill. Abraham, however, did not refuse, and it was accounted unto him for righteousness.[14]

37. Abraham received concubines, and they bore him children; and it was accounted unto him for righteousness, because they were given unto him, and he abode in my law; as Isaac also and Jacob did none other things than that which they were commanded; and because they did none other things than that which they were commanded, they have entered into their exaltation, according to the promises, and sit upon thrones, and are not angels but are gods.

38. David also received many wives and concubines, and also Solomon and Moses my servants, as also many others of my servants, from the beginning of creation until this time; and in nothing did they sin save in those things which they received not of me.[15]

39. David's wives and concubines were given unto him of me, by the hand of Nathan, my servant, and others of the prophets who had the keys of this power; and in none of these things did he sin against me save in the case of Uriah and his wife; and, therefore he hath fallen from his exaltation, and received his portion; and he shall not inherit them out of the world, for I gave them unto another, saith the Lord.

40. I am the Lord thy God, and I gave unto thee, my servant Joseph, an appointment, and restore all things. Ask what ye will, and it shall be given unto you according to my word.

41. And as ye have asked concerning adultery, verily, verily, I say unto you, if a man receiveth a wife in the new and everlasting covenant, and if she be with another man, and I have not appointed

unto her by the holy anointing she hath committed adultery and shall be destroyed.

42. If she be not in the new and everlasting covenant, and she be with another man, she has committed adultery.

43. And if her husband be with another woman, and he was under a vow, he hath broken his vow and hath committed adultery.

44. And if she hath not committed adultery, but is innocent and hath not broken her vow, and she knoweth it, and I reveal it unto you, my servant Joseph, then shall you have power, by the power of my Holy Priesthood, to take her and give her unto him that hath not committed adultery but hath been faithful; for he shall be made ruler over many.

45. For I have conferred upon you the keys and power of the priesthood, wherein I restore all things, and make known unto you all things in due time.

46. And verily, verily, I say unto you, that whatsoever you seal on earth shall be sealed in heaven; and whatsoever you bind on earth, in my name and by my word, saith the Lord, it shall be eternally bound in the heavens; and whosesoever sins you remit on earth shall be remitted eternally in the heavens; and whosesoever sins you retain on earth shall be retained in heaven.[16]

47. And again, verily I say, whomsoever you bless I will bless, and whomsoever you curse I will curse, saith the Lord; for I, the Lord, am thy God.

48. And again, verily I say unto you, my servant Joseph, that whatsoever you give on earth, and to whomsoever you give any one on earth, by my word and according to my law, it shall be visited with blessings and not cursings, and with my power, saith the Lord, and shall be without condemnation on earth and in heaven.

49. For I am the Lord thy God, and will be with thee even unto the end of the world, and through all eternity; for verily I seal upon you your exaltation, and prepare a throne for you in the kingdom of my Father, with Abraham your father.

50. Behold, I have seen your sacrifices, and will forgive all your sins; I have seen your sacrifices in obedience to that which I have told you. Go, therefore, and I make a way for your escape, as I accepted the offering of Abraham of his son Isaac.

Notes

1. The "new and everlasting covenant" is the fulness of the gospel. It is *everlasting* in the sense that it was had from the days of

Adam. It is *new* inasmuch as it is introduced for the first time in centuries, is a restoration after a period of apostasy.

2. The "Holy Spirit of Promise" is the Holy Spirit promised to the Saints, or, in other words, the Holy Ghost or third member of the Godhead. Latter-day Saints believe that the Holy Ghost has specific functions, such as revelator, testifier, discerner, and comforter. In addition, the Holy Ghost is a *sealer,* and as such seals the promise of salvation upon those who are just and true.

3. John 14:6.

4. Joseph Smith explained that this verse was the true meaning of the Lord's denunciation of the Sadducees in Matthew 22 and Luke 20. That is to say, "they" who neither marry nor are given in marriage in the resurrection are they who did not have their marriage performed by one having proper priesthood authority—power to bind on earth and in heaven, power to perform the ceremony beyond time and thus seal the union for eternity. (Cf. Mt 16:19.)

5. "In the celestial glory there are three heavens or degrees; and in order to obtain the highest, a man must enter into this order of the priesthood [meaning the new and everlasting covenant of marriage]; and if he does not, he cannot obtain it. He may enter into the other, but that is the end of his kingdom; he cannot have an increase." (*Doctrine and Covenants,* 131:1–4.)

6. Here again is taught the doctrine of man becoming as God.

7. Cf. Matthew 7:14.

8. Cf. John 17:3.

9. Cf. Matthew 7:13.

10. This is a difficult and perplexing verse. It has specific reference to a couple who have (1) entered into the new and everlasting covenant of marriage—that is, have been married in a Mormon temple; and (2) have been faithful to all covenants, such that the Lord had granted to them the promise of salvation (sealed them by the Holy Spirit of Promise). The matter of their being "destroyed in the flesh" (cf. 1 Cor. 5:5) is a doctrinal issue about which little has been said by Church authorities, and thus is a subject whose whole meaning is uncertain.

11. See, for example, Genesis 15:5; 17:1–14.

12. Joseph Smith taught that through "eternal marriage" the blessings of Abraham, Isaac, and Jacob are made available.

13. Genesis 16:1–3. Note in this revelation that *God* initiated the polygamous relationship.

14. Note again the 1842 letter from Joseph Smith to Nancy Rigdon. Smith explained: "Whatever God requires is right."

15. See 2 Samuel 11, 12; I Kings 11:1–6.
16. Cf. Matthew 16:18–19.

16. READING THE SIGNS OF THE TIMES:
AN APPENDIX (1831)

In prefacing this revelation the Prophet Joseph Smith wrote: "At this time there were many things which the Elders desired to know relative to preaching the Gospel to the inhabitants of the earth, and concerning the gathering; and in order to walk by the true light, and be instructed from on high, on the 3rd of November, 1831, I inquired of the Lord and received the following important revelation, which has since been added to the book of Doctrine and Covenants, *and called the Appendix." (*History of the Church *1:229.) It is now Section 133 of that volume of LDS scripture.*

Hearken, O ye people of my church, saith the Lord your God, and hear the word of the Lord concerning you—

2. The Lord who shall suddenly come to his temple;[1] the Lord who shall come down upon the world with a curse to judgment; yea, upon all the nations that forget God, and upon all the ungodly among you.

3. For he shall make bare his holy arm in the eyes of all the nations, and all the ends of the earth shall see the salvation of their God.

4. Wherefore, prepare ye, prepare ye, O my people; sanctify yourselves; gather ye together, O ye people of my church, upon the land of Zion, all you that have not been commanded to tarry.

5. Go ye out from Babylon. Be ye clean that bear the vessels of the Lord.[2]

6. Call your solemn assemblies, and speak often one to another. And let every man call upon the name of the Lord.

7. Yea, verily I say unto you again, the time has come when the voice of the Lord is unto you: Go ye out of Babylon; gather ye out from among the nations, from the four winds, from one end of heaven to the other.

8. Send forth the elders of my church unto the nations which are afar off; unto the islands of the sea; send forth unto foreign lands; call upon all nations, first upon the Gentiles, and then upon the Jews.

9. And behold, and lo, this shall be their cry, and the voice of the Lord unto all people: Go ye forth unto the land of Zion, that the borders of my people may be enlarged, and that her stakes may be strengthened,[3] and that Zion may go forth unto the regions round about.

10. Yea, let the cry go forth among all people: Awake and arise and go forth to meet the Bridegroom; behold and lo, the bridegroom cometh; go ye out to meet him.[4] Prepare yourselves for the great day of the Lord.

11. Watch, therefore, for ye know neither the day nor the hour.

12. Let them, therefore, who are among the Gentiles flee unto Zion.

13. And let them who be of Judah flee unto Jerusalem, unto the mountains of the Lord's house.

14. Go ye out from among the nations, even from Babylon, from the midst of wickedness, which is spiritual Babylon.

15. But verily, thus saith the Lord, let not your flight be in haste, but let all things be prepared before you; and he that goeth, let him not look back lest sudden destruction shall come upon him.

16. Hearken and hear, O ye inhabitants of the earth. Listen, ye elders of my church together, and hear the voice of the Lord; for he calleth upon all men, and he commandeth all men everywhere to repent.

17. For behold, the Lord God hath sent forth the angel crying through the midst of heaven, saying: Prepare ye the way of the Lord, and make his paths straight, for the hour of his coming is nigh—

18. When the Lamb shall stand upon Mount Zion, and with him a hundred and forth-four thousand,[5] having his Father's name written on their foreheads.

19. Wherefore, prepare ye for the coming of the Bridegroom; go ye, go ye out to meet him.

20. For behold, he shall stand upon the mount of Olivet, and upon the mighty ocean, even the great deep, and upon the islands of the sea, and upon the land of Zion.

21. And he shall utter his voice out of Zion, and he shall speak from Jerusalem, and his voice shall be heard among all people;

22. And it shall be a voice as the voice of many waters, and as the voice of a great thunder, which shall break down the mountains, and the valleys shall not be found.

23. He shall command the great deep, and it shall be driven back into the north countries, and the islands shall become one land;

24. And the land of Jerusalem and the land of Zion shall be turned back into their own place, and the earth shall be like as it was in the days before it was divided.

25. And the Lord, even the Savior, shall stand in the midst of his people, and shall reign over all flesh.

26. And they who are in the north countries shall come in remembrance before the Lord; and their prophets shall hear his voice, and shall no longer stay themselves; and they shall smite the rocks, and the ice shall flow down at their presence.[6]

27. And an highway shall be cast up in the midst of the great deep.

28. Their enemies shall become a prey unto them,

29. And in the barren deserts there shall come forth pools of living water; and the parched ground shall no longer be a thirsty land.

30. And they shall bring forth their rich treasures unto the children of Ephraim, my servants.

31. And the boundaries of the everlasting hills shall tremble at their presence.

32. And there shall they fall down and be crowned with glory, even in Zion, by the hands of the servants of the Lord, even the children of Ephraim.

33. And they shall be filled with songs of everlasting joy.

34. Behold, this is the blessing of the everlasting God upon the tribes of Israel, and the richer blessing upon the head of Ephraim and his fellows.

35. And they also of the tribe of Judah, after their pain, shall be sanctified in holiness before the Lord, to dwell in his presence day and night, forever and ever.

36. And now, verily saith the Lord, that these things might be known among you, O inhabitants of the earth, I have sent forth mine angel flying through the midst of heaven, having the everlasting gospel, who hath appeared unto some and hath committed it unto man, who shall appear unto many that dwell on the earth.

37. And this gospel shall be preached unto every nation, and kindred, and tongue, and people.[7]

38. And the servants of God shall go forth, saying with a loud voice: Fear God and give glory to him, for the hour of his judgment is come;

39. And worship him that made heaven, and earth, and the sea, and the fountains of waters—[8]

40. Calling upon the name of the Lord day and night, saying: O

that thou wouldst rend the heavens, that thou wouldst come down, that the mountains might flow down at thy presence.

41. And it shall be answered upon their heads; for the presence of the Lord shall be as the melting fire that burneth, and as the fire which causeth the waters to boil.[9]

42. O Lord, thou shalt come down to make thy name known to thine adversaries, and all nations shall tremble at thy presence.

43. When thou doest terrible things, things they look not for;

44. Yea, when thou comest down, and the mountains flow down at thy presence, thou shalt meet him who rejoiceth and worketh righteousness, who remembereth thee in thy ways.

45. For since the beginning of the world have not men heard nor perceived by the ear, neither hath any eye seen, O God, besides thee, how great things thou hast prepared for him that waiteth for thee.

46. And it shall be said: Who is this that cometh down from God in heaven with dyed garments; yea, from the regions which are not known, clothed in his glorious apparel, traveling in the greatness of his strength?

47. And he shall say: I am he who spake in righteousness, mighty to save.

48. And the Lord shall be red in his apparel, and his garments like him that treadeth in the wine-vat.[10]

49. And so great shall be the glory of his presence that the sun shall hide his face in shame, and the moon shall withhold its light, and the stars shall be hurled from their places.

50. And his voice shall be heard: I have trodden the wine-press alone, and have brought judgment upon all people; and none were with me;

51. And I have trampled them in my fury, and I did tread upon them in mine anger, and their blood have I sprinkled upon my garments, and stained all my raiment; for this was the day of vengeance which was in my heart.

52. And now the year of my redeemed is come; and they shall mention the loving kindness of their Lord, and all that he has bestowed upon them according to his goodness, and according to his loving kindness, forever and ever.

53. In all their afflictions he was afflicted.[11] And the angel of his presence saved them; and in his love, and in his pity, he redeemed them, and bore them, and carried them all the days of old;

54. Yea, and Enoch also, and they who were with him; the prophets who were before him; and Noah also, and they who were before him; and Moses also, and they who were before him;

55. And from Moses to Elijah, and from Elijah to John, who were with Christ in his resurrection, and the holy apostles, with Abraham, Isaac, and Jacob, shall be in the presence of the Lamb.

56. And the graves of the saints shall be opened;[12] and they shall come forth and stand on the right hand of the Lamb, when he shall stand upon Mount Zion, and upon the holy city, the New Jerusalem; and they shall sing the song of the Lamb, day and night forever and ever.

57. And for this cause, that men might be made partakers of the glories which were to be revealed, the Lord sent forth the fulness of his gospel, his everlasting covenant, reasoning in plainness and simplicity—

58. To prepare the weak for those things which are coming on the earth, and for the Lord's errand in the day when the weak shall confound the wise, and the little one become a strong nation, and two shall put their tens of thousands to flight.

59. And by the weak things of the earth the Lord shall thrash the nations by the power of his Spirit.

60. And for this cause these commandments were given; they were commanded to be kept from the world in the day that they were given, but now are to go forth unto all flesh—

61. And this according to the mind and will of the Lord, who ruleth over all flesh.

62. And unto him that repenteth and sanctifieth himself before the Lord shall be given eternal life.

63. And upon them that hearken not to the voice of the Lord shall be fulfilled that which was written by the prophet Moses, that they should be cut off from among the people.[13]

64. And also that which was written by the prophet Malachi: For, behold, the day cometh that shall burn as an oven, and all the proud, yea, and all that do wickedly, shall be stubble; and the day that cometh shall burn them up, saith the Lord of hosts, that it shall leave them neither root nor branch.[14]

65. Wherefore, this shall be the answer of the Lord unto them:

66. In that day when I came unto mine own, no man among you received me, and you were driven out.

67. When I called again there was none of you to answer; yet my arm was not shortened at all that I could not redeem, neither my power to deliver.

68. Behold, at my rebuke I dry up the sea. I make the rivers a wilderness; their fish stink, and die for thirst.

69. I clothe the heavens with blackness, and make sackcloth their covering.

70. And this shall ye have of my hand—ye shall lie down in sorrow.

71. Behold, and lo, there are none to deliver you; for ye obeyed not my voice when I called to you out of the heavens; ye believed not my servants, and when they were sent unto you ye received them not.

72. Wherefore, they sealed up the testimony and bound up the law, and ye were delivered over unto darkness.

73. These shall go away into outer darkness, where there is weeping, and wailing, and gnashing of teeth.

74. Behold the Lord your God hath spoken it. Amen.

Notes

1. Malachi 3:1.
2. Isaiah 52:11.
3. Isaiah 54:2.
4. Matthew 25:6.
5. Revelation 14:1.
6. This is a reference to the dramatic return of the ten "lost" tribes of Israel, the northern kingdom carried away captive by the Assyrians in 721 B.C.E.
7. Matthew 24:14.
8. Revelation 14:6–7.
9. Cf. 2 Peter 3:10.
10. Cf. Revelation 19:13.
11. Isaiah 63:9.
12. Cf. Matthew 27:52–53.
13. Deuteronomy 18:19; Acts 3:23.
14. Malachi 4:1.

VI.

TRANSLATIONS

1. THE BOOK OF MORMON STORY BEGINS (1830)

The Book of Mormon saga begins with the call of Lehi to prophetic duties. In the story, Lehi is a contemporary with Jeremiah, (ca. 600 B.C.E.) and, like his prophetic colleague, is called of God to preach repentance and prophesy of the destruction of Jerusalem by the Babylonians. The text which follows constitutes Chapter One of the book of First Nephi.

I, Nephi, having been born of goodly parents, therefore I was taught somewhat in all the learning of my father; and having seen many afflictions in the course of my days, nevertheless, having been highly favored of the Lord in all my days; yea, having had a great knowledge of the goodness and the mysteries of God, therefore I make a record of my proceedings in my days.

2. Yea, I make a record in the language of my father, which consists of the learning of the Jews and the language of the Egyptians.[1]

3. And I know that the record which I make is true; and I make it with mine own hand; and I make it according to my knowledge.

4. For it came to pass in the commencement of the first year of the reign of Zedekiah, king of Judah, (my father, Lehi, having dwelt at Jerusalem in all his days); and in that same year there came many prophets, prophesying unto the people that they must repent, or the great city Jerusalem must be destroyed.

5. Wherefore it came to pass that my father, Lehi, as he went forth prayed unto the Lord, yea, even with all his heart, in behalf of his people.

6. And it came to pass as he prayed unto the Lord, there came a pillar of fire and dwelt upon a rock before him; and he saw and heard much; and because of the things which he saw and heard he did quake and tremble exceedingly.

7. And it came to pass that he returned to his own house at Jerusalem; and he cast himself upon his bed, being overcome with the Spirit and the things which he had seen.

8. And being thus overcome with the Spirit, he was carried away in a vision, even that he saw the heavens open, and he thought he saw God sitting upon his throne, surrounded with numberless concourses of angels in the attitude of singing and praising their God.

9. And it came to pass that he saw one descending out of the midst of heaven, and he beheld that his luster was above that of the sun at noon-day.

10. And he also saw twelve others following him, and their brightness did exceed that of the stars in the firmament.[2]

11. And they came down and went forth upon the face of the earth; and the first came and stood before my father, and gave unto him a book, and bade him that he should read.

12. And it came to pass that as he read, he was filled with the Spirit of the Lord.

13. And he read, saying: Wo, wo, unto Jerusalem, for I have seen thine abominations! Yea, and many things did my father read concerning Jerusalem—that it should be destroyed, and the inhabitants thereof; many should perish by the sword, and many should be carried away captive into Babylon.

14. And it came to pass that when my father had read and seen many great and marvelous things, he did exclaim many things unto the Lord; such as: Great and marvelous are thy works, O Lord God Almighty! Thy throne is high in the heavens, and thy power, and goodness, and mercy are over all the inhabitants of the earth, and, because thou art merciful, thou wilt not suffer those who come unto thee that they shall perish!

15. And after this manner was the language of my father in the praising of his God; for his soul did rejoice, and his whole heart was filled, because of the things which he had seen, yea, which the Lord had shown unto him.

16. And now I, Nephi, do not make a full account of the things which my father hath written, for he hath written many things which he saw in visions and in dreams; and he also hath written many things which he prophesied and spake unto his children, of which I shall not make a full account.

17. But I shall make an account of my proceedings in my days. Behold, I make an abridgment of the record of my father, upon plates which I have made with mine own hands; wherefore, after I have abridged the record of my father then will I make an account of mine own life.

18. Therefore, I would that ye should know, that after the Lord had shown so many marvelous things unto my father, Lehi, yea, concerning the destruction of Jerusalem, behold he went forth among the people, and began to prophesy and to declare unto them concerning the things which he had both seen and heard.

19. And it came to pass that the Jews did mock him because of the things which he testified of them; for he truly testified of their wickedness and their abominations; and he testified that the things which he saw and heard, and also the things which he read in the book, manifested plainly of the coming of a Messiah, and also the redemption of the world.

20. And when the Jews heard these things they were angry with him; yea, even as with the prophets of old, whom they had cast out, and stoned, and slain; and they also sought his life, that they might take it away. But behold, I, Nephi, will show unto you that the tender mercies of the Lord are over all those whom he hath chosen, because of their faith, to make them mighty even unto the power of deliverance.

Notes

1. Old LDS tradition holds that the "learning of the Jews and the language of the Egyptians" describes a Hebrew cultural background and an Egyptian script. (See John L. Sorenseon, *An Ancient American Setting for the Book of Mormon* [Salt Lake City: Deseret Book Co. and Foundation for Ancient Research and Mormon Studies, 1985], pp. 74–76.)

2. This seems to be a reference to Jesus Christ and his twelve apostles.

2. THE CONDESCENSION OF THE GREAT GOD (1830)

Among the central messages of the Book of Mormon prophets from the beginning is the coming of Jesus Christ as Messiah and Savior of mankind. The Book of Mormon is thus one of the scriptural sources for the Latter-day Saint belief in "Christ's Eternal Gospel," the concept that Christian prophets have taught Christian doctrines and participated in Christian ordinances (sacraments) since the days of Adam. In the chapter which follows, Nephi, the son of Lehi, has a visionary experience in which he is able to see the birth and ministry of Jesus of Nazareth some 600 years ahead of time. His father Lehi had had a similar experience before him, and now Nephi becomes an additional witness. The following is the eleventh chapter of the book of First Nephi.

For it came to pass after I had desired to know the things that my father had seen, and believing that the Lord was able to make them known unto me, as I sat pondering in mine heart I was caught away in the Spirit of the Lord, yea, into an exceedingly high mountain, which I never had before seen, and upon which I never had before set my foot.

2. And the Spirit said unto me: Behold, what desirest thou?

3. And I said: I desire to behold the things which my father saw.

4. And the Spirit said unto me: Believest thou that thy father saw the tree of which he hath spoken?[1]

5. And I said: Yea, thou knowest that I believe all the words of my father.

6. And when I had spoken these words, the Spirit cried with a loud voice, saying: Hosanna to the Lord, the most high God; for he is God over all the earth, yea, even above all. And blessed art thou, Nephi, because thou believest in the Son of the most high God; wherefore, thou shalt behold the things which thou has desired.

7. And behold this thing shall be given unto thee for a sign, that after thou hast beheld the tree which bore the fruit which thy father tasted, thou shalt also behold a man descending out of heaven, and him shall ye witness; and after ye have witnessed him ye shall bear record that it is the Son of God.

8. And it came to pass that the Spirit said unto me: Look! And I looked and beheld a tree; and it was like unto the tree which my father had seen; and the beauty thereof was far beyond, yea, exceeding of all beauty; and the whiteness thereof did exceed the whiteness of the driven snow.

9. And it came to pass after I had seen the tree, I said unto the Spirit: I behold thou hast shown unto me the tree which is precious above all.

10. And he said unto me: What desirest thou?

11. And I said unto him: To know the interpretation thereof—

for I spake unto him as a man speaketh; for I beheld that he was in the form of a man; yet nevertheless, I knew that it was the Spirit of the Lord; and he spake unto me as a man speaketh with another.

12. And it came to pass that he said unto me: Look! And I looked as if to look upon him, and I saw him not; for he had gone from before my presence.

13. And it came to pass that I looked and beheld the great city of Jerusalem, and also other cities. And I beheld the city of Nazareth; and in the city of Nazareth I beheld a virgin, and she was exceedingly fair and white.

14. And it came to pass that I saw the heavens open; and an angel came down and stood before me; and he said unto me: Nephi, what beholdest thou?

15. And I said unto him: A virgin, most beautiful and fair above all other virgins.

16. And he said unto me: Knowest thou the condescension of God?

17. And I said unto him: I know that he loveth his children; nevertheless, I do not know the meaning of all things.

18. And he said unto me: Behold, the virgin whom thou seest is the mother of the Son of God,[2] after the manner of the flesh.

19. And it came to pass that I beheld that she was carried away in the Spirit; and after she had been carried away in the Spirit for the space of a time the angel spake unto me, saying: Look!

20. And I looked and beheld the virgin again, bearing a child in her arms.

21. And the angel said unto me: Behold the Lamb of God, yea, even the Son of the Eternal Father![3] Knowest thou the meaning of the tree which thy father saw?

22. And I answered him, saying: Yea, it is the love of God, which sheddeth itself abroad in the hearts of the children of men; wherefore, it is the most desirable above all things.

23. And he spake unto me, saying: Yea, and the most joyous to the soul.

24. And after he had said these words, he said unto me: Look! And I looked, and I beheld the Son of God going forth among the children of men; and I saw many fall down at his feet and worship him.

25. And it came to pass that I beheld that the rod of iron, which my father had seen, was the word of God, which led to the fountain of living waters, or to the tree of life; which waters are a representation of the love of God.

26. And the angel said unto me again: Look and behold the condescension of God!

27. And I looked and beheld the Redeemer of the world, of whom my father had spoken; and I also beheld the prophet who should prepare the way before him. And the Lamb of God went forth and was baptized of him; and after he was baptized, I beheld the heavens open, and the Holy Ghost come down out of heaven and abide upon him in the form of a dove.

28. And I beheld that he went forth ministering unto the people, in power and great glory; and the multitudes were gathered together to hear him; and I beheld that they cast him out from among them.

29. And I also beheld twelve others following him. And it came to pass they were carried away in the Spirit from before my face, and I saw them not.

30. And it came to pass that the angel spake unto me again, saying: Look! And I looked, and I beheld the heavens open again, and I saw angels descending upon the children of men; and they did minister unto them.

31. And he spake unto me again, saying: Look! And I looked, and I beheld the Lamb of God going forth among the children of men. And I beheld multitudes of people who were sick, and who were afflicted with all manner of diseases, and with devils and unclean spirits; and the angel spake and showed all these things unto me. And they were healed by the power of the Lamb of God; and the devils and the unclean spirits were cast out.

32. And it came to pass that the angel spake unto me again, saying: Look! And I looked and beheld the Lamb of God, that he was taken by the people; yea, the Son of the everlasting God[4] was judged of the world; and I saw and bear record.

33. And I, Nephi, saw that he was lifted up upon the cross and slain for the sins of the world.

34. And after he was slain I saw the multitudes of the earth, that they were gathered together to fight against the apostles of the Lamb; for thus were the twelve called by the angel of the Lord.

35. And the multitude of the earth was gathered together; and I beheld that they were in a large and spacious building, like unto the building which my father saw. And the angel of the Lord spake unto me again, saying: Behold the world and the wisdom thereof; yea, behold the house of Israel hath gathered together to fight against the twelve apostles of the Lamb.

36. And it came to pass that I saw and bear record, that the great and spacious building was the pride of the world; and it fell, and

the fall thereof was exceedingly great. And the angel of the Lord spake unto me again, saying: Thus shall be the destruction of all nations, kindreds, tongues, and people, that shall fight against the twelve apostles of the Lamb.

Notes

1. In chapter eight of First Nephi, Lehi had a dream in which he saw a straight and narrow path leading to a beautiful tree (the tree of life), whose fruit was "most desirable above all other things."
2. The first edition of the Book of Mormon (1830) reads: "The virgin whom thou seest is the *mother of God,* after the manner of the flesh."
3. 1830 edition: "Behold the Lamb of God, yea, even *the Eternal Father!"*
4. 1830 edition: "Yea, the *everlasting God* was judged of the world."

3. "O HOW GREAT THE GOODNESS OF OUR GOD" (1830)

One of the greatest philosopher-theologians in the Book of Mormon is Jacob, son of Lehi and younger brother of Nephi. In the chapter which follows (Chapter Nine of Second Nephi), Jacob speaks of the greatness of the "Plan of Our God" for the redemption of mankind, and of the blessings of the Atonement of Christ.

And now, my beloved brethren, I have read these things that ye might know concerning the covenants of the Lord that he has covenanted with all the house of Israel—

2. That he has spoken unto the Jews, by the mouth of his holy prophets, even from the beginning down, from generation to generation, until the time comes that they shall be restored to the true church and fold of God; when they shall be gathered home to the lands of their inheritance and shall be established in all their lands of promise.[1]

3. Behold, my beloved brethren, I speak unto you these things that ye may rejoice, and lift up you heads forever, because of the blessings which the Lord God shall bestow upon your children.

4. For I know that ye have searched much, many of you, to

know of things to come; wherefore I know that ye know that our flesh must waste away and die; nevertheless in our bodies we shall see God.

5. Yea, I know that ye know that in the body he shall show himself unto those at Jerusalem, from whence we came; for it is expedient that it should be among them; for it behooveth the great Creator that he suffereth himself to become subject unto man in the flesh, and die for all men, that all men might become subject unto him.

6. For as death hath passed upon all men, to fulfil the merciful plan of the great Creator, there must needs be a power of resurrection, and the resurrection must needs come unto man by reason of the fall; and the fall came by reason of transgression; and because man became fallen they were cut off from the presence of the Lord.

7. Wherefore, it must needs be an infinite atonement—save it should be an infinite atonement this corruption could not put on incorruption. Wherefore, the first judgment which came upon man must needs have remained to an endless duration. And if so, this flesh must have laid down to rot and to crumble to its mother earth, to rise no more.

8. O the wisdom of God, his mercy and grace! For behold, if the flesh should rise no more our spirits must become subject to that angel who fell from before the presence of the Eternal God, and became the devil, to rise no more.[2]

9. And our spirits must have become like unto him, and we become devils, angels to a devil, to be shut out from the presence of our God, and to remain with the father of lies, in misery, like unto himself; yea, to that being who beguiled our first parents, who transformeth himself nigh unto an angel of light, and stirreth up the children of men unto secret combinations of murder and all manner of secret works of darkness.

10. O how great the goodness of our God, who prepareth a way for our escape from the grasp of this awful monster; yea, that monster, death and hell, which I call the death of the body, and also the death of the spirit.

11. And because of the way of deliverance of our God, the Holy One of Israel,[3] this death, of which I have spoken, which is the temporal, shall deliver up its dead; which death is the grave.

12. And this death of which I have spoken, which is the spiritual death, shall deliver up its dead; which spiritual death is hell; wherefore, death and hell must deliver up their dead, and hell must deliver

up its captive spirits, and the grave must deliver up its captive bodies, and the bodies and the spirits of men will be restored one to the other;[4] and it is by the power of the resurrection of the Holy One of Israel.

13. O how great the plan of our God! For on the other hand, the paradise of God must deliver up the spirits of the righteous, and the grave deliver up the body of the righteous; and the spirit and the body is restored to itself again, and all men become incorruptible, and immortal, and they are living souls, having a perfect knowledge like unto us in the flesh, save it be that our knowledge shall be perfect.

14. Wherefore, we shall have a perfect knowledge of all our guilt, and our uncleanness, and our nakedness; and the righteous shall have a perfect knowledge of their enjoyment, and their righteousness, being clothed with purity, yea, even with the robe of righteousness.

15. And it shall come to pass that when all men shall have passed from this first death unto life, insomuch as they have become immortal, they must appear before the judgment-seat of the Holy One of Israel; and then cometh the judgment, and then must they be judged according to the holy judgment of God.

16. And assuredly, as the Lord liveth, for the Lord God hath spoken it, and it is his eternal word, which cannot pass away, that they who are righteous shall be righteous still, and they who are filthy shall be filthy still; wherefore, they who are filthy are the devil and his angels; and they shall go away into everlasting fire, prepared for them; and their torment is as a lake of fire and brimstone, whose flame ascendeth up forever and ever and has no end.

17. O the greatness and the justice of our God! For he executeth all his words, and they have gone forth out of his mouth, and his law must be fulfilled.

18. But, behold the righteous, the saints of the Holy One of Israel, they who have believed in the Holy One of Israel, they who have endured the crosses of the world, and despised the shame of it, they shall inherit the kingdom of God, which was prepared for them from the foundation of the world, and their job shall be full forever.

19. O the greatness of the mercy of our God, the Holy One of Israel! For he delivereth his saints from that awful monster the devil, and death, and hell, and that lake of fire and brimstone, which is endless torment.[5]

20. O how great the holiness of our God! For he knoweth all things, and there is not anything save he knows it.

21. And he cometh into the world that he may save all men if

they will hearken unto his voice; for behold, he suffereth the pains of all men, yea, the pains of every living creature, both men, women, and children, who belong to the family of Adam.

22. And he suffereth this that the resurrection might pass upon all men, that all might stand before him at the great and judgment day.

23. And he commandeth all men that they must repent, and be baptized in his name, having perfect faith in the Holy One of Israel, or they cannot be saved in the kingdom of God.

24. And if they will not repent and believe in his name, and be baptized in his name, and endure to the end, they must be damned; for the Lord God, the Holy One of Israel, has spoken it.

25. Wherefore, he has given a law; and where there is no law given there is no punishment; and where there is no punishment there is no condemnation; and where there is no condemnation the mercies of the Holy One of Israel have claim upon them, because of the atonement; for they are delivered by the power of him.

26. For the atonement satisfieth the demands of his justice upon all those who have not the law given to them, that they are delivered from that awful monster, death and hell, and the devil, and the lake of fire and brimstone, which is endless torment; and they are restored to that God who gave them breath, which is the Holy One of Israel.

27. But wo unto him that has the law given, yea, that has all the commandments of God, like unto us, and that transgresseth them, and that wasteth the days of his probation, for awful is his state!

28. O that cunning plan of the evil one! O the vainness, and the frailties, and the foolishness of men! When they are learned they think they are wise, and they hearken not unto the counsel of God, for they set it aside, supposing they know of themselves, wherefore, their wisdom is foolishness and it profiteth them not. And they shall perish.

29. But to be learned is good if they hearken unto the counsels of God.

30. But wo unto the rich, who are rich as to the things of the world. For because they are rich they despise the poor, and they persecute the meek, and their hearts are upon their treasures; wherefore, their treasure is their god. And behold, their treasure shall perish with them also.

31. And wo unto the deaf that will not hear; for they shall perish.

32. Wo unto the blind that will not see; for they shall perish also.

33. Wo unto the uncircumcised of heart, for a knowledge of their iniquities shall smite them at the last day.

34. Wo unto the liar, for he shall be thrust down to hell.

35. Wo unto the murderer who deliberately killeth, for he shall die.

36. Wo unto them who commit whoredoms, for they shall be thrust down to hell.

37. Yea, wo unto those that worship idols, for the devil of all devils delighteth in them.

38. And, in fine, wo unto all those who die in their sins; for they shall return to God, and behold his face, and remain in their sins.

39. O, my beloved brethren, remember the awfulness in transgressing against that Holy God, and also the awfulness of yielding to the enticings of that cunning one. Remember, to be carnally-minded is death, and to be spiritually-minded is life eternal.[6]

40. O, my beloved brethren, give ear to my words. Remember the greatness of the Holy One of Israel. Do not say that I have spoken hard things against you; for if ye do, ye will revile against the truth; for I have spoken the words of your Maker. I know that the words of truth are hard against all uncleanness; but the righteous fear them not, for they love the truth and are not shaken.

41. O then, my beloved brethren, come unto the Lord, the Holy One. Remember that his paths are righteous. Behold, the way for man is narrow, but it lieth in a straight course before him, and the keeper of the gate is the Holy One of Israel; and he employeth no servant there; and there is none other way save it be by the gate; for he cannot be deceived, for the Lord God is his name.

42. And whoso knocketh, to him will he open; and the wise, and the learned, and they that are rich, who are puffed up because of their learning, and their wisdom, and their riches—yea, they are they whom he despiseth; and save they shall cast these things away, and consider themselves fools before God, and come down in the depths of humility, he will not open unto them.

43. But the things of the wise and the prudent shall be hid from them forever—yea, that happiness which is prepared for the saints.

44. O, my beloved brethren, remember my words. Behold, I take off my garments, and I shake them before you; I pray the God of my salvation that he view me with his all-searching eye; wherefore, ye shall know at the last day, when all men shall be judged of their works, that the God of Israel did witness that I shook your iniquities from my soul, and that I stand with brightness before him, and am rid of your blood.

45. O, my beloved brethren, turn away from your sins; shake off the chains of him that would bind you fast; come unto that God who is the rock of your salvation.

46. Prepare your souls for that glorious day when justice shall be administered unto the righteous, even the day of judgment, that ye may not shrink with awful fear; that ye may not remember your awful guilt in perfectness, and be constrained to exclaim: Holy, holy are thy judgments, O Lord God Almighty—but I know my guilt; I transgressed thy law, and my transgressions are mine; and the devil hath obtained me, that I am a prey to his awful misery.

47. But behold, my brethren, is it expedient that I should awake you to an awful reality of these things? Would I harrow up your souls if your minds were pure? Would I be plain unto you according to the plainness of the truth if ye were freed from sin?

48. Behold, if ye were holy I would speak unto you of holiness; but as ye are not holy, and ye look upon me as a teacher, it must needs be expedient that I teach you the consequences of sin.

49. Behold, my soul abhorreth sin, and my heart delighteth in righteousness; and I will praise the holy name of my God.

50. Come, my brethren, every one that thirsteth, come ye to the waters; and he that hath no money, come buy and eat; yea, come buy wine and milk without money and without price.

51. Wherefore, do not spend money for that which is of no worth, nor your labor for that which cannot satisfy. Hearken diligently unto me, and remember the words which I have spoken; and come unto the Holy One of Israel, and feast upon that which perisheth not, neither can be corrupted, and let your soul delight in fatness.

52. Behold, my beloved brethren, remember the words of your God; pray unto him continually by day, and give thanks unto his holy name by night. Let your hearts rejoice.

53. And behold how great the covenants of the Lord, and how great his condescensions unto the children of men; and because of his greatness, and his grace and mercy, he has promised unto us that our seed shall not utterly be destroyed, according to the flesh, but that he would preserve them; and in future generations they shall become a righteous branch unto the house of Israel.

54. And now, my brethren, I would speak unto you more; but on the morrow I will declare unto you the remainder of my words. Amen.

Notes

1. In the Book of Mormon, the gathering of the Jews and of all Israel consisted of (a) coming to the knowledge of the true Messiah and associating with his followers; and (b) gathering to the physical locations commanded by the leaders of his church.
2. Cf. 1 Corinthians 15:12–17.
3. Jesus Christ is known in the Book of Mormon as the Holy One of Israel.
4. Cf. Revelation 20:12–14.
5. Joseph Smith did not believe in the literal burning of hell, but rather in the torment of disappointment in the mind of man. (*History of the Church,* 6:314.)
6. See Romans 8:6.

4. JESUS CHRIST VISITS THE NEPHITES (1830)

Book of Mormon prophets from the beginning spoke not only of the coming of Jesus to Palestine, but also of a visit to the people in America after his ascension in the Old World. The book of Third Nephi records that just prior to his appearance in the western hemisphere many upheavals in nature (storms, earthquakes, natural disasters) took place. In the first chapter quoted below (from Third Nephi, Chapter Eleven), approximately 2500 people in number witness the descent of the Messiah and attend to his initial teachings. In the second chapter (Third Nephi, Chapter Twenty-Seven), Jesus preaches concerning the name of his Church and the nature of his gospel.

1. And now it came to pass that there were a great multitude gathered together, of the people of Nephi, round about the temple which was in the land Bountiful; and they were marveling and wondering one with another, and were showing one to another the great and marvelous change which had taken place.
2. And they were also conversing about this Jesus Christ, of whom the sign had been given concerning his death.
3. And it came to pass that while they were thus conversing one with another, they heard a voice as if it came out of heaven; and they cast their eyes round about, for they understood not the voice which they heard; and it was not a harsh voice, neither was it a loud voice; nevertheless, and notwithstanding it being a small voice it did pierce them that did hear to the center, insomuch that there was no part of

their frame that it did not cause to quake; yea, it did pierce them to the very soul, and did cause their hearts to burn.

4. And it came to pass that again they heard the voice, and they understood it not.

5. And again the third time they did hear the voice, and did open their ears to hear it; and their eyes were towards the sound thereof; and they did look steadfastly towards heaven, from whence the sound came.

6. And behold, the third time they did understand the voice which they heard; and it said unto them:

7. Behold my Beloved Son, in whom I am well pleased, in whom I have glorified my name—hear ye him.[1]

8. And it came to pass, as they understood they cast their eyes up again towards heaven; and behold, they saw a Man descending out of heaven; and he was clothed in a white robe; and he came down and stood in the midst of them; and the eyes of the whole multitude were turned upon him, and they durst not open their mouths, even one to another, and wist not what it meant, for they thought it was an angel that had appeared unto them.

9. And it came to pass that he stretched forth his hand and spake unto the people, saying:

10. Behold, I am Jesus Christ, whom the prophets testified shall come into the world.

11. And behold, I am the light and the life of the world; and I have drunk out of that bitter cup which the Father hath given me, and have glorified the Father in taking upon me the sins of the world, in the which I have suffered the will of the Father in all things from the beginning.

12. And it came to pass that when Jesus had spoken these words the whole multitude fell to the earth; for they remembered that it had been prophesied among them that Christ should show himself unto them after his ascension into heaven.

13. And it came to pass that the Lord spake unto them saying:

14. Arise and come forth unto me, that ye may thrust your hands into my side, and also that ye may feel the prints of the nails in my hands and in my feet, that ye may know that I am the God of Israel, and the God of the whole earth, and have been slain for the sins of the world.

15. And it came to pass that the multitude went forth, and thrust their hands into his side, and did feel the prints of the nails in his hands and in his feet; and this they did do, going forth one by one until they had all gone forth, and did see with their eyes and did feel

with their hands, and did know of a surety and did bear record, that it was he, of whom it was written by the prophets, that should come.

16. And when they had all gone forth and had witnessed for themselves, they did cry out with one accord, saying:

17. Hosanna! Blessed be the name of the Most High God! And they did fall down at the feet of Jesus, and did worship him.

18. And it came to pass that he spake unto Nephi (for Nephi was among the multitude) and he commanded him that he should come forth.

19. And Nephi arose and went forth, and bowed himself before the Lord and did kiss his feet.

20. And the Lord commanded him that he should arise. And he arose and stood before him.

21. And the Lord said unto him: I give unto you power that ye shall baptize this people when I am again ascended into heaven.

22. And again the Lord called others, and said unto them likewise; and he gave unto them power to baptize. And he said unto them: On this wise shall ye baptize; and there shall be no disputations among you.

23. Verily I say unto you, that whoso repenteth of his sins through your words, and desireth to be baptized in my name, on this wise shall ye baptize them—Behold, ye shall go down and stand in the water, and in my name shall ye baptize them.

24. And now behold, these are the words which ye shall say, calling them by name, saying:

25. Having authority given me of Jesus Christ, I baptize you in the name of the Father, and of the Son, and of the Holy Ghost. Amen.[2]

26. And then shall ye immerse them in the water, and come forth again out of the water.

27. And after this manner shall ye baptize in my name; for behold, verily I say unto you, that the Father, and the Son, and the Holy Ghost are one; and I am in the Father, and the Father in me, and the Father and I are one.

28. And according as I have commanded you thus shall ye baptize. And there shall be no disputations among you, as there have hitherto been; neither shall there be disputations among you concerning the points of my doctrine, as there have hitherto been.

29. For verily, verily I say unto you, he that hath the spirit of contention is not of me, but is of the devil, who is the father of contention, and he stirreth up the hearts of men to contend with anger, one with another.

30. Behold, this is not my doctrine, to stir up the hearts of men with anger, one against another; but this is my doctrine, that such things should be done away.

31. Behold, verily, verily, I say unto you, I will declare unto you my doctrine.

32. And this is my doctrine, and it is the doctrine which the Father hath given unto me; and I bear record of the Father, and the Father beareth record of me, and the Holy Ghost beareth record of the Father and me; and I bear record that the Father commandeth all men, everywhere, to repent and believe in me.

33. And whoso believeth in me, and is baptized, the same shall be saved; and they are they who shall inherit the kingdom of God.

34. And whoso believeth not in me, and is not baptized, shall be damned.

35. Verily, verily, I say unto you, that this is my doctrine, and I bear record of it from the Father; and whoso believeth in me believeth in the Father also; and unto him will the Father bear record of me, for he will visit him with fire and with the Holy Ghost.

36. And thus will the Father bear record of me, and the Holy Ghost will bear record unto him of the Father and me; for the Father, and I, and the Holy Ghost are one.

37. And again I say unto you, ye must repent, and become as a little child,[3] and be baptized in my name, or ye can in nowise receive these things.

38. And again I say unto you, ye must repent, and be baptized in my name, and become as a little child, or ye can in nowise inherit the kingdom of God.

39. Verily, verily, I say unto you, that this is my doctrine, and whoso buildeth upon this buildeth upon my rock, and the gates of hell shall not prevail against them.

40. And whoso shall declare more or less than this, and establish it for my doctrine, the same cometh of evil, and is not built upon my rock; but he buildeth upon a sandy foundation, and the gates of hell stand open to receive such when the floods come and the winds beat upon them.

41. Therefore, go forth unto this people, and declare the words which I have spoken, unto the ends of the earth.

And it came to pass that as the disciples of Jesus were journeying and were preaching the things which they had both heard and seen, and were baptizing in the name of Jesus, it came to pass that the disciples were gathered together and were united in mighty prayer and fasting.

2. And Jesus again showed himself unto them, for they were praying unto the Father in his name; and Jesus came and stood in the midst of them, and said unto them: What will ye that I shall give unto you?

3. And they said unto him: Lord, we will that thou wouldst tell us the name whereby we shall call this church; for there are disputations among the people concerning this matter.

4. And the Lord said unto them: Verily, verily, I say unto you, why is it that the people should murmur and dispute because of this thing?

5. Have they not read the scriptures, which say ye must take upon you the name of Christ, which is my name? For by this name shall ye be called at the last day;

6. And whoso taketh upon him my name, and endureth to the end, the same shall be saved at the last day.

7. Therefore, whatsoever ye shall do, ye shall do it in my name; therefore ye shall call the church in my name; and ye shall call upon the Father in my name that he will bless the church for my sake.

8. And how be it my church save it be called in my name? For if a church be called in Moses' name then it be Moses' church; or if it be called in the name of a man then it be the church of a man; but if it be called in my name then it is my church, if it so be that they are built upon my gospel.

9. Verily I say unto you, that ye are built upon my gospel; therefore ye shall call whatsoever things ye do call, in my name; therefore if ye call upon the Father, for the church, if it be in my name the Father will hear you;

10. And if it so be that the church is built upon my gospel then will the Father show forth his own works in it.

11. But if it be not built upon my gospel, and is built upon the works of men, or upon the works of the devil, verily I say unto you they have joy in their works for a season, and by and by the end cometh and they are hewn down and cast into the fire, from whence there is no return.

12. For their works do follow them, for it is because of their works that they are hewn down; therefore remember the things that I have told you.

13. Behold I have given unto you my gospel, and this is the gospel which I have given unto you—that I came into the world to do the will of my Father, because my Father sent me.

14. And my Father sent me that I might be lifted up upon the cross; and after that I had been lifted up upon the cross, that I might draw all men unto me, that as I have been lifted up by men even so should men be lifted up by the Father, to stand before me, to be judged of their works, whether they be good or whether they be evil—

15. And for this cause have I been lifted up; therefore, according to the power of the Father I will draw all men unto me, that they may be judged according to their works.

16. And it shall come to pass, that whoso repenteth and is baptized in my name shall be filled; and if he endureth to the end, behold, him will I hold guiltless before my Father at that day when I shall stand to judge the world.

17. And he that endureth not unto the end, the same is he that is also hewn down and cast into the fire, from whence they can no more return, because of the justice of the Father.

18. And this is the word which he hath given unto the children of men. And for this cause he fulfilleth the words which he hath given, and he lieth not, but fulfilleth all his words.

19. And no unclean thing can enter into his kingdom; therefore nothing entereth into his rest save it be those who have washed their garments in my blood, because of their faith, and the repentance of all their sins, and their faithfulness unto the end.

20. Now this is the commandment: Repent, all ye ends of the earth, and come unto me and be baptized in my name, that ye may be sanctified by the reception of the Holy Ghost, that ye may stand spotless before me at the last day.

21. Verily, verily, I say unto you, this is my gospel; and ye know the things that ye must do in my church; for the works which ye have seen me do that shall ye also do; for that which ye have seen me do even that shall ye do;

22. Therefore, if ye do these things blessed are ye, for ye shall be lifted up at the last day.

23. Write the things which ye have seen and heard, save it be those which are forbidden.

24. Write the works of this people, which shall be, even as hath been written, of that which hath been.

25. For behold, out of the books which have been written, and which shall be written, shall this people be judged, for by them shall their works be known unto men.

26. And behold, all things are written by the Father; therefore out of the books which shall be written shall the world be judged.[4]

27. And know ye that ye shall be judges of this people, according to the judgment which I shall give unto you, which shall be just. Therefore, what manner of men ought ye to be? Verily I say unto you, even as I am.

28. And now I go unto the Father. And verily I say unto you, whatsoever things ye shall ask the Father in my name shall be given unto you.

29. Therefore, ask, and ye shall receive; knock, and it shall be opened unto you; for he that asketh, receiveth; and unto him that knocketh, it shall be opened.[5]

30. And now, behold, my joy is great, even unto fulness, because of you, and also this generation; yea, and even the Father rejoiceth, and also all the holy angels, because of you and this generation; for none of them are lost.

31. Behold, I would that ye should understand; for I mean them who are now alive of this generation; and none of them are lost; and in them I have fulness of joy.

32. But behold, it sorroweth me because of the fourth generation from this generation,[6] for they are led away captive by him even as was the son of perdition;[7] for they will sell me for silver and for gold, and for that which moth doth corrupt and which thieves can break through and steal.[8] And in that day will I visit them, even in turning their works upon their own heads.

33. And it came to pass that when Jesus had ended these sayings he said unto his disciples: Enter ye in at the strait gate; for strait is the gate, and narrow is the way that leads to life, and few there be that find it; but wide is the gate, and broad the way which leads to death, and many there be that travel therein, until the night cometh, wherein no man can work.

Notes

1. Cf. Matthew 3:17; 17:5.
2. Cf. Matthew 28:19.
3. Cf. Matthew 18:3.
4. Revelation 20:12.
5. Matthew 7:7.
6. The Book of Mormon story ends in 421 C.E. with the destruction of the Nephite nation.
7. John 17:12.
8. Matthew 6:19.

5. A VISION GIVEN TO MOSES (1830)

*In June of 1830 Joseph Smith began his work of "inspired transla-
tion" of the King James Bible. Among the first things recorded by a
scribe were "Selections from the Book of Moses," what Latter-day
Saints recognize as the "new translation" of the early chapters of
Genesis. As a sort of preface to the whole translation, there is an
initial chapter containing "the words of God, which he spake unto
Moses at a time when Moses was caught up into an exceedingly high
mountain." This is an account for which there is no biblical corollary
whatsoever, an occasion to be located chronologically between the
burning bush episode and the encounter with Pharaoh (see verses 17
and 26 in the following). The text below is known as Moses 1 in the*
Pearl of Great Price.

The words of God, which he spake unto Moses at a time when
Moses was caught up into an exceedingly high mountain,

2. And he saw God face to face, and he talked with him, and
the glory of God was upon Moses; therefore Moses could endure his
presence.

3. And God spake unto Moses, saying: Behold, I am the Lord
God Almighty, and Endless is my name; for I am without beginning
of days or end of years; and is not this endless?

4. And, behold, thou art my son; wherefore look, and I will
show thee the workmanship of mine hands; but not all, for my works
are without end, and also my words, for they never cease.

5. Wherefore, no man can behold all my works, except he
behold all my glory; and no man can behold all my glory, and afterwards remain in the flesh on the earth.

6. And I have a work for thee, Moses, my son; and thou art in
the similitude of mine Only Begotten; and mine Only Begotten is and
shall be the Savior,[1] for he is full of grace and truth; but there is no
God beside me, and all things are present with me, for I know them
all.

7. And now, behold, this one thing I show unto thee, Moses,
my son, for thou art in the world, and now I show it unto thee.

8. And it came to pass that Moses looked, and beheld the
world upon which he was created; and Moses beheld the world and
the ends thereof, and all the children of men which are, and which
were created; of the same he greatly marveled and wondered.

9. And the presence of God withdrew from Moses, that his

glory was not upon Moses; and Moses was left unto himself. And as he was left unto himself, he fell unto the earth.

10. And it came to pass that it was for the space of many hours before Moses did again receive his natural strength like unto man; and he said unto himself: Now, for this cause I know that man is nothing, which thing I never had supposed.

11. But now mine own eyes have beheld God; but not my natural, but my spiritual eyes, for my natural eyes could not have beheld; for I should have withered and died in his presence; but his glory was upon me; and I beheld his face, for I was transfigured before him.

12. And it came to pass that when Moses had said these words, behold, Satan came tempting him, saying: Moses, son of man, worship me.

13. And it came to pass that Moses looked upon Satan and said: Who art thou? For behold, I am a son of God, in the similitude of his Only Begotten; and where is thy glory that I should worship thee?

14. For behold, I could not look upon God, except his glory should come upon me, and I were transfigured before him. But I can look upon thee in the natural man. Is it not so, surely?

15. Blessed be the name of my God, for his Spirit hath not altogether withdrawn from me, or else where is thy glory, for it is darkness unto me? And I can judge between thee and God; for God said unto me: Worship God, for him only shalt thou serve.

16. Get thee hence, Satan; deceive me not; for God said unto me: Thou art after the similitude of mine Only Begotten.

17. And he also gave me commandments when he called unto me out of the burning bush, saying: Call upon God in the name of mine Only Begotten, and worship me.

18. And again Moses said: I will not cease to call upon God, I have other things to inquire of him: for his glory has been upon me, wherefore I can judge between him and thee. Depart hence, Satan.

19. And now, when Moses had said these words, Satan cried with a loud voice, and ranted[2] upon the earth, and commanded, saying: I am the Only Begotten, worship me.

20. And it came to pass that Moses began to fear exceedingly; and as he began to fear, he saw the bitterness of hell. Nevertheless, calling upon God, he received strength, and he commanded, saying: Depart from me, Satan, for this one God only will I worship, which is the God of glory.

21. And now Satan began to tremble, and the earth shook; and Moses received strength, and called upon God, saying: In the name of the Only Begotten, depart hence, Satan.

22. And it came to pass that Satan cried with a loud voice, with weeping, and wailing, and gnashing of teeth; and he departed hence, even from the presence of Moses, that he beheld him not.

23. And now of this thing Moses bore record; but because of wickedness it is not had among the children of men.

24. And it came to pass that when Satan had departed from the presence of Moses, that Moses lifted up his eyes unto heaven, being filled with the Holy Ghost, which beareth record of the Father and the Son;

25. And calling upon the name of God, he beheld his glory again, for it was upon him; and he heard a voice, saying: Blessed art thou, Moses, for I, the Almighty, have chosen thee, and thou shalt be made stronger than many waters; for they shall obey thy command as if thou wert God.[3]

26. And lo, I am with thee, even unto the end of thy days; for thou shalt deliver my people from bondage, even Israel my chosen.

27. And it came to pass, as the voice was still speaking, Moses cast his eyes and beheld the earth, yea, even all of it; and there was not a particle of it which he did not behold, discerning it by the spirit of God.

28. And he beheld also the inhabitants thereof, and there was not a soul which he beheld not; and he discerned them by the Spirit of God; and their numbers were great, even numberless as the sand upon the sea shore.

29. And he beheld many lands; and each land was called earth, and there were inhabitants on the face thereof.

30. And it came to pass the Moses called upon God, saying: Tell me, I pray thee, why these things are so, and by what thou madest them?

31. And behold, the glory of the Lord was upon Moses, so that Moses stood in the presence of God, and talked with him face to face. And the Lord God said unto Moses: For mine own purpose have I made these things. Here is wisdom and it remaineth in me.

32. And by the word of my power, have I created them, which is mine Only Begotten Son, who is full of grace and truth.

33. And worlds without number have I created; and I also created them for mine own purpose; and by the Son I created them,[4] which is mine Only Begotten.

34. And the first man of all men have I called Adam, which is many.

35. But only an account of this earth, and the inhabitants thereof, give I unto you. For behold, there are many worlds that have

passed away by the word of my power. And there are many that now stand, and innumerable are they unto man; but all things are numbered unto me, for they are mine and I know them.

36. And it came to pass that Moses spake unto the Lord, saying: Be merciful unto thy servant, O God and tell me concerning this earth, and the inhabitants thereof, and also the heavens, and then thy servant will be content.

37. And the Lord God spake unto Moses, saying: The heavens, they are many, and they cannot be numbered unto man; but they are numbered unto me, for they are mine.

38. And as one earth shall pass away, and the heavens thereof even so shall another come; and there is no end to my works, neither to my words.

39. For behold, this is my work and my glory—to bring to pass the immortality and eternal life of man.[5]

40. And now, Moses, my son, I will speak unto thee concerning this earth upon which thou standest; and thou shalt write the things which I shall speak.[6]

41. And in a day when the children of men shall esteem my words as naught and take many of them from the book which thou shalt write, behold, I will raise up another like unto thee;[7] and they shall be had again among the children of men—among as many as shall believe.

42. (These words were spoken unto Moses in the mount, the name of which shall not be known among the children of men. And now they are spoken unto you. Show them not unto any except them that believe. Even so. Amen.)

Notes

1. Note again the Christocentric nature of this literature.
2. Editions of the "Pearl of Great Price" prior to 1981 have this passage as: "Satan cried with a loud voice, and *rent* upon the earth."
3. Cf. Exodus 7:1.
4. Hebrews 1:1–3.
5. This verse—a capsule statement of God's (and thus man's) purpose—is the most frequently quoted scriptural verse in Latter-day Saint history.
6. This seems to have reference to the Mosaic creation account in Genesis.
7. Mormons believe this to be a reference to Joseph Smith, the one

called "to preside over the whole church, and to be like unto Moses." (*Doctrine and Covenants,* 107:91; cf. 28:2.)

6. THE CALL AND MINISTRY OF ENOCH (1830)

As noted in the Introduction, the Joseph Smith Translation of the call and ministry of Enoch is a detailed 100+ verse section now a part of the Book of Moses in the "Pearl of Great Price." In the chapter preceding the one quoted below, Enoch is assured by the Lord that despite his speech defect and overall lack of confidence, God can make strong things out of weak but humble and trusting vessels. The following is Chapter Seven of the Book of Moses.

And it came to pass that Enoch continued his speech, saying: Behold, our father Adam taught these things,[1] and many have believed and become the sons of God, and many have believed not, and have perished in their sins, and are looking forth with fear, in torment, for the fiery indignation of the wrath of God to be poured out upon them.

2. And from that time forth Enoch began to prophesy, saying unto the people, that: As I was journeying and stood upon the place Mahujah, and cried unto the Lord, there came a voice out of heaven, saying—Turn ye, and get ye upon the mount Simeon.

3. And it came to pass that I turned and went up on the mount; and as I stood upon the mount, I beheld the heavens open, and I was clothed upon with glory;

4. And I saw the Lord; and he stood before my face, and he talked with me, even as a man talketh one with another, face to face; and he said unto me: Look, and I will show unto thee the world for the space of many generations.

5. And it came to pass that I beheld in the valley of Shum, and lo, a great people which dwelt in tents, which were the people of Shum.

6. And again the Lord said unto me: Look; and I looked towards the north, and I beheld the people of Canaan, which dwelt in tents.

7. And the Lord said unto me: Prophesy; and I prophesied, saying: Behold the people of Canaan, which are numerous, shall go forth in battle array against the people of Shum, and shall slay them that they shall utterly be destroyed; and the people of Canaan shall

divide themselves in the land, and the land shall be barren and unfruitful, and none other people shall dwell there but the people of Canaan;

8. For behold, the Lord shall curse the land with much heat, and the barrenness thereof shall go forth forever; and there was a blackness came upon all the children of Canaan,[2] that they were despised among all people.

9. And it came to pass that the Lord said unto me: Look; and I looked, and I beheld the land of Sharon, and the land of Enoch, and the land of Omner, and the land of Heni, and the land of Shem, and the land of Haner, and the land of Hanannihah, and all the inhabitants thereof;

10. And the Lord said unto me: Go to this people, and say unto them—Repent, lest I come out and smite them with a curse, and they die.

11. And he gave unto me a commandment that I should baptize in the name of the Father, and of the Son, which is full of grace and truth, and of the Holy Ghost, which beareth record of the Father and the Son.

12. And it came to pass that Enoch continued to call upon all the people, save it were the people of Canaan, to repent;

13. And so great was the faith of Enoch that he led the people of God, and their enemies came to battle against them; and he spake the word of the Lord, and the earth trembled, and the mountains fled, even according to his command; and the rivers of water were turned out of their course; and the roar of the lions was heard out of the wilderness; and all nations feared greatly, so powerful was the word of Enoch, and so great was the power of the language which God had given him.

14. There also came up a land out of the depth of the sea, and so great was the fear of the enemies of the people of God, that they fled and stood afar off and went upon the land which came up out of the depth of the sea.

15. And the giants of the land, also stood afar off; and there went forth a curse upon all people that fought against God;

16. And from that time forth there were wars and bloodshed among them; but the Lord came and dwelt with his people, and they dwelt in righteousness.

17. The fear of the Lord was upon all nations, so great was the glory of the Lord, which was upon his people. And the Lord blessed the land, and they were blessed upon the mountains, and upon the high places, and did flourish.

18. And the Lord called his people ZION, because they were of

one heart and one mind, and dwelt in righteousness; and there was no poor among them.

19. And Enoch continued his preaching in righteousness unto the people of God. And it came to pass in his days, that he built a city that was called the City of Holiness, even ZION.

20. And it came to pass that Enoch talked with the Lord; and he said unto the Lord; Surely Zion shall dwell in safety forever. But the Lord said unto Enoch: Zion have I blessed, but the residue of the people have I cursed.

21. And it came to pass that the Lord showed unto Enoch all the inhabitants of the earth; and he beheld, and lo, Zion, in process of time, was taken up into heaven. And the Lord said unto Enoch: Behold mine abode forever.

22. And Enoch also beheld the residue of the people which were the sons of Adam; and they were a mixture of all the seed of Adam save it was the seed of Cain, for the seed of Cain were black, and had not place among them.

23. And after that Zion was taken up into heaven, Enoch beheld, and lo, all the nations of the earth were before him;

24. And there came generation upon generation; and Enoch was high and lifted up, even in the bosom of the Father, and of the Son of Man; and behold, the power of Satan was upon all the face of the earth.

25. And he saw angels descending out of heaven; and he heard a loud voice saying: Wo, wo be unto the inhabitants of the earth.

26. And he beheld Satan; and he had a great chain in his hand, and it veiled the whole face of the earth with darkness; and he looked up and laughed, and his angels rejoiced.

27. And Enoch beheld angels descending out of heaven, bearing testimony of the Father and Son; and the Holy Ghost fell on many and they were caught up by the powers of heaven into Zion.

28. And it came to pass that the God of heaven looked upon the residue of the people, and he wept; and Enoch bore record of it, saying: How is it that the heavens weep, and shed forth their tears as the rain upon the mountains?

29. And Enoch said unto the Lord: How is it that thou canst weep, seeing thou art holy, and from all eternity to all eternity?

30. And were it possible that man could number the particles of the earth, yea, millions of earths like this, it would not be a beginning to the number of thy creations; and thy curtains are stretched out still; and yet thou art there, and thy bosom is there; and also thou art just; thou art merciful and kind forever;

31. And thou hast taken Zion to thine own bosom, from all thy creations, from all eternity to all eternity; and naught but peace, justice, and truth is the habitation of thy throne; and mercy shall go before thy face and have no end; how is it thou canst weep?

32. The Lord said unto Enoch: Behold these thy brethren; they are the workmanship of mine own hands, and I gave unto them their knowledge, in the day I created them; and in the Garden of Eden, gave I unto man his agency;[3]

33. And unto thy brethren have I said, and also given commandment, that they should love one another, and that they should choose me, their Father; but behold, they are without affection, and they hate their own blood;

34. And the fire of mine indignation is kindled against them; and in my hot displeasure will I send in the floods[4] upon them, for my fierce anger is kindled against them.

35. Behold, I am God; Man of Holiness[5] is my name; Man of Counsel is my name; and Endless and Eternal is my name, also.

36. Wherefore, I can stretch forth mine hands and hold all the creations which I have made; and mine eye can pierce them also, and among all the workmanship of mine hands there has not been so great wickedness as among thy brethren.

37. But behold, their sins shall be upon the heads of their fathers; Satan shall be their father, and misery shall be their doom; and the whole heavens shall weep over them, even all the workmanship of mine hands; wherefore should not the heavens weep, seeing these shall suffer?

38. But behold, these which thine eyes are upon shall perish in the floods; and behold, I will shut them up; a prison have I prepared for them.[6]

39. And That which I have chosen hath pled before my face. Wherefore, he suffereth for their sins; inasmuch as they will repent in the day that my Chosen shall return unto me, and until that day they shall be in torment;

40. Wherefore, for this shall the heavens weep, yea, and all the workmanship of mine hands.

41. And it came to pass that the Lord spake unto Enoch, and told Enoch all the doings of the children of men; wherefore Enoch knew, and looked upon their wickedness, and their misery, and wept and stretched forth his arms, and his heart swelled wide as eternity;[7] and his bowels yearned; and all eternity shook.

42. And Enoch also saw Noah, and his family; that the posterity of all the sons of Noah should be saved with a temporal salvation;

43. Wherefore Enoch saw that Noah built an ark; and that the Lord smiled upon it, and held it in his own hand; but upon the residue of the wicked the floods came and swallowed them up.

44. And as Enoch saw this, he had bitterness of soul, and wept over his brethren, and said unto the heavens: I will refuse to be comforted; but the Lord said unto Enoch: Lift up your heart, and be glad; and look.

45. And it came to pass that Enoch looked; and from Noah, he beheld all the families of the earth; and he cried unto the Lord, saying: When shall the day of the Lord come? When shall the blood of the Righteous be shed, that all they that mourn may be sanctified and have eternal life?

46. And the Lord said: It shall be in the meridian of time, in the days of wickedness and vengeance.

47. And behold, Enoch saw the day of the coming of the Son of Man, even in the flesh; and his soul rejoiced, saying: The Righteous is lifted up, and the Lamb is slain from the foundation of the world;[8] and through faith I am in the bosom of the Father, and behold, Zion is with me.

48. And it came to pass that Enoch looked upon the earth; and he heard a voice from the bowels thereof, saying: Wo, wo is me, the mother of men; I am pained, I am weary, because of the wickedness of my children. When shall I rest, and be cleansed from the filthiness which is gone forth out of me? When will my Creator sanctify me, that I may rest, and righteousness for a season abide upon my face?

49. And when Enoch heard the earth mourn, he wept, and cried unto the Lord, saying: O Lord, wilt thou not have compassion upon the earth? Wilt thou not bless the children of Noah?

50. And it came to pass that Enoch continued his cry unto the Lord, saying: I ask thee, O Lord, in the name of thine Only Begotten, even Jesus Christ, that thou wilt have mercy upon Noah and his seed, that the earth might never more be covered by the floods.

51. And the Lord could not withhold; and he covenanted with Enoch, and sware unto him with an oath, that he would stay the floods;[9] that he would call upon the children of Noah;

52. And he sent forth an unalterable decree, that a remnant of his seed should always be found among all nations, while the earth should stand;

53. And the Lord said: Blessed is he through whose seed Messiah shall come; for he saith—I am Messiah, the King of Zion, the Rock of Heaven, which is broad as eternity; whoso cometh in at the gate and climbeth up by me shall never fall; wherefore, blessed are

they of whom I have spoken, for they shall come forth with songs of everlasting joy.

54. And it came to pass that Enoch cried unto the Lord, saying: When the Son of Man cometh in the flesh, shall the earth rest? I pray thee, show me these things.

55. And the Lord said unto Enoch: Look, and he looked and beheld the Son of Man lifted up on the cross, after the manner of men;

56. And he heard a loud voice; and the heavens were veiled; and all the creations of God mourned; and the earth groaned; and the rocks were rent; and the saints arose, and were crowned at the right hand of the Son of Man, with crowns of glory;[10]

57. And as many of the spirits as were in prison came forth, and stood on the right hand of god; and the remainder were reserved in chains of darkness until the judgment of the great day.

58. And again Enoch wept and cried unto the Lord; saying: When shall the earth rest?

59. And Enoch beheld the Son of Man ascend up unto the Father; and he called unto the Lord, saying: Wilt thou not come again upon the earth? Forasmuch as thou art God, and I know thee, and thou hast sworn unto me, and commanded me that I should ask in the name of thine Only Begotten; thou hast made me, and given unto me a right to thy throne, and not of myself, but through thine own grace; wherefore, I ask thee if thou wilt not come again on the earth.

60. And the Lord said unto Enoch: As I live, even so will I come in the last days, in the days of wickedness and vengeance, to fulfil the oath which I have made unto you concerning the children of Noah;

61. And the day shall come that the earth shall rest, but before that day the heavens shall be darkened, and a veil of darkness shall cover the earth; and the heavens shall shake, and also the earth; and great tribulations shall be among the children of men, but my people will I preserve;

62. And righteousness will I send down out of heaven;[11] and truth will I send forth out of the earth, to bear testimony of mine Only Begotten; his resurrection from the dead; yea, and also the resurrection of all men;[12] and righteousness and truth will I cause to sweep the earth as with a flood, to gather out mine elect from the four quarters of the earth, unto a place which I shall prepare, an Holy City, that my people may gird up their loins, and be looking forth for the time of my coming; for there shall be my tabernacle, and it shall be called Zion, a New Jerusalem.[13]

63. And the Lord said unto Enoch: Then shalt thou and all thy

city meet them there, and we will receive them into our bosom, and they shall see us; and we will fall upon their necks, and they shall fall upon our necks, and we will kiss each other;

64. And there shall be mine abode, and it shall be Zion, which shall come forth out of all the creations which I have made; and for the space of a thousand years the earth shall rest.

65. And it came to pass that Enoch saw the day of the coming of the Son of Man, in the last days, to dwell on the earth in righteousness for the space of a thousand years;

66. But before that day he saw great tribulations among the wicked; and he also saw the sea, that it was troubled, and men's hearts failing them, looking forth with fear for the judgments of the Almighty God, which should come upon the wicked.

67. And the Lord showed Enoch all things, even unto the end of the world; and he saw the day of the righteous, the hour of their redemption, and received a fulness of joy;

68. And all the days of Zion, in the days of Enoch, were three hundred and sixty-five years.

69. And Enoch and all his people walked with God, and he dwelt in the midst of Zion; and it came to pass that Zion was not, for God received it up into his own bosom; and from thence went forth the saying, ZION IS FLED.[14]

Notes

1. Matters dealing with the coming of Christ, his atonement for original sin, and the importance of spiritual rebirth. (Moses 6:51–62.)

2. Latter-day Saint traditions hold that the curse upon Cain (Gen 4) was the denial of the rights of priesthood for Cain and his descendants, the mark of the curse being a black skin (see verse 22). Descendants of Cain settled in the land of Canaan.

3. For some reason, the publication committee responsible for printing the first edition of Joseph Smith's translation of the Bible in 1867 decided to use an earlier manuscript version of this passage. A later revision (known as Old Testament Manuscript #3) reads: "They are the workmanship of mine own hands, and I gave unto them their *intelligence,* in the day I created them; and in the Garden of Eden, *man had his agency.*" (See Matthews, "A Plainer Translation," p. 157.)

4. Enoch here becomes witness of the flood in the days of Noah (three generations later).

5. For Joseph Smith, then, Jesus Christ was the Son of Man of Holiness or, simply, the Son of Man.
6. Cf. 1 Peter 3:18–20.
7. From Old Testament Manuscript #3: "Wherefore Enoch knew, and looked upon their wickedness, and their misery, and wept and stretched forth his arms, *and he beheld eternity.*" (Matthews, "A Plainer Translation," p. 158.)
8. Cf. Revelation 13:8.
9. Note here that the promise to never again destroy the earth by flood was made to Enoch. Later in this account (JST, Genesis 9:21–25) the covenant is re-confirmed with Noah.
10. Cf. Matthew 27:51–53.
11. Psalms 85:11.
12. The Latter-day Saints believe this to be a reference to the Book of Mormon.
13. Joseph Smith taught that the "New Jerusalem" is to be established in Independence (Jackson County), Missouri. (See *Doctrine and Covenents,* 57:1–3; 84:2–4.)
14. See Hebrews 11:5.

7. THE EARLY MINISTRY OF ABRAHAM (1842)

Joseph Smith and a number of Church members in Kirtland, Ohio, acquired some Egyptian artifacts in the summer of 1835. Among these were two papyrus documents which the Prophet indicated contained writings from both Abraham and Joseph of old. (History of the Church, 2:236.) Smith began work on the documents at the time and labored intermittently at the task of translating them for the next seven years. The translation, now comprising "The Book of Abraham" in the Pearl of Great Price, *was published in issues of the* Times and Seasons *in 1842 (March 1, March 15, May 16). The following, which corresponds approximately to the time period of Genesis 11–12, are Chapters One and Two of the Book of Abraham.*

In the land of the Chaldeans, at the residence of my fathers, I Abraham,[1] saw that it was needful for me to obtain another place of residence;

2. And, finding there was greater happiness and peace and rest for me, I sought for the blessings of the fathers, and the right whereunto I should be ordained to administer the same; having been

myself a follower of righteousness, desiring also to be one who possessed great knowledge, and to be a greater follower of righteousness, and to possess a greater knowledge, and to be a father of many nations, a prince of peace, and desiring to receive instructions, and to keep the commandments of God, I became a rightful heir, a High Priest, holding the right belonging to the fathers.

3. It was conferred upon me from the fathers; it came down from the fathers, from the beginning of time, yea, even from the beginning, or before the foundation of the earth, down to the present time, even the right of the firstborn, or the first man, who is Adam, or first father,[2] through the fathers unto me.

4. I sought for mine appointment unto the Priesthood according to the appointment of God unto the fathers concerning the seed.

5. My fathers, having turned from their righteousness, and from the holy commandments which the Lord their God had given unto them, unto the worshiping of the gods of the heathen, utterly refused to hearken to my voice;

6. For their hearts were set to do evil, and were wholly turned to the god of Elkenah, and the god of Libnah, and the god of Mahmackrah, and the god of Korash, and the god of Pharaoh, king of Egypt;

7. Therefore they turned their hearts to the sacrifice of the heathen in offering up their children unto these dumb idols, and hearkened not unto my voice, but endeavored to take away my life by the hand of the priest of Elkenah. The priest of Elkenah was also the priest of Pharaoh.

8. Now, at this time it was the custom of the priest of Pharaoh, the king of Egypt, to offer up upon the altar which was built in the land of Chaldea, for the offering unto these strange gods, men, women, and children.

9. And it came to pass that the priest made an offering unto the god of Pharaoh, and also unto the god of Shagreel, even after the manner of the Egyptians. Now the god of Shagreel was the sun.

10. Even the thank-offering of a child did the priest of Pharaoh offer upon the altar which stood by the hill called Potiphar's Hill, at the head of the plain of Olishem.

11. Now, this priest had offered upon this altar three virgins at one time, who were the daughters of Onitah, one of the royal descent directly from the loins of Ham. These virgins were offered up because of their virtue; they would not bow down to worship gods of wood or of stone, therefore they were killed upon this altar, and it was done after the manner of the Egyptians.

12. And it came to pass that the priests laid violence upon me, that they might slay me also, as they did those virgins upon this altar; and that you may have a knowledge of this altar, I will refer you to the representation at the commencement of this record.[3]

13. It was made after the form of a bedstead, such as was had among the Chaldeans, and it stood before the gods of Elkenah, Libnah, Mahmackrah, Korash, and also a god like unto that of Pharaoh, king of Egypt.

14. That you may have an understanding of these gods, I have given you the fashion of them in the figures at the beginning, which manner of figures is called by the Chaldeans Rahleenos, which signified hieroglyphics.

15. And as they lifted up their hands upon me, that they might offer me up and take away my life, behold, I lifted up my voice unto the Lord my God, and the Lord hearkened and heard, and he filled me with the vision of the Almighty, and the angel of his presence stood by me, and immediately unloosed my bands;

16. And his voice was unto me: Abraham, Abraham, behold, my name is Jehovah, and I have heard thee, and have come down to deliver thee, and to take thee away from thy father's house, and from all thy kinsfolk, into a strange land which thou knowest not of;

17. And this because they have turned their hearts away from me, to worship the god of Elkenah, and the god of Libnah, and the god of Mahmackrah, and the god of Korash, and the god of Pharaoh, king of Egypt; therefore I have come down to visit them, and to destroy him who hath lifted up his hand against thee, Abraham, my son, to take away thy life.

18. Behold, I will lead thee by my hand, and I will take thee, to put upon thee my name, even the Priesthood of thy father, and my power shall be over thee.

19. As it was with Noah so shall it be with thee; but through thy ministry my name shall be known in the earth forever, for I am thy God.

20. Behold, Potiphar's Hill was in the land of Ur, of Chaldea. And the Lord broke down the altar of Elkenah, and of the gods of the land, and utterly destroyed them, and smote the priest that he died; and there was great mourning in Chaldea, and also in the court of Pharaoh; which Pharaoh signifies king by royal blood.

21. Now this king of Egypt was a descendant from the loins of Ham, and was a partaker of the blood of the Canaanites by birth.

22. From this descent sprang all the Egyptians and thus the blood of the Canaanites was preserved in the land.

23. The land of Egypt being first discovered by a woman, who was the daughter of Ham, and the daughter of Egyptus, which in the Chaldean signifies Egypt, which signifies that which is forbidden;

24. When this woman discovered the land it was under water, who afterward settled her sons in it; and thus, from Ham, sprang that race which preserved the curse in the land.

25. Now the first government of Egypt was established by Pharaoh, the eldest son of Egyptus, the daughter of Ham, and it was after the manner of the government of Ham, which was patriarchal.

26. Pharaoh, being a righteous man, established his kingdom and judged his people wisely and justly all his days, seeking earnestly to imitate that order established by the fathers in the first generations, in the days of the first patriarchal reign, even in the reign of Adam, and also of Noah, his father, who blessed him with the blessings of the earth and with the blessings of wisdom, but cursed him as pertaining to the Priesthood.

27. Now, Pharaoh being of that lineage by which he could not have the right of Priesthood,[4] notwithstanding the Pharaohs would fain claim it from Noah, through Ham, therefore my father was led away by their idolatry;

28. But I shall endeavor, hereafter, to delineate the chronology running back from myself to the beginning of the creation, for the records have come into my hands, which I hold unto this present time.

29. Now, after the priest of Elkenah was smitten that he died, there came a fulfilment of those things which were said unto me concerning the land of Chaldea, that there should be a famine in the land.

30. Accordingly a famine prevailed throughout all the land of Chaldea, and my father was sorely tormented because of the famine, and he repented of the evil which he had determined against me, to take away my life.

31. But the records of the fathers, even the patriarchs, concerning the right of Priesthood, the Lord my God preserved in mine own hands; therefore a knowledge of the beginning of the creation, and also of the planets, and of the stars, as they were made known unto the fathers, have I kept even unto this day, and I shall endeavor to write some of these things upon this record, for the benefit of my posterity that shall come after me.[5]

Now the Lord God caused the famine to wax sore in the land of Ur, insomuch that Haran, my brother, died; but Terah, my father, yet lived in the land of Ur, of the Chaldees.

2. And it came to pass that I, Abraham, took Sarai to wife, and Nehor, my brother, took Milcah to wife, who was the daughter of Haran.[6]

3. Now the Lord had said unto me: Abraham, get thee out of thy country, and from thy kindred, and from thy father's house, unto a land that I will show thee.

4. Therefore I left the land of Ur, of the Chaldees, to go into the land of Canaan; and I took Lot, my brother's son, and his wife, and Sarai my wife; and also my father followed after me, unto the land which we denominated Haran.

5. And the famine abated; and my father tarried in Haran and dwelt there, as there were many flocks in Haran; and my father turned again unto his idolatry, therefore he continued in Haran.

6. But I, Abraham, and Lot, my brother's son, prayed unto the Lord and the Lord appeared unto me, and said unto me: Arise, and take Lot with thee; for I have purposed to take thee away out of Haran, and to make of thee a minister to bear my name in a strange land which I will give unto thy seed after thee for an everlasting possession, when they hearken to my voice.

7. For I am the Lord thy God; I dwell in heaven; the earth is my footstool; I stretch my hand over the sea, and it obeys my voice; I cause the wind and the fire to be my chariot; I say to the mountains— Depart hence—and behold, they are taken away by a whirlwind, in an instant, suddenly.

8. My name is Jehovah, and I know the end from the beginning; therefore my hand shall be over thee.

9. And I will make of thee a great nation, and I will bless thee above measure, and make thy name great among all nations, and thou shalt be a blessing unto thy seed after thee, that in their hands they shall bear this ministry and Priesthood unto all nations;

10. And I will bless them through thy name; for as many as receive this Gospel shall be called after thy name, and shall be accounted thy seed, and shall rise up and bless thee, as their father;

11. And I will bless them that bless thee, and curse them that curse thee; and in thee (that is, in thy Priesthood) and in thy seed (that is, thy Priesthood), for I give unto thee a promise that this right shall continue in thee, and in thy seed after thee (that is to say, the literal seed, or the seed of the body) shall all the families of the earth

be blessed, even with the blessings of the Gospel, which are the blessings of salvation, even of life eternal.[7]

12. Now, after the Lord had withdrawn from speaking to me, and withdrawn his face from me, I said in my heart: Thy servant has sought thee earnestly; now I have found thee;

13. Thou didst send thine angel to deliver me from the gods of Elkenah, and I will do well to hearken unto thy voice, therefore let thy servant rise up and depart in peace.

14. So I, Abraham, departed as the Lord had said unto me, and Lot with me; and I, Abraham, was sixty and two years old[8] when I departed out of Haran.

15. And I took Sarai, whom I took to wife when I was in Ur, in Chaldea, and Lot, my brother's son, and all our substance that we had gathered, and the souls that we had won in Haran, and came forth in the way to the land of Canaan, and dwelt in tents as we came on our way;

16. Therefore, eternity was our covering and our rock and our salvation, as we journeyed from Haran by the way of Jershon, to come to the land of Canaan.

17. Now I, Abraham, built an altar in the land of Jershon, and made an offering unto the Lord, and prayed that the famine might be turned away from my father's house, that they might not perish.

18. And then we passed from Jershon through the land unto the place of Sechem; it was situated in the plains of Moreh, and we had already come into the borders of the land of the Canaanites, and I offered sacrifice there in the plains of Moreh, and called on the Lord devoutly, because we had already come into the land of this idolatrous nation.

19. And the Lord appeared unto me in answer to my prayers, and said unto me: Unto thy seed will I give this land.[9]

20. And I, Abraham, arose from the place of the altar which I had built unto the Lord, and removed from thence unto a mountain on the east of Bethel, and pitched my tent there, Bethel on the west, and Hai on the east; and there I built another altar unto the Lord, and called again upon the name of the Lord.

21. And I, Abraham, journeyed, going on still towards the south; and there was a continuation of a famine in the land; and I, Abraham, concluded to go down into Egypt, to sojourn there, for the famine became very grievous.

22. And it came to pass when I was come near to enter into Egypt, the Lord said unto me:[10] Behold, Sarai, thy wife, is a very fair woman to look upon;

23. Therefore it shall come to pass, when the Egyptians shall see her, they will say—She is his wife; and they will kill you, but they will save her alive; therefore see that ye do on this wise:

24. Let her say unto the Egyptians, she is thy sister, and thy soul shall live.

25. And it came to pass that I, Abraham, told Sarai, my wife, all that the Lord had said unto me—Therefore say unto them, I pray thee, thou art my sister, that it may be well with me for thy sake, and my soul shall live because of thee.

Notes

1. Note that this document (as contrasted with Genesis) is a first-person account.
2. Other early documents have this passage as "even the right of the firstborn, or the first man, who is Adam, *our* first father." (See pre-1981 editions of the *Pearl of Great Price*.)
3. A diagram accompanies the text in the *Pearl of Great Price*.
4. In summary, then, Ham, the son of Noah, married Egyptus outside the covenant; she had been a descendant of Cain, and thus her posterity was not entitled to the priesthood. The daughter of Ham, also called Egyptus, named her oldest son "Pharoah," a name which subsequently became a dynastic title.

   Though at this point the Latter-day Saints are unable to isolate a specific time (or document) when Joseph Smith specified that blacks should not receive the priesthood, these passages (together with those noted earlier in Moses 7) may provide a possible scriptural basis for the Mormon position regarding blacks and the Priesthood—a position maintained until June of 1978.
5. The Book of Abraham (chapters four and five) also contains an account of the Creation.
6. An earlier account read: "I, Abraham, took Sarai to wife, and Nehor, my brother, took Milcah to wife, *who were the daughters* of Haran." (*Times and Seasons,* 3:705.)
7. Cf. Genesis 12:2–3; 15:5; 17:1–4.
8. The account in Genesis says that Abraham was seventy-five years old. (Gen 12:4.)
9. Genesis 13:15; 17:18.
10. Note that it is *God* who initiates this plan.

8. A REVELATION CONCERNING MELCHIZEDEK (1831)

It is interesting to note that two of the most enigmatic figures of antiquity—Enoch and Melchizedek—receive considerable attention from Joseph Smith in his writings and translations. Melchizedek, mentioned briefly in the Old Testament context of Abraham and the battle of the kings, as well as in the New Testament book of Hebrews, is, in the passage below, described extensively. This passage is the basis for an LDS tradition that Melchizedek and the city of Salem, like Enoch and his city, were translated and taken into heaven without experiencing death. The following excerpt is from the Joseph Smith Translation of the 14th chapter of Genesis.

25. And Melchizedek lifted up his voice and blessed Abram.

26. Now Melchizedek was a man of faith, who wrought righteousness; and when a child he feared God, and stopped the mouths of lions, and quenched the violence of fire.[1]

27. And thus, having been approved of God, he was ordained an high priest after the order of the covenant which God made with Enoch,

28. It being after the order of the Son of God; which order came, not by man, nor the will of man; neither by father nor mother; neither by beginning of days nor end of years; but of God;[2]

29. And it was delivered unto men by the calling of his own voice, according to his own will, unto as many as believed on his name.

30. For God having sworn unto Enoch and unto his seed with an oath by himself; that every one being ordained after this order and calling should have power, by faith, to break mountains, to divide the seas, to dry up waters, to turn them out of their course;

31. To put at defiance the armies of nations, to divide the earth, to break every band, to stand in the presence of God, to do all things according to his will, according to his command, subdue principalities and powers; and this by the will of the Son of God which was from before the foundation of the world.

32. And men having this faith, coming up unto this order of God, were translated and taken up into heaven.

33. And now, Melchizedek was a priest of this order; therefore he obtained peace in Salem, and was called the Prince of peace.[3]

34. And his people wrought righteousness, and obtained heaven, and sought for the city of Enoch which God had before taken, separat-

ing it from the earth, having reserved it unto the latter days, or the end of the world;

35. And hath said, and sworn with an oath, that the heavens and the earth should come together; and the sons of God should be tried so as by fire.

36. And this Melchizedek, having thus established righteousness, was called the king of heaven by his people, or, in other words, the King of peace.

37. And he lifted up his voice, and he blessed Abram, being the high priest, and the keeper of the storehouse of God;

38. Him whom God had appointed to receive tithes for the poor.

39. Wherefore, Abram paid unto him tithes of all that he had, of all the riches which he possessed, which God had given him more than that which he had need.

40. And it came to pass, that God blessed Abram, and gave unto him riches, and honor, and lands for an everlasting possession; according to the covenant which he had made, and according to the blessing wherewith Melchizedek had blessed him.

Notes

1. Compare Hebrews 11:33–34.
2. Note that it is the order of the priesthood which Melchizedek bore which is "without father, without mother, without descent, having neither beginning of days, nor end of life." (Heb 7:3.)
3. Abraham thus sought to be a "prince of peace" like Melchizedek, his contemporary. (See Abraham 1:2.)

9. THE PROPHECIES CONCERNING JOSEPH OF EGYPT (1833)

The following is an extract from the Joseph Smith Translation of the 50th chapter of Genesis, beginning with verse 24. The reader will notice the lengthy insertion regarding the prophecies of Joseph concerning Moses, Aaron, and a "choice seer" of the latter days.

24. And Joseph said unto his brethren, I die, and go unto my fathers; and I go down to my grave with joy. The God of my father Jacob be with you, to deliver you out of affliction in the days of your bondage; for the Lord hath visited me, and I have obtained a promise of the Lord, that out of the fruit of my loins, the Lord God will raise up a righteous branch out of my loins; and unto thee, whom my father

Jacob hath named Israel, a prophet; (not the Messiah who is called Shilo;[1]) and this prophet shall deliver my people out of Egypt in the days of thy bondage.

25. And it shall come to pass that they shall be scattered again; and a branch shall be broken off, and shall be carried into a far country; nevertheless they shall be remembered in the covenants of the Lord, when the Messiah cometh; for he shall be made manifest unto them in the latter days, in the Spirit of power; and shall bring them out of darkness into light; out of hidden darkness, and out of captivity unto freedom.

26. A seer shall the Lord my God raise up, who shall be a choice seer unto the fruit of my loins.

27. Thus saith the Lord God of my fathers unto me, A choice seer will I raise up out of the fruit of thy loins,[2] and he shall be esteemed highly among the fruit of thy loins; and unto him will I give commandment that he shall do a work for the fruit of thy loins, his brethren.

28. And he shall bring them to the knowledge of the covenants which I have made with thy fathers; and he shall do whatsoever work I shall command him.

29. And I will make him great in mine eyes, for he shall do my work; and he shall be great like unto him whom I have said I would raise up unto you, to deliver my people, O house of Israel, out of the land of Egypt; for a seer will I raise up to deliver my people out of the land of Egypt; and he shall be called Moses. And by this name he shall know that he is of thy house; for he shall be nursed by the king's daughter, and shall be called her son.

30. And again, a seer will I raise up out of the fruit of thy loins, and unto him will I give power to bring forth my word unto the seed of thy loins; and not to the bringing forth of my word only, saith the Lord, but to the convincing them of my word, which shall have already gone forth among them in the last days;

31. Wherefore the fruit of thy loins shall write,[3] and the fruit of the loins of Judah shall write;[4] and that which shall be written by the fruit of thy loins, and also that which shall be written by the fruit of thy loins of Judah, shall grow together unto the confounding of false doctrines, and laying down of contentions, and establishing peace among the fruit of thy loins, and bringing them to a knowledge of their fathers in the latter days; and also to the knowledge of my covenants, saith the Lord.

32. And out of weakness shall he be made strong, in that day

when my work shall go forth among all my people, which shall restore them, who are of the house of Israel, in the last days.

33. And that seer will I bless, and they that seek to destroy him shall be confounded; for this promise I give unto you; for I will remember you from generation to generation; and his name shall be called Joseph, and it shall be after the name of his father; and he shall be like unto you; for the thing which the Lord shall bring forth by his hand shall bring my people unto salvation.

34. And the Lord sware unto Joseph that he would preserve his seed forever, saying, I will raise up Moses, and a rod shall be in his hand, and he shall gather together my people, and he shall lead them as a flock, and he shall smite the waters of the Red Sea with his rod.

35. And he shall have judgment, and shall write the word of the Lord. And he shall not speak many words, for I will write unto him my law by the finger of mine own hand. And I will make a spokesman for him, and his name shall be called Aaron.

36. And it shall be done unto thee in the last days also, even as I have sworn. Therefore, Joseph said unto his brethren, God will surely visit you, and bring you out of this land, unto the land which he sware unto Abraham, and unto Isaac, and to Jacob.

37. And Joseph confirmed many other things unto his brethren, and took an oath of the children of Israel, saying unto them, God will surely visit you, and ye shall carry up my bones from hence.

38. So Joseph died when he was an hundred and ten years old; and they embalmed him, and they put him in a coffin in Egypt; and he was kept from burial by the children of Israel, that he might be carried up and laid in the sepulchre with his father. And thus they remembered the oath which they sware unto him.

Notes

1. Cf. Genesis 49:10.
2. Mormons view this as an ancient prophecy of Joseph Smith.
3. The Book of Mormon, a record of a people who were descendants of the tribe of Joseph.
4. The Bible, a record of the Jews.

10. AN EXTRACT FROM THE
SERMON ON THE MOUNT [JST, MATTHEW 7] (1831)

The following excerpted text will demonstrate some of the major changes in the JST of Matthew 7. The JST places an even stronger emphasis on the Sermon on the Mount as an apostolic preparation, an address directed almost exclusively to the Twelve.

4. And again, ye shall say unto them, Why is it that thou beholdest the mote that is in thy brother's eye, but considerest not the beam that is in thine own eye?

5. Or how wilt thou say to thy brother, Let me pull out the mote out of thine eye; and canst not behold a beam in thine own eye?

6. And Jesus said unto his disciples, Beholdest thou the Scribes, and the Pharisees, and the Priests, and the Levites? They teach in their synagogues, but do not observe the law, nor the commandments; and all have gone out of the way, and are under sin.

7. Go thou and say unto them, Why teach ye men the law and the commandments, when ye yourselves are the children of corruption?

8. Say unto them, Ye hypocrites, first cast out the beam out of thine own eye; and then shalt thou see clearly to cast out the mote out of thy brother's eye.

9. Go ye into the world, saying unto all, Repent, for the kindom of heaven has come nigh unto you.

10. And the mysteries of the kingdom ye shall keep within yourselves; for it is not meet to give that which is holy unto the dogs; neither cast ye your pearls unto swine, lest they trample them under their feet.

11. For the world cannot receive that which ye, yourselves, are not able to bear; wherefore ye shall not give your pearls unto them, lest they turn again and rend you.

12. Say unto them, Ask of God; ask, and it shall be given you; seek, and ye shall find; knock, and it shall be opened unto you.

13. For every one that asketh, receiveth; and he that seeketh, findeth; and unto him that knocketh, it shall be opened.

14. And then said his disciples unto him, they will say unto us, We ourselves are righteous, and need not that any man should teach us. God, we know, heard Moses and some of the prophets; but us he will not hear.

15. And they will say, We have the law for our salvation, and that is sufficient for us.

16. Then Jesus answered, and said unto his disciples, thus shall ye say unto them.

17. What man among you, having a son, and he shall be standing out, and shall say, Father, open thy house that I may come in and sup with thee, will not say, Come in, my son; for mine is thine, and thine is mine?

11. JESUS' PROPHECIES OF DESTRUCTION AND THE PAROUSIA [JST, MATTHEW 24] (1831)

In his translation of Matthew 24, Joseph Smith placed a line of demarcation (see verse 21) between those prophecies pertaining to the destruction of Jerusalem and the Jews in 70 C.E. and the signs incident to Christ's Second Coming in glory. The following is known as "Joseph Smith-Matthew" in the "Pearl of Great Price."

For I say unto you, that ye shall not see me henceforth and know that I am he of whom it is written by the prophets, until ye shall say: Blessed is he who cometh in the name of the Lord, in the clouds of heaven, and all the holy angels with him. Then understood his disciples that he should come again on the earth, after that he was glorified and crowned on the right hand of God.

2. And Jesus went out, and departed from the temple; and his disciples came to him, for to hear him, saying: Master, show us concerning the buildings of the temple, as thou hast said—They shall be thrown down, and left unto you desolate.

3. And Jesus said unto them: See ye not all these things, and do ye not understand them? Verily I say unto you, there shall not be left here, upon this temple, one stone upon another that shall not be thrown down.

4. And Jesus left them, and went upon the Mount of Olives. And as he sat upon the Mount of Olives, the disciples came unto him privately, saying: Tell us when shall these things be which thou has said concerning the destruction of the temple, and the Jews; and what is the sign of thy coming, and of the end of the world, or the destruction of the wicked, which is the end of the world?

5. And Jesus answered, and said unto them: Take heed that no man deceive you;

6. For many shall come in my name, saying—I am Christ—and shall deceive many;

7. Then shall they deliver you up to be afflicted, and shall kill you, and ye shall be hated of all nations, for my name's sake;

8. And then shall many be offended, and shall betray one another, and shall hate one another;

9. And many false prophets shall arise, and shall deceive many;

10. And because iniquity shall abound, the love of many shall wax cold;

11. But he that remaineth steadfast and is not overcome, the same shall be saved.

12. When you, therefore, shall see the abomination of desolation, spoken of by Daniel the prophet, concerning the destruction of Jerusalem, then you shall stand in the holy place; whoso readeth let him understand.

13. Then let them who are in Judea flee into the mountains;

14. Let him who is on the housetop flee, and not return to take anything out of his house;

15. Neither let him who is in the field return back to take his clothes;

16. And wo unto them that are with child, and unto them that give suck in those days;

17. Therefore, pray ye the Lord that your flight be not in the winter, neither on the Sabbath day;

18. For then, in those days, shall be great tribulation on the Jews, and upon the inhabitants of Jerusalem, such as was not before sent upon Israel, of God, since the beginning of their kingdom until this time; no, nor ever shall be sent again upon Israel.

19 All things which have befallen them are only the beginning of the sorrows which shall come upon them.

20. And except those days should be shortened, there should none of their flesh be saved; but for the elect's sake, according to the covenant, those days shall be shortened.

21. Behold, these things I have spoken unto you concerning the Jews; and again, after the tribulation of those days which shall come upon Jerusalem, if any man shall say unto you, Lo, here is Christ, or there, believe him not;

22. For in those days there shall also arise false Christs, and false prophets, and shall show great signs and wonders, insomuch, that, if

possible, they shall deceive the very elect, who are the elect according to the covenant.

23. Behold, I speak these things unto you for the elect's sake; and you also shall hear of wars, and rumors of wars; see that ye be not troubled, for all I have told you must come to pass; but the end is not yet.

24. Behold, I have told you before;

25. Wherefore, if they shall say unto you: Behold, he is in the desert; go not forth: Behold, he is in the secret chambers; believe it not;

26. For as the light of the morning cometh out of the east, and shineth even unto the west, and covereth the whole earth, so shall also the coming of the Son of Man be.

27. And now I show unto you a parable. Behold, wheresoever the carcass is, there will the eagles be gathered together; so likewise shall mine elect be gathered from the four quarters of the earth.

28. And they shall hear of wars, and rumors of wars.

29. Behold I speak for mine elect's sake; for nation shall rise against nation, and kingdom against kingdom; there shall be famines, and pestilences, and earthquakes, in divers places.

30. And again, because iniquity shall abound, the love of men shall wax cold; but he that shall not be overcome, the same shall be saved.

31. And again, this Gospel of the Kingdom shall be preached in all the world, for a witness unto all nations, and then shall the end come, or the destruction of the wicked;

32. And again shall the abomination of desolation, spoken of by Daniel the prophet, be fulfilled.[1]

33. And immediately after the tribulation of those days, the sun shall be darkened, and the moon shall not give her light, and the stars shall fall from heaven, and the powers of heaven shall be shaken.

34. Verily, I say unto you, this generation, in which these things shall be shown forth, shall not pass away until all I have told you shall be fulfilled.[2]

35. Although, the days will come, that heaven and earth shall pass away; yet my words shall not pass away, but all shall be fulfilled.

36. And, as I said before, after the tribulation of those days, and the powers of the heavens shall be shaken, then shall appear the sign of the Son of Man in heaven, and then shall all the tribes of the earth mourn; and they shall see the Son of Man coming in the clouds of heaven, with power and great glory;

37. And whoso treasureth up my word, shall not be deceived, for the Son of Man shall come, and he shall send his angels before him with the great sound of a trumpet, and they shall gather together the remainder of his elect from the four winds, from one end of heaven to the other.

38. Now learn a parable of the figtree—When its branches are yet tender, and it begins to put forth leaves, you know that summer is nigh at hand;

39. So likewise, mine elect, when they shall see all these things, they shall know that he is near, even at the doors;

40. But of that day, and hour, no one knoweth; no, not the angels of God in heaven, but my Father only.

41. But as it was in the days of Noah, so it shall be also at the coming of the Son of Man;

42. For it shall be with them, as it was in the days which were before the flood; for until the day that Noah entered into the ark they were eating and drinking; marrying and giving in marriage;

43. And knew not until the flood came, and took them all away; so shall also the coming of the Son of Man be.

44. Then shall be fulfilled that which is written, that in the last days, two shall be in the field, the one shall be taken, and the other left;

45. Two shall be grinding at the mill, the one shall be taken, and the other left;

46. And what I say unto one, I say unto all men; watch, therefore, for you know not at what hour your Lord doth come.

47. But know this, if the good man of the house had known in what watch the thief would come, he would have watched, and would not have suffered his house to have been broken up, but would have been ready.

48. Therefore be ye also ready, for in such an hour as ye think not, the Son of Man cometh.

49. Who, then, is a faithful and wise servant, whom his lord hath made ruler over his household, to give them meat in due season?

50. Blessed is that servant whom his lord, when he cometh, shall find so doing; and verily I say unto you, he shall make him ruler over all his goods.

51. But if that evil servant shall say in his heart: My lord delayeth his coming,

52. And shall begin to smite his fellow-servants, and to eat and drink with the drunken,

53. The lord of that servant shall come in a day when he looketh not for him, and in an hour that he is not aware of,

54. And shall cut him asunder, and shall appoint him his portion with the hypocrites; there shall be weeping and gnashing of teeth.

55. And thus cometh the end of the wicked, according to the prophecy of Moses,[3] saying: They shall be cut off from among the people; but the end of the earth is not yet, but by and by.

Notes

1. A revelation in the *Doctrine and Covenants* speaks of the "abomination of desolation" in the last days as the destruction of wickedness at the time of Christ's coming in glory. (*Doctrine and Covenants,* 88:85.)
2. Cf. Matthew 24:34.
3. Deuteronomy 18:19; Acts 3:23.

VII.

PRAYERS

1. A DEDICATORY PRAYER FOR THE TEMPLE (1836)

Joseph Smith explained that one of the primary reasons for gathering to Zion was to build a temple, a holy place where God could endow those who participate therein with power from on high. In 1833 work went forward on a temple in Kirtland, Ohio. The Latter-day Saints literally gave all that they had for the construction of "the House of the Lord," and felt that their sacrifices were more than rewarded: the winter and spring of 1836 proved to be a "pentecostal" era for the Mormons, as they became convinced that the "latter-day glory" had begun to be manifest. During a fifteen-week period from January 21, to May 1, 1836, more Saints claimed visions of heavenly beings, more persons spoke in tongues and interpreted, and more prophesied than during any other comparable recorded period in LDS history. The following dedicatory prayer for the Kirtland Temple was given by revelation to Joseph Smith and some of the leaders of the Church, and was offered for the first time on Sunday, March 27, 1836. It is found in Personal Writings of Joseph Smith, pp. 174–80, and is also contained in the Doctrine and Covenants *(section 109). The following, given for convenience in reading, is the edited version as now found in the* Doctrine and Covenants.

Thanks be to thy name, O Lord God of Israel, who keepest covenant and showest mercy unto thy servants who walk uprightly before thee, with all their hearts—

2. Thou who hast commanded thy servants to build a house to thy name in this place [Kirtland].

3. And now thou beholdest, O Lord, that thy servants have done according to thy commandment.

4. And now we ask thee, Holy Father, in the name of Jesus Christ, the Son of thy bosom, in whose name alone salvation can be administered to the children of men,[1] we ask thee, O Lord, to accept of this house, the workmanship of the hands of us, thy servants, which thou didst command us to build.

5. For thou knowest that we have done this work through great tribulation; and out of our poverty we have given of our substance to build a house to thy name, that the Son of Man might have a place to manifest himself to his people.

6. And as thou has said in a revelation, given to us, calling us thy friends, saying—Call your solemn assembly, as I have commanded you;

7. And as all have not faith, seek ye diligently and teach one another words of wisdom; yea, seek ye out of the best books words of wisdom, seek learning even by study and also by faith;

8. Organize yourselves; prepare every needful thing, and establish a house, even a house of prayer, a house of fasting, a house of faith, a house of learning, a house of glory, a house of order, a house of God;

9. That your incomings may be in the name of the Lord, that your outgoings may be in the name of the Lord, that all your salutations may be in the name of the Lord, with uplifted hands upon the Most High—[2]

10. And now, Holy Father, we ask thee to assist us, in calling our solemn assembly, that it may be done to thine honor and to thy divine acceptance;

11. And in a manner that we may be found worthy, in thy sight, to secure a fulfillment of the promises which thou hast made unto us, thy people, in the revelations given unto us;

12. That thy glory may rest down upon thy people, and upon this thy house, which we now dedicate to thee, that it may be sanctified and consecrated to be holy, and that thy holy presence may be continually in this house;

13. And that all people who shall enter upon the threshhold of the Lord's house may feel the power, and feel constrained to acknowledge that thou hast sanctified it, and that it is thy house, a place of holiness.

14. And do thou grant, Holy Father, that all those who shall worship in this house may be taught words of wisdom out of the best books, and that they may seek learning even by study, and also by faith, as thou hast said;

15. And that they may grow up in thee, and receive a fulness of the Holy Ghost, and be organized according to thy laws, and be prepared to obtain every needful thing;

16. And that this house may be a house of prayer, a house of fasting, a house of faith, a house of glory and of God, even thy house;

17. That all the incomings of thy people, into this house, may be in the name of the Lord;

18. That all their outgoings from this house may be in the name of the Lord;

19. And that all their salutations may be in the name of the Lord, with holy hands, uplifted to the Most High;

20. And that no unclean thing shall be permitted to come into thy house to pollute it;

21. And when thy people transgress, any of them, they may speedily repent and return unto thee, and find favor in thy sight, and be restored to the blessings which thou hast ordained to be poured out upon those who shall reverence thee in thy house.

22. And we ask thee, Holy Father, that thy servants may go forth from this house armed with power, and that thy name may be upon them, and thy glory be round about them, and thine angels have charge over them;

23. And from this place they may bear exceedingly great and glorious tidings, in truth, unto the ends of the earth, that they may know that this is thy work, and that thou hast put forth thy hand, to fulfil that which thou hast spoken by the mouths of the prophets, concerning the last days.

24. We ask thee, Holy Father, to establish the people that shall worship, and honorably hold a name and standing in this thy house, to all generations and for eternity;

25. That no weapon formed against them shall prosper;[3] that he who diggeth a pit for them shall fall into the same himself;

26. That no combination of wickedness shall have power to rise up and prevail over thy people upon whom thy name shall be put in this house;

27. And if any people shall rise against this people, that thine anger be kindled against them;

28. And if they shall smite this people thou wilt smite them; thou wilt fight for thy people as thou didst in the day of battle, that they may be delivered from the hands of all their enemies.

29. We ask thee, Holy Father, to confound, and astonish, and to bring to shame and confusion, all those who have spread lying reports abroad, over the world, against thy servant or servants, if they will not repent, when the everlasting gospel shall be proclaimed in their ears;

30. And that all their works may be brought to naught, and be swept away by the hail, and by the judgments which thou wilt send upon them in thine anger, that there may be an end to lyings and slanders against thy people.

31. For thou knowest, O Lord, that thy servants have been innocent before thee in bearing record of thy name, for which they have suffered these things.

32. Therefore we plead before thee for a full and complete deliverance from under this yoke;

33. Break it off, O Lord, break it off from the necks of thy servants, by thy power, that we may rise up in the midst of this generation and do thy work.

34. O Jehovah, have mercy upon this people, and as all men sin forgive the transgressions of thy people, and let them be blotted out forever.

35. Let the anointing of thy ministers be sealed upon them with power from on high.

36. Let it be fulfilled upon them, as upon those on the day of Pentecost; let the gift of tongues be poured out upon thy people, even cloven tongues as of fire, and the interpretation thereof.

37. And let thy house be filled, as with a rushing mighty wind, with thy glory.[4]

38. Put upon thy servants the testimony of the covenant, that when they go out and proclaim thy word they may seal up the law, and prepare the hearts of thy saints for all those judgments thou art about to send, in thy wrath, upon the inhabitants of the earth, because of their transgressions, that thy people may not faint in the day of trouble.

39. And whatsoever city thy servants shall enter, and the people of that city receive their testimony, let thy peace and thy salvation be upon that city; that they may gather out of that city the righteous, that they may come forth to Zion, or to her stakes, the places of thine appointment, with songs of everlasting joy;

40. And until this be accomplished, let not thy judgments fall upon that city.

41. And whatsoever city thy servants shall enter, and the people of that city receive not the testimony of thy servants, and thy servants warn them to save themselves from this untoward generation, let it be upon that city according to that which thou hast spoken by the mouths of thy prophets.[5]

42. But deliver thou, O Jehovah, we beseech thee, thy servants from their hands, and cleanse them from their blood.

43. O Lord, we delight not in the destruction of our fellow men; their souls are precious before thee;

44. But thy word must be fulfilled. Help thy servants to say, with thy grace assisting them: Thy will be done, O Lord, and not ours.[6]

45. We know that thou hast spoken by the mouth of thy prophets terrible things concerning the wicked, in the last days—that thou wilt pour out thy judgments, without measure;

46. Therefore, O Lord, deliver thy people from the calamity of the wicked; enable thy servants to seal up the law, and bind up the testimony, that they may be prepared against the day of burning.

47. We ask thee, Holy Father, to remember those who have been driven by the inhabitants of Jackson County, Missouri, from the lands of their inheritance, and break off, O Lord, this yoke of affliction that has been put upon them.

48. Thou knowest, O Lord, that they have been greatly oppressed and afflicted by wicked men; and our hearts flow out with sorrow because of their grievous burdens.

49. O Lord, how long wilt thou suffer this people to bear this affliction, and the cries of their innocent ones to ascend up in thine ears, and their blood come up in testimony before thee, and not make a display of thy testimony in their behalf?

50. Have mercy, O Lord, upon the wicked mob, who have driven thy people, that they may cease to spoil, that they may repent of their sins if repentance is to be found;

51. But if they will not, make bare thine arm, O Lord, and redeem that which thou didst appoint a Zion unto thy people.

52. And if it cannot be otherwise, that the cause of thy people may not fail before thee may thine anger be kindled, and thine indignation fall upon them, that they may be wasted away, both root and branch,[7] from under heaven;

53. But inasmuch as they will repent, thou art gracious and merciful, and wilt turn away thy wrath when thou lookest upon the face of thine Anointed.

54. Have mercy, O Lord, upon all these nations of the earth; have mercy upon the rulers of our land; may those principles, which were so honorably and nobly defended, namely, the constitution of our land, by our fathers, be established forever.

55. Remember the kings, the princes, the nobles, and the great ones of the earth, and all people, and the churches, all the poor, the needy, and afflicted ones of the earth;

56. That their hearts may be softened when thy servants shall go out from thy house, O Jehovah, to bear testimony of thy name; that their prejudices may give way before the truth, and thy people may obtain favor in the sight of all;

57. That all the ends of the earth may know that we, thy servants, have heard thy voice, and that thou hast sent us;

58. That from among all these, thy servants, the sons of Jacob, may gather out the righteous to build a holy city to thy name, as thou hast commanded them.

59. We ask thee to appoint unto Zion other stakes[8] besides this one which thou hast appointed, that the gathering of thy people may roll on in great power and majesty, that thy work may be cut short in righteousness.

60. Now these words, O Lord, we have spoken before thee, concerning the revelations and commandments which thou hast given unto us, who are identified with the Gentiles.

61. But thou knowest that thou hast a great love for the children of Jacob, who have been scattered upon the mountains for a long time in a cloudy and dark day.

62. We therefore ask thee to have mercy upon the children of Jacob that Jerusalem, from this hour, may begin to be redeemed;

63. And the yoke of bondage may begin to be broken off from the house of David;

64. And the children of Judah[9] may begin to return to the lands which thou didst give to Abraham, their father.

65. And cause that the remnants of Jacob, who have been cursed and smitten because of their transgression, be converted from their wild and savage condition to the fulness of the everlasting gospel;

66. That they may lay down their weapons of bloodshed, and cease their rebellions.

67. And may all the scattered remnants of Israel, who have been driven to the ends of the earth, come to a knowledge of the truth, believe in the Messiah, and be redeemed from oppression, and rejoice before thee.

68. O Lord, remember thy servants, Joseph Smith, Jun., and all

his afflictions and persecutions—how he has covenanted with Jehovah, and vowed to thee, O Mighty God of Jacob—and the commandments which thou hast given unto him, and that he hath sincerely striven to do thy will.

69. Have mercy, O Lord, upon his wife and children that they may be exalted in thy presence, and preserved by thy fostering hand.

70. Have mercy upon all their immediate connections, that their prejudices may be broken up and swept away as with a flood; that they may be converted and redeemed with Israel, and know that thou art God.

71. Remember, O Lord, the presidents, even all the presidents of thy church, that thy right hand may exalt them, with all their immediate families, and their immediate connections, that their names may be perpetuated and had in everlasting remembrance from generation to generation.

72. Remember all thy church, O Lord, with all their families, and all their immediate connections, with all their sick and afflicted ones, with all the poor and meek of the earth; that the kingdom, which thou hast set up without hands, may become a great mountain and fill the whole earth;[10]

73. That thy church may come forth out of the wilderness of darkness, and shine forth fair as the moon, clear as the sun, and terrible as an army with banners;

74. And be adorned as a bride for that day when thou shalt unveil the heavens, and cause the mountains to flow down at thy presence, and the valleys to be exalted, the rough places made smooth; that thy glory may fill the earth;

75. That when the trump shall sound for the dead, we shall be caught up in the cloud to meet thee, that we may ever be with the Lord;

76. That our garments may be pure, that we may be clothed upon with robes of righteousness, with palms in our hands, and crowns of glory upon our heads, and reap eternal joy for all our sufferings.

77. O Lord God Almighty, hear us in these our petitions, and answer us from heaven, thy holy habitation, where thou sittest enthroned with glory, honor, power, majesty, might, dominion, truth, justice, judgment, mercy, and an infinity of fulness, from everlasting to everlasting.

78. O hear, O hear, O hear us, O Lord! And answer these petitions, and accept the dedication of this house unto thee, the work of our hands, which we have built unto thy name;

79. And also this church, to put upon it thy name. And help us by the power of thy Spirit, that we may mingle our voices with those bright, shining seraphs around thy throne with acclamations of praise, singing Hosanna to God and the Lamb!

80. And let these, thine anointed ones, be clothed with salvation, and thy saints shout aloud for joy. Amen, and Amen.

Notes

1. Acts 4:12.
2. For verses 6–9, see *Doctrine and Covenants,* 88:117–20.
3. Isaiah 54:17.
4. See Acts 2.
5. Matthew 10:14–15.
6. Cf. Matthew 26:39; Mark 14:36; Luke 22:42.
7. Cf. Malachi 4:1.
8. The word *stake,* used in Isaiah 54:2, came to represent an ecclesiastical unit composed of a number of congregations, somewhat akin to a diocese.
9. That is, the Jews.
10. See Daniel 2:31–45.

2. A PRAYER FOR THE COMING KINGDOM (1831)

Joseph Smith and the Latter-day Saints believed the Church of Jesus Christ of Latter-day Saints to be the fulfillment of the prophetic dream of King Nebuchadnezzar that in the last days "shall the God of heaven set up a kingdom, which shall never be destroyed," a kingdom which shall eventually "stand for ever." (Dan 2:44) The Church was the kingdom of God on earth, whose mission was to prepare men and women for the coming kingdom of heaven. This prayer was written in October of 1831 in Hiram, Ohio, and now constitutes section 65 of the Doctrine and Covenants.

Hearken, and lo, a voice as of one sent down from on high, who is mighty and powerful, whose going forth is unto the ends of the earth, yea, whose voice is unto men—Prepare ye the way of the Lord, make his paths straight.

2. The keys of the kingdom of God are committed unto man on the earth, and from thence shall the gospel roll forth unto the ends of

the earth, as the stone which is cut[1] out of the mountain without hands shall roll forth, until it has filled the whole earth.[2]

3. Yea, a voice crying—Prepare ye the way of the Lord,[3] prepare ye the supper of the Lamb, make ready for the Bridegroom.[4]

4. Pray unto the Lord, call upon his holy name, make known his wonderful works among the people.

5. Call upon the Lord, that his kingdom may go forth upon the earth, that the inhabitants thereof may receive it, and be prepared for the days to come, in the which the Son of Man shall come down in heaven, clothed in the brightness of his glory, to meet the kingdom of God which is set up on the earth.

6. Wherefore, may the kingdom of God go forth, that the kingdom of heaven may come,[5] that thou, O God, mayest be glorified in heaven so on earth, that thine enemies may be subdued; for thine is the honor, power and glory, forever and ever. Amen.

Notes

1. From the "Kirtland Revelation Book": The Stone "which is *hewed* out of the mountain."
2. Daniel 2:31–45.
3. Cf. Malachi 3:1; Matthew 3:3.
4. Cf. Matthew 22:1–14; Revelation 19:9.
5. Matthew 6:9–10.

BIBLIOGRAPHY

LATTER-DAY SAINT SCRIPTURES

The Book of Mormon. Salt Lake City: The Church of Jesus Christ of Latter-day Saints, 1981.

The Doctrine and Covenants. Salt Lake City: The Church of Jesus Christ of Latter-day Saints, 1981.

The Holy Bible. Salt Lake City: The Church of Jesus Christ of Latter-day Saints, 1979.

Holy Scriptures, Inspired Version (Joseph Smith Translation). Independence, Mo.: Herald Publishing Company, 1974.

The Pearl of Great Price. Salt Lake City: The Church of Jesus Christ of Latter-day Saints, 1981.

HISTORICAL AND DOCTRINAL SOURCES

Ahlstrom, Syndney E., ed. *Theology in America.* Indianapolis: The Bobbs-Merrill Company, Inc., 1967.

Anderson, Bernhard W. *Understanding the Old Testament,* 3rd ed. Englewood Cliffs, New Jersey: Prentice-Hall, Inc., 1975.

Andrus, Hyrum L. *Doctrinal Themes of the Doctrine and Covenants.* Provo, Utah: Brigham Young University Press, 1970.

————. *Doctrines of the Kingdom.* Salt Lake City: Bookcraft Publishers, 1973.

Andrus, Hyrum L. and Andrus, Helen Mae. *They Knew the Prophet.* Salt Lake City: Bookcraft Publishers, 1974.

Arrington, Leonard J. and Bitton, Davis. *The Mormon Experience.* New York: Alfred A. Knopf, 1979.

Arrington, Leonard J.; Fox, Feramorz; and May, Dean L. *Building the City of God: Community and Cooperation Among the Mormons.* Salt Lake City: Deseret Book Company, 1976.

255

Bachman, Daniel. "New Light on An Old Hypothesis: The Ohio Origins of the Revelation on Eternal Marriage." *Journal of Mormon History,* Vol. 5 (1978).

Backman, Milton V., Jr. *American Religions and the Rise of Mormonism.* Salt Lake City: Deseret Book Company, 1970.

———. "Awakenings in the Burned-Over District: New Light on the Historical Setting of the First Vision." *Brigham Young University Studies,* Spring 1966.

———. "Truman Coe's 1836 Description of Mormonism." *Brigham Young University Studies,* Vol. 17, no. 3 (Spring 1977).

Barrett, Ivan J. *Joseph Smith and the Restoration.* Provo, Utah: Brigham Young University Press, 1973.

Bedell, George C.; Sandon, Leo, Jr.,; and Wellborn, Charles. *Religion in America.* New York: Macmillan, 1975.

Bellah, Robert N. "American Society and the Mormon Community." *Reflections on Mormonism.* Provo, Utah: Religious Studies Center, Brigham Young University, 1978.

Benson, Ezra Taft. "Born of God." Conference Report, October 1985. Salt Lake City: The Church of Jesus Christ of Latter-day Saints.

Boston Quarterly Review, 3 vols. Boston: Cambridge Press, 1840.

Brodie, Fawn M. *No Man Knows My History: The Life of Joseph Smith the Mormon Prophet.* New York: Alfred A. Knopf, 1945.

Bushman, Richard. *Joseph Smith and the Beginnings of Mormonism.* Urbana/Chicago: University of Illinois Press, 1984.

Campbell, Alexander. *The Christian Baptist,* 7 Vols., 13th ed., Rev. D. S. Burnet. Bethany, West Va.: H. S. Bosworth, 1861.

Cheesman, Paul R. *The Keystone of Mormonism: Little Known Truths About the Book of Mormon.* Salt Lake City: Deseret Book Co., 1973.

Christianson, James R. "A Ray of Light in an Hour of Darkness." *Studies in Scripture, Vol. 1: The Doctrine and Covenants,* ed. Robert L. Millet and Kent P. Jackson. Sandy, Utah: Randall Book Co., 1984.

Clark, James R., comp. *Messages of the First Presidency,* 6 Vols. Salt Lake City: Bookcraft Publishers, 1965–1975.

Collier, Fred C. *Unpublished Revelations of the Prophets and Presidents of the Church of Jesus Christ of Latter-day Saints.* Salt Lake City: Collier's Publishing Company, 1979.

Conference Reports. Salt Lake City: The Church of Jesus Christ of Latter-day Saints, 1830–1986.

Cook, Lyndon W. *Joseph Smith and the Law of Consecration.* Provo, Utah: Grandin, 1985.

———. *The Revelations of the Prophet Joseph Smith.* Salt Lake City, Utah: Deseret Book Co., 1985.

Cowley, Matthias F. *Wilford Woodruff.* Salt Lake City: Bookcraft Publishers, 1964.

Cross, Whitney R. *The Burned Over District.* Ithaca, New York: Cornell University Press, 1950.

Davies, W. D. "Israel, The Mormons and the Land." *Reflections on Mormonism.* Provo, Utah: Religious Studies Center, Brigham Young University, 1978.

DeGroot, A. T. and Garrison, W. E. *The Disciples of Christ.* St. Louis: Bethany Press, 1958.

Denny, Frederick M. and Taylor, Rodney L. ed., *The Holy Book in Comparative Perspective.* Columbia, South Carolina: University of South Carolina Press, 1985.

Deseret Evening News, October 2, 1875.

de Tocqueville, Alexis. *Democracy in America.* New York: Doubleday, 1969.

Ehat, Andrew F. and Cook, Lyndon W., ed. *The Words of Joseph Smith.* Provo, Utah: Religious Studies Center, Brigham Young University, 1980.

Emerson, Ralph Waldo. *The Dial.* New York: Russell and Russell, Inc., 1961.

The Evening and Morning Star. Independence, Mo.: The Church of Jesus Christ of Latter-day Saints, 1832–34.

Fish, Carl Russell. *The Rise of the Common Man.* New York: Macmillan, 1927.

Foster, Lawrence. *Religion and Sexuality.* New York: Oxford University Press, 1981.

Godfrey, Kenneth W. "Causes of Non-Mormon Conflict in Hancock County, Illinois, 1839–1846." Ph.D. Dissertation, Brigham Young University, 1967.

Hansen, Klaus J. *Mormonism and the American Experience.* Chicago: University of Chicago Press, 1981.

Herberg, Will. *Protestant, Catholic, Jew.* New York: Doubleday & Company, 1960.

Hill, Marvin S. "The Role of Christian Primitivism in the Origin and Development of the Mormon Kingdom." Ph.D. Dissertation, University of Chicago, 1968.

Hills, Margaret T. *The English Bible in America.* New York: The American Bible Society, 1961.

Howard, Richard P. *Restoration Scriptures.* Independence, Mo.: Herald Publishing House, 1969.

The Improvement Era. Salt Lake City: The Church of Jesus Christ of Latter-day Saints.

Jackson, Kent P. "Latter-day Saints: A Dynamic Scriptural Process." *The Holy Book in Comparative Perspective,* ed. Frederick M. Denny and Rodney L. Taylor. Columbia, South Carolina: University of South Carolina Press, 1985.

Jackson, Kent P. and Millet, Robert L., ed. *Studies in Scripture, Vol. 3: Genesis to 2 Samuel.* Sandy, Utah: Randall Book Co., 1985.

Jamison, Leland A. and Smith, James Ward, eds. *The Shaping of American Religion,* 4 Vols. Princeton: Princeton University, 1961.

Jennings, Warren A. "Zion is Fled: The Expulsion of the Mormons From Jackson County, Missouri." Ph.D. Dissertation, University of Florida, 1962.

Jessee, Dean C. "The Early Accounts of Joseph Smith's First Vision." *Brigham Young University Studies,* Spring 1969.

———, ed. *The Personal Writings of Joseph Smith.* Salt Lake City: Deseret Book Co., 1984.

Johnson, Benjamin F. Letter to George A. Gibbs, April to October 1903. Typescript in Harold B. Lee Library, Brigham Young University.

Journal of Discourses, 26 Vols. Liverpool, England: F.D. Richards and Sons, 1855–86.

Juvenile Instructor. Salt Lake City: The Church of Jesus Christ of Latter-day Saints.

The Latter-day Saint Millennial Star. Liverpool, England: The Church of Jesus Christ of Latter-day Saints.

Ludlow, Daniel H. *Latter-day Prophets Speak.* Salt Lake City: Bookcraft Publishers, 1951.

Lyon, T. Edgar. "Doctrinal Development of the Church During the Nauvoo Soujourn, 1839–1846." *Brigham Young University Studies,* Vol. 15, no. 4 (Summer 1975).

McConkie, Bruce R. *A New Witness for the Articles of Faith.* Salt Lake City: Deseret Book Co., 1985.

———. *Let Every Man Learn His Duty.* Salt Lake City: Deseret Book Company, 1976.

————. *The Millennial Messiah.* Salt Lake City: Deseret Book Company, 1982.

————. *Mormon Doctrine,* 2nd ed. Salt Lake City: Bookcraft Publishers, 1966.

————. *The Mortal Messiah,* 3 Books. Salt Lake City: Deseret Book Company, 1978–1981.

McConkie, Joseph F. "The Principle of Revelation." *Studies in Scripture, Vol. 1: The Doctrine and Covenants,* ed. Robert L. Millet and Kent P. Jackson. Sandy, Utah: Randall Book Co., 1984.

McKay, David O. *Gospel Ideals.* Salt Lake City: The Improvement Era, 1953.

McKiernan, F. Mark. *The Voice of One Crying in the Wilderness: Sidney Rigdon, Religious Reformer.* Lawrence, Kansas: Coronado Press, 1971.

McLellin, William E. Letter dated May 7, 1877.

Matthews, Robert J. *"A Plainer Translation": Joseph Smith's Translation of the Bible, A History and Commentary.* Provo, Utah: Brigham Young University Press, 1975.

Millet, Robert L. "The Development of the Concept of Zion in Mormon Theology," Ph.D. Dissertation, Flordia State University, 1983.

Millet, Robert L. and Jackson, Kent P., ed. *Studies in Scripture, Vol. 1: The Doctrine and Covenants.* Sandy, Utah: Randall Book Co., 1984.

————. *Studies in Scripture, Vol. 2: The Pearl of Great Price.* Sandy, Utah: Randall Book Co., 1985.

Millet, Robert L. and McConkie, Joseph Fielding. *The Life Beyond.* Salt Lake City: Bookcraft, 1986.

Nibley, Hugh W. *Nibley on the Timely and the Timeless.* Provo, Utah: Religious Studies Center, Brigham Young University, 1978.

————. "Our Glory and Our Condemnation." BYU Last Lecture Series, 1971–72.

————. "What is Zion? A Distant View." BYU Lecture Series, 1972–73.

Niebuhr, H. Richard. *Christ and Culture.* New York: Harper & Row, Publishers, 1951.

Novak, Michael. *The Spirit of Democratic Capitalism.* New York: Simon & Schuster, 1982.

Nyman, Monte S. and Millet, Robert L., ed. *The Joseph Smith Translation: The Restoration of Plain and Precious Things.* Provo,

Utah: Religious Studies Center, Brigham Young University, 1985.

O'Callaghan, E. B. *A List of Editions of the Holy Scriptures and Parts Thereof, Printed in America Previous to 1860.* Albany: Munsell & Rowland, 1861.

O'Dea, Thomas F. *The Mormons.* Chicago: University of Chicago Press, 1957.

Olsen, Steven L. "Zion: The Structure of a Theological Revolution." *Sunstone,* November–December 1981.

Packer, Boyd K. *The Holy Temple.* Salt Lake City: Bookcraft Publishers, 1980.

Peterson, H. Donl. "The Birth and Development of the Pearl of Great Price." *Studies in Scripture, Vol. 2: The Pearl of Great Price,* ed. Robert L. Millet and Kent P. Jackson, Sandy, UT: Randall Book Co., 1985.

Peterson, Paul H. "An Historical Analysis of the Word of Wisdom," Master's Thesis, Brigham Young University, 1972.

Pratt, Parley P. *Autobiography of Parley P. Pratt.* Salt Lake City: Deseret Book Co., 1976.

————. *Key to the Science of Theology,* 9th ed. Salt Lake City: Deseret Book Company, 1965.

Quincy, Josiah. *Figures of the Past.* Boston: Roberts Brothers, 1883.

Rich, Russell R. *Ensign to the Nations.* Provo, Utah: Brigham Young University Press, 1972.

Roberts, B. H. *A Comprehensive History of the Church of Jesus Christ of Latter-day Saints,* 6 Vols. Salt Lake City: The Church of Jesus Christ of Latter-day Saints, 1930.

Shipps, Jan. *Mormonism: The Story of a New Religious Tradition.* Urbana/Chicago: University of Illinois Press, 1985.

Smith, Hyrum M. and Sjodahl, Janne M. *Doctrine and Covenants Commentary.* Salt Lake City: Deseret Book Co., 1965.

Smith, Joseph. *History of the Church of Jesus Christ of Latter-day Saints,* 7 Vols., ed. B. H. Roberts. Salt Lake City: Deseret Book Company, 1957.

————. *Lectures on Faith.* Salt Lake City: Deseret Book Co., 1985.

Smith, Joseph F. *Gospel Doctrine.* Salt Lake City: Deseret Book Company, 1971.

Smith, Joseph Fielding, comp. *Teachings of the Prophet Joseph Smith.* Salt Lake City: Deseret Book Co., 1976.

————. *Doctrines of Salvation,* 3 Vols., comp. Bruce R. McConkie. Salt Lake City: Bookcraft Publishers, 1954–56.

Smith, Timothy L. "The Book of Mormon in a Biblical Culture." *Journal of Mormon History,* Vol. 7 (1980).

Times and Seasons, 6 Vols. Nauvoo, Illinois: The Church of Jesus Christ of Latter-day Saints, 1839–46.

Van Wagoner, Richard and Walker, Steven C. "Joseph Smith: the Gift of Seeing." *Dialogue,* Vol. 15, no. 2 (Summer 1982).

Von Rad, Gerhard. *Old Testament Theology,* 2 Vols. New York: Harper & Row Publishers, 1962.

Whitney, Helen Mar. "Scenes and Incidents in Nauvoo." *Woman's Exponent,* November 1, 1881.

Whitney, Orson F. *History of Utah,* 2 Vols. Salt Lake City: George Q. Cannon & Sons, 1892.

Widtsoe, John A., comp. *Discourses of Brigham Young.* Salt Lake City: Deseret Book Co., 1978.

Young, Joseph. "Vocal Music." *History of the Organization of the Seventies.* Salt Lake City: Deseret Steam Printing Establishment, 1878.

Young Woman's Journal. Salt Lake City: The Church of Jesus Christ of Latter-day Saints.

INDEX

Other Volumes in This Series

LINCOLN CHRISTIAN COLLEGE AND SEMINARY